# *Philosophy of Economics*

(MATH/NEWTONIAN LAWS)

VS

(POSITIVISM - NOMINALISM / HUMES

SKEPT EMP OF

ECO , PSY , POL )

VS

(VIRTUAL PARTICLES QNT PHY )

# International Library of Philosophy

*Editor*: Ted Honderich
*Grote Professor of the Philosophy of Mind and Logic*
*University College London*

Recent books in the series include:

*\*Content and Consciousness*   Daniel C. Dennett
*State Punishment*   Nicola Lacey
*Needs*   Garrett Thompson
*Modern Anti-Realism and Manufactured Truth*   Gerald Vision
*\*Wittgenstein's Philosophy of Psychology*   Malcolm Budd
*Scientism: Philosophy and the Infatuation with Science*   Tom Sorell
*The Immaterial Self: A Defence of the Cartesian Dualist
Conception of the Mind*   John Foster

\* Also available in paperback

# Philosophy of Economics

*On the Scope of Reason in
Economic Inquiry*

Subroto Roy

London and New York

First published 1989

First published in paperback in 1991
by Routledge
11 New Fetter Lane, London EC4P 4EE

Simultaneously published in the USA and Canada
by Routledge
a division of Routledge, Chapman and Hall, Inc.
29 West 35th Street, New York, NY 10001

Typeset in 10/12 Times by Columns of Reading

Printed in Great Britain
by TJ Press (Padstow) Ltd, Padstow, Cornwall

*British Library Cataloguing in Publication Data*
Roy, Subroto
Philosophy of economics : on the scope of reason in
economic inquiry. *Subroto Roy.* — (International library
of philosophy)
1. Economics — philosophical perspectives
I. Title   II. Series
330.01

*Library of Congress Cataloging in Publication Data*
Roy, Subroto
Philosophy of economics: on the scope of reason in
economic inquiry / Subroto Roy.
p.   cm.—(International library of philosophy)
Bibliography: p.
Includes index.
1. Economics—Philosophy.  I. Title.  II. Series.
HB72.R69   1991
330′.01—dc20   90–26359

ISBN 0–415–06028–1

To R. A. R.

# Contents

# *Preface*

The publication of this work marks the end of an adventure of more than a decade and a half, most of the writing being done between 17 December 1980 and 22 May 1987. It has been quite perilous at times, especially as a foreigner in the West, and over the years many teachers, colleagues, friends, and members of family have contributed to the author's learning with their thoughts and actions. A number of senior scholars in economics and philosophy, especially Professor Frank Hahn, Professor James Buchanan, Professor Milton Friedman, Professor Max Black, Professor Sidney Alexander, Professor Amartya Sen, Professor Peter Bauer, Professor T. W. Hutchison and Dr C. J. Bliss, have lent their support to the work as it developed, even when they may have not known of its final form, or disagreed with its content, or been themselves a subject of its criticism. Most especially, the work has been honoured in the last six years with the unwavering encouragement of Professor T. W. Schultz of the University of Chicago. And Professor Ted Honderich of University College London has shown it the kindest consideration, without which publication would have been much delayed. Finally, a large debt will be seen to be owed to the philosophical work of Mr Renford Bambrough of St. John's College, Cambridge; however, he should not be considered responsible for the use that has been made here of his writings.

*HONOLULU*
*15 AUGUST 1988*

ix

# 1

# *Introduction*

In this book, some of the central philosophical questions facing the modern economist will be raised. Most attention will be given to the question of the appropriate relationship between the positive and the normative, as well as to its parent question of the appropriate scope of objective reasoning in the making of evaluative judgements. Closely related is the question of the appropriate role of the economic expert in society, while slightly more distant questions have to do with the significance of interpersonal comparisons of utility, with the philosophical status of the concepts and theorems of mathematical economics, and with how judgements of probability should be understood. It is this family of questions which will be the concern of the present work.

Economics is a science with potentially important practical bearing upon the lives of men and nations. The state of the modern world may have been affected more profoundly and subtly by the use or misuse of economic knowledge than by many another science[1]. Yet anyone familiar with the intellectual history of the field will know it to have seen more conflicts, and often conflicts of a more destructive kind, than may be reasonably expected or tolerated in the development of a scholarly discipline. The reader will be familiar with the many explicit and implicit divisions of opinion that have occurred upon theories and methods and evidence and policies, which have sometimes torn apart individual university departments and even threatened the integrity of the science itself. Indeed the modern economist in a

1

despondent mood might be inclined to say of the state of his discipline as David Hume once said of philosophy: 'There is nothing which is not the subject of debate, and in which men of learning are not of contrary opinions. The most trivial question escapes not our controversy, and in the most momentous we are not able to give any certain decision. Disputes are multiplied, as if everything was uncertain, and they are settled with the utmost warmth, as if everything was certain.'[2]

At the same time as there have been deep and persistent divisions on substantive questions of economic theory and method and evidence and policy, there has been a deliberate or inadvertent consensus about the answer to an important question in the theory of knowledge. Modern economists happen to have been practically unanimous in their opinion on the possible scope of objective reasoning in the making of judgements, and thus in their opinion on the appropriate relationship between the positive and the normative. A broad consensus has developed to the effect that while common reasoning can have some scope in evaluative discussion, it is quite possible in practice and in principle for this scope to become exhausted. At such a point of the exhaustion of reason, only sheer and unadulterated subjective differences will be found to remain between people. Put another way, it has been believed possible for judgements ultimately to become immune to rational question and criticism.

Many of the pioneers of twentieth century economic thought, Kenneth J. Arrow, Milton Friedman, F. A. Hayek, Sir John Hicks, Oskar Lange, Gunnar Myrdal, Lionel Robbins, Joan Robinson, Paul Samuelson, Joseph Schumpeter, Jan Tinbergen, to name but a few, who between themselves would represent all of the main schools of contemporary economics, may be found to have shared such a thesis in the theory of knowledge, differing amongst themselves only upon the relatively minor question of the precise amount of room reasoning should be considered to have: some saying a great amount, others saying almost none, but all agreeing that whatever the exact amount it is a *finite* amount, both actually and potentially. The theory of demand, the theory of macroeconomic policy, the theory of welfare economics, the theory of social choice – each has in whole or in part rested upon an epistemological premise of this kind. If such a consensus can be shown to have existed, the reader may agree it to be something of a remarkable fact, since it would be difficult indeed to find a single substantive proposition of theory or method or evidence or policy to which a similar measure of consensus among modern economists might obtain.

One of the objects of the present work will be to argue that the fact that there have been tremendous disharmonies on substantive economic questions, may not be independent of the fact there has been this kind of harmony in the theory of knowledge among many of the pioneers of twentieth century economics as well as the many more who have followed them. If the epistemological point hitherto accepted as true happens in fact to be false, it becomes possible that the scope of objective reasoning on substantive questions has been artificially prevented from being extended as far as it could have and should have been. Evaluative judgements are clearly of indefinite variety: attitudes towards goods or people, expectations of the future, recommendations to buy or sell, advice to a friend or a student or a government, etc. – roughly, all judgements taken by an individual or social agent about a right or optimal course of action in given circumstances. We shall find the consensus has been that it is possible for reasoning to come to a necessary halt in the process of coming to such judgements, whether the maker of the judgement is a public body or a private individual acting in the capacity of consumer or voter. A large amount (and possibly the whole amount) of what may deserve to be within the domain of common and objective reasoning comes to be placed instead under the rule of subjective will and caprice. Not only must we live with the fact that discussions between citizens or economists or politicians or spouses or siblings or nation-states *do* frequently come to end without resolution, because there happens to be a lack of patience or tolerance or perseverance or good humour or whatever, but also that such outcomes may be written into the script from the start. In any normative discussion, we are to be permitted to call a unilateral halt merely by declaring 'Well that is a value judgement of mine' or 'That is a personal opinion of mine', with the implication that any further questioning is out of bounds and unacceptable. Given a theory which allows us in this way to declare as we please what to call objective science and what to call subjective opinion, and given that it may be but human nature to be sceptical of the other fellow's dogma while

3

being oblivious to one's own, we may have some explanation of how the consensus among economists in the theory of knowledge may have caused and preserved a state of affairs in which rival substantive dogmas can thrive – because the processes of common reasoning and even communication itself may have been allowed too often to come to a virtual standstill (or move at a snail's pace). 'Disputes are multiplied, as if everything was uncertain, and they are settled with the utmost warmth, as if everything was certain.'

The gist of the present work will be that the present consensus in the theory of economic knowledge is logically inconsistent. It is therefore untenable and deserves to be abandoned. *Men can aspire to, and in fact do attain and possess, certain and objective knowledge in an indefinite number of contexts. At the same time, there is no proposition of any kind held by anyone which must be thought of as necessarily closed to further question on grounds of reason or evidence.* This simple maxim is something that may be found to hold in any field of human inquiry or endeavour one cares to mention – mathematics or medicine, ethics or physics, history or probability, logic or theology – and it will be our purpose in this work to examine its consequences in the context of economics in particular.

**2.** Our study is one in what may be called theory of economic knowledge, and it may be worth a moment to consider what may be meant by this.

Bertrand Russell said of pure mathematics that it was a subject 'in which we do not know what we are talking about'[3] – meaning that the pure mathematician does not normally intend to refer in theorems to substantive factual truths about the world. The epistemology or theory of knowledge of a discipline may be thought of similarly as being not concerned with either affirming or denying, corroborating or refuting the substantive propositions that happen to be made within the discipline. The study of the theory of economic knowledge may be thought of as not making any commitment one way or another to the substantive propositions which are to be found within the department of economics itself. Instead it is a more abstract undertaking, which seeks to examine certain kinds of questions from *outside* the department in the practical hope of dissolving or at least

4

clarifying the character of substantive questions and controversies that may be occurring within. For example, to ask whether a criterion of truth and falsity *can* be applied to economic propositions, or whether objective knowledge is *possible* in the field, or how the kinds of propositions made in economics are to be *justified*, or how they compare and contrast with propositions made in other departments of inquiry – these would be the kinds of question we might see asked in the theory of economic knowledge; from which too the importance can be seen of generally abstaining from making substantive commitments in the process.

Much of the present work, especially Parts I and II, may be understood to be an attempt to provide a theory of economic knowledge of this kind. Thus the reader will not find in it commitments made to any substantive economic propositions. There is no theorem reported of the existence or efficiency of some new kind of economic equilibrium, no new model or evidence offered of the influence of the supply of money on prices, no new theory of how the expectations of economic agents may be formed or fulfilled or disappointed, no new evidence or explanation of why some country may be experiencing rapid growth or high inflation or increasing unemployment. No new result *within* economic science; one might almost say, nothing substantive! The present work will offer no more than 'a machine to think with' on certain philosophical aspects of economics; it intends to leave economics as it is – and yet in so doing to have shown the way out of some of the philosophical difficulties that are encountered in its study. 'For the clarity that we are aiming at is indeed *complete* clarity. But this simply means that the philosophical problems should *completely* disappear.'[4]

Yet the practical purpose of making an investigation of this kind may be stated quite readily. For suppose, for the sake of argument, we granted the truth of our simple maxim and assumed that the epistemological concepts 'knowledge' and 'doubt', and their allied concepts 'objectivity' and 'freedom', should not be seen as incompatible in the project of inquiry. What consequences would follow from accepting such a viewpoint? Clearly first of all, we would be placed in a happy position of being able to say that no matter how deep or persistent the actual disagreements between economists or between citizens on economic questions happened to be, there *is* knowledge to be had in the study of economics. Not just high sophistry or rhetoric or political posturing or the opinions and prejudices of different people – but certain and objective *knowledge* about those actions, events, and phenomena that are part of the economic context. We would be able to say, in other words, there are at least some propositions in economics which are *true*, and which moreover can be *known* to be true.

An important ambiguity is possible here in asking whether there is knowledge about a given matter, insofar as such a question can be taken either as asking whether it is possible for there to be any knowledge about the matter, or as asking whether it is known that someone actually possesses such knowledge and how that has been determined. Defining as an expert someone who has the most reasonable and justifiable answer to give to a question, we need to distinguish, in other words, the relatively cool logical question of *whether* there can be any such thing as expert knowledge from the more heated political question of *who* is supposed to be such an expert and how we are supposed to know that. For instance, a question like 'Is there a proof to Fermat's last theorem?' can be understood either in the manner of the pure mathematician, as asking whether there *can* be a proof to the proposition it is impossible $x^n + y^n = z^n$ for positive integers $x$, $y$, $z$, $n$, and $n > 2$; or in the manner of the historian of mathematics, as asking whether any human being has come up with such a proof, as Fermat said he had done but of which no record exists. Among the great thinkers, Plato is the most influential to have crossed these wires in suggesting it possible not only for there to be objective knowledge about mathematics and ethics and statesmanship, but also for a special and closed set of experts to come to be identified to whom such knowledge should be thought of as being exclusively given. Plato's theory can be and has been interpreted as giving license to elitism and dictatorship, yet the natural protest which the ideas of these would evoke in most of us may lead to an equal and opposite error of denying the very possibility of knowledge because we feared or wished to reject the idea of being ruled by a closed set of self-described experts. Once these wires are uncrossed, we may see it to be quite possible to maintain that there *can* be objective knowledge and expertise in economics, without making any commitments toward specifying who should be considered an expert on some economic issue, or how we are supposed to determine that, or for that matter claiming any such knowledge or expertise for ourselves.

A second consequence of our simple maxim may seem more troubling. For by its second part, we should also have to say that even while there is objective knowledge in economics, there is nevertheless no proposition in the field which must be thought of as being necessarily closed to further question. Not the proposition that every human act is a rational act, nor the proposition that economic agents continually maximize utility, or are well modelled as doing so, nor the proposition that the market economy cannot be expected to reach full employment and needs to be and can be actively supplemented by macro-economic policy, nor the proposition that the growth of money is necessary and sufficient for inflation, nor the proposition that free trade will maximize world output given factor immobility, nor the proposition that externalities imply a possible scope for taxes and subsidies, nor the proposition that the histories of nations is a history of class struggle. By the second part of the maxim, there is *no* axiom or theorem of economic theory, *no* finding of economic history, *no* estimate of the value of an economic coefficient, *no* prediction of the course of an economic variable, *no* proposal of economic policy, which must be thought of as being closed to further question. None whatsoever. 'No statement is immune to revision' (Quine).[5]

Taken together, then, the net consequence of supposing objectivity and freedom, knowledge and doubt, to be compatible concepts deserving of equal respect, is that we shall be able to chart a course which steers us clear of two perennial and opposing hazards besetting all projects of human inquiry, *viz.*, Scepticism and Dogmatism – the modern origins of which were traced by the American philosopher Charles Sanders Peirce to the cartesian proposal that philosophy 'must begin with universal doubt, whereas scholasticism had never questioned fundamentals.'[6] In the pages to follow, we *will* be denying universal doubt *and* we shall be free to question fundamentals. In an indefinite number of contexts, there is certain and objective knowledge to be had. Scepticism, understood technically as a logical thesis denying that we can possibly have or know that we have certain knowledge, is therefore a false thesis. At the same time, there is no proposition which is necessarily closed to question. Dogmatism, understood technically as a logical thesis implying there can be or must be some propositions which are absolutely and incorrigibly true, is therefore an equally false thesis. In place of a theory of knowledge restricting the scope of common reasoning to the finite or even the potentially finite, it is possible to have a theory of knowledge extending this scope to the potentially infinite. In particular, while normative proposals in economics or elsewhere may be supposed to be objectively better or worse depending on the soundness of the positive grounds given in their support, *there are no unquestionable normative proposals – because there are no unquestionable positive grounds*. The simple practical result of making the present investigation is that it will permit a sure and safe course to be found between Scepticism and Dogmatism for any project of economic inquiry.

**3.** Would such a simple and straightforward thesis be new to economics in any way? To what extent has the argument which has been summarized above and which will be developed in the chapters to follow not been expressed before? The reader may wish an answer to such a question, and the author presently takes this to be as follows.

With respect to the general debate which has occurred about knowledge and scepticism especially in moral philosophy, there will be little if anything in the present work which is a direct or novel contribution to it. While the philosophers have not been concerned with political economy at all, we shall be passive participants to their discussions, listening in to see what can be learned for our purposes and not intending to add to them directly. It may be remembered of course that it has not been long since economics formally broke away from philosophy to become a specialized discipline in its own right, in the belief that the concerns of economics are of a more concrete and practical kind than those of philosophy.[7] Since then we have made many highly abstract and theoretical claims, while also becoming scornful of philosophical thinking and believing ourselves to be exempt from its influences. Yet serious philosophical thought constitutes a mature and magnificent conversation which it would be foolish for any serious science to be deaf to. Moreover, it has been quite

8

widely believed that there have been significant advances in philosophical understanding in the present century, and we are responsible to take such a claim seriously. It will be one of the aims of the present work to apply what may be learned from these discussions towards resolving, or at least clarifying, some of the main substantive disputations in modern economic science.

There are two broad traditions of moral philosophy relevant to our subject-matter, one deriving from Aristotle, the other from Hume (and a line of sceptics before him). Even though it would be unwise to expect agreement within either tradition, we may for convenience speak of an aristotelian and a humean tradition respectively.[8] With respect to the discussions among economists on the relationship of the positive to the normative, we shall find an eminent consensus to have appeared on the humean side. This work will declare for the other side, and in so doing will have to dissent from the humean consensus upon which all of the theory of social choice and much of the theory of welfare economics and theory of economic policy have appeared to rest. As far as is known by the author, there seem to have been but two published dissents on similar lines among economists in recent decades: those of Sidney Alexander and Amartya Sen. Of these, Professor Sen's dissent has been very short and hesitant, and he would seem to have withdrawn it in other writings. Professor Alexander's dissent has been clear and vigorous, but unlike his work on the balance of payments, his philosophical work has not received attention, and the present work was mostly developed in complete ignorance of its existence.[9]

By the end of this work however, a clear choice should have been set out for the reader on the question of the relationship of the positive to the normative – between the consequences of accepting the humean consensus among economists and the consequences of the position of Professor Alexander and the author and possibly Professor Sen. The simple maxim 'Objective knowledge is possible and yet there is no proposition which is closed to question' should not undermine its own content by being closed to question itself – instead it is supposed to refer and apply to itself as well. It may be true and deserving of our belief but it is not self-evidently so, and will have to earn its credentials at the common bar of reason. Ultimately it will have to be the reader's individual judgement to decide whether it has been successfully shown that, contrary to what has been supposed by many of the pioneers of twentieth-century economics, no conflict must arise between knowledge and doubt, objectivity and freedom. The history of the discussion may accord to our side the advantage J. S. Mill had seen to be enjoyed by all minority opinions: if the opinion of one or a few is false then not much will be lost by believing in it, while if it proves better able to stand the tests of time then much may be gained by allowing it to replace error. Put differently, it may seem quite risky that the pioneers of modern economic science have placed all their philosophical eggs in the humean basket – just in case it is Hume himself who happens to be mistaken.

**4.** In Part I of the work will be found described the received theory of economic knowledge and its possible justification, as well as an account of the logical difficulties that arise with it. Chapter 2 has the task of documenting as fully as possible the existence of a humean consensus among economists in recent decades. Chapter 3 then examines the kinds of reasons that may incline us to be persuaded to such a view, and which may go toward explaining how it has seemed to be an attractive theory to so many economists. These reasons appear to have been of two different but related sorts.

First the concept of value as used in ordinary life and ethics may have become confounded with the concept of economic value or scarcity or *rareté* in Walras's term. Where economists have referred to a theory of value, they may have meant to refer more accurately to a theory of relative prices as determined by conditions of scarcity. The advance of the original neoclassicals in the late nineteenth century was to establish the importance of subjective estimations of economic agents to the determination of the relative prices of goods – as opposed to, say, how much labour went into different production processes as the classical economists might have said, or how much intrinsic value God had placed in the goods as the scholastics might have said. While it is clear by now that such an observation is broadly correct, it would be a mistake to go from a premise that market prices are determined in part by subjective estimations to a conclusion that the relative prices thus determined in any sense establish an order of how goods deserve to be valued or not. Goods are indeed valued the way they are because people happen to value them. Yet equally, in most cases, people seem to value goods in the way they do because the goods deserve to be thus valued – for example, because, like food or clothing or shelter, the goods are conducive to some valuable human purpose.

Secondly, it is possible the consensus has been motivated by a desire to find an effective shield against dogmatism and tyranny. For example, the context of an open parliamentary democracy presupposed by the modern theory of economic policy may have derived out of the experience of the great tyrannies of twentieth century history. There may have been a natural and understandable desire that the choices and decisions of citizens in the capacity of voters or consumers should be treated with the fullest due respect, and a humean scepticism may have been adopted because it has been believed to be something which is necessary and sufficient for this kind of respect to be shown. This would be an outstanding reason for adopting a humean point of view, and one which any critic must be required to account for. Yet it also places in relief the contradiction that is present within the humean theory. For example, a theory of economic policy which has to rely upon an assumption of the polity being open and democratic would have to be silent about the conduct of economic policy in societies which were demonstrably not open or democratic, making it a theory very special and contingent in its range of application. Moreover, to give the defence of political or economic or religious freedom as a reason for holding a subjectivist epistemology would be to have left freedom entirely defenceless and toothless from those who would attack it *from within precisely the same subjectivist framework*. For example, if we confounded a general right to express an opinion freely with an idea that what such an opinion expresses is itself a matter of subjective opinion, then clearly, by the same token, an opinion that opinions should be freely expressed might also be considered merely subjective, and therefore no better or worse than its contrary. Within a subjectivist theory of knowledge, there ultimately can be nothing to choose between freedom and tyranny.

Chapter 4 is a survey of these kinds of logical difficulties with the humean position stated in Chapters 2 and 3. Its main result will be that the anti-dogmatic campaign of the humean cannot succeed, and in fact comes to make the Sceptic resemble the Dogmatist more than anything else. It is possible that this happens because both Sceptic and Dogmatist are sharing the same deductivist model of justification, to the effect that we cannot know a proposition to be true or right unless we have deduced it as the conclusion of a set of premises of whose truth or rightness we are certain. The Sceptic sees the threat of infinite regress that is implicit in such a model, and then denies we can be certain of anything. The Dogmatist sees the potential regress too, but responds to it by calling a halt at some arbitrary point, denying the need or possibility of going any further. In Part II a fresh picture will be given which attempts to preserve the truths the Sceptic and Dogmatist would each like us to take notice of, while correcting for the distortions both would force upon us by their unequivocal adoption of a deductivist model of justification. Chapter 5 reframes the main philosophical problems of Part I in terms of the ancient dualism between Nominalism and Realism, and brings to light a possible resolution of this which has been advanced by a number of modern philosophers. Chapter 6 develops the argument further and applies it to the question of the appropriate role of expertise in a democracy. Taken together, Part II contains the main outlines of a fresh theory of economic knowledge with which to replace the flawed and inconsistent theory to which so many economists have thus far subscribed.

Part III of the work consists of a series of diverse illustrations and possible applications of the theory of knowledge developed in Part II. Chapters 7 to 10 all give examples of how inquiry and criticism can be seen to proceed in economics without sacrifice of either objectivity or freedom. Chapter 7 examines an actual debate on a concrete question of microeconomic policy, which may be compared and contrasted with the more academic examples of later chapters. Chapter 8 examines aspects of the division in macroeconomics and monetary theory since J. M. Keynes's *General Theory of Employment, Interest and Money*. Chapter 9 considers a question with wide and general reference to economic theory: how the relationship between mathematical economics and real economic phenomena might be best understood. This has been the subject of long and bitter disputation, and some light is attempted to be shed on it from the vantage point of the philosophy of mathematics. It is possible that certain views in the philosophy of mathematics have been presupposed in modern mathematical economics; once these are exposed and aired, some of the conceptual problems which have been faced in this discussion may come to be dissolved. The theory of probability and expected utility and the theory of general equilibrium are used as brief illustrations. Finally, in Chapter 10, the possible philosophical sources of the controversy surrounding the question of interpersonal comparisons of utility are described, and a possible resolution suggested. This is argued to have bearing on the received understanding of the foundations of welfare economics.

**5.** It will be found in the present work, then, that we shall be denying universal doubt on the one hand, while yet being free to question fundamentals on the other. Such a project will entail a critical examination of the philosophical premises and assumptions advanced by some of the most distinguished contemporary scholars in our field, and it is to be hoped the spirit in which the present criticism is offered will not be misunderstood. Every generation holds a peculiar advantage over preceding generations in having available to it what has gone before, while not being able to anticipate the criticisms of its own beliefs that will certainly come in the future. This kind of advantage that the present holds over the past may be thought of as being quite arbitrary, and we can expect it to carry with it a responsibility of taking what has gone before into serious account. Since no individual is able to do so on his own, we find every generation as a whole attempting to provide itself with critical discussions, which, when integrated over time, constitute the grand and unending conversation we call the history of human thought. It is with such a model in mind of a continuing and self-critical tradition of scholarship that we shall seek to address the questions raised at the beginning about the foundations of economic knowledge, while making no pretence whatsoever to finality, and instead leaving the entire treatment as open as it can be made to the examination and criticism of others.

# PART I

# 2

# *Hume and the Economists*

There has been a broad and long-standing consensus among economists about the character of the relationship between positive and normative propositions, as well as about the related question of the appropriate scope and limits of economic expertise in society. Joining in this consensus have been many of the pioneers of twentieth-century economic thought including Kenneth J. Arrow, Milton Friedman, F. A. Hayek, Sir John Hicks, Oskar Lange, Gunnar Myrdal, Lionel Robbins, Joan Robinson, Paul Samuelson, Joseph Schumpeter, and Jan Tinbergen. Many others are likely to be found in explicit or implicit agreement, while a survey by Professor T. W. Hutchison suggests that some of the most renowned figures of nineteenth-century economics should probably be included as well.[1] The main purpose of this chapter will be to provide enough documentary evidence to show that such a consensus has in fact existed. When we think of how many deep and wide differences there have been over the years in the field that was once called political economy and is now called economic science, differences on questions of method and theory and evidence and recommendations of policy, the existence of such a consensus may seem quite a remarkable fact.

Very briefly, what appears to have been accepted is that it is possible to identify a body of progressively changing knowledge called 'positive economics', which is the main contribution of economists to human knowledge and understanding in general. It consists of such things as the microeconomic and macroeconomic

17

descriptions of present and past states of an economy, conditional predictions of such states in the future, hypothetical or substantive explanations of what economic causes may have what economic effects, the deduction and analysis of theorems of economic significance, and so on. That is to say, positive economics has been supposed to consist of the domain of propositions in an economic context which have to do in one way or another with questions of what *is* the case, or with what has been the case in the past or may be expected to be the case in the future. In contrast, evaluative or prescriptive or 'normative' propositions, having in one way or another to do with what *ought* to be done or not done by a government or a private economic agent, have been believed to fall into quite a different category. These have been believed to amount sooner or later to being expressions of subjective personal opinion, either on the part of individual economists or of those whom they may happen to be advising.

Most economists who have considered the matter have allowed that there is usually at least some scope, and sometimes much scope, for common reasoning on logical and empirical grounds to be brought to bear in normative discussion; making it possible that at least some of the disagreements between economists or citizens or politicians on normative questions can come to be objectively resolved. But it has been believed possible also for the processes of common reasoning to become exhausted in discussions of normative questions like those of economic policy or ethics or jurisprudence, in a way they are not supposed to become exhausted in discussions of positive questions like those of economic theory or econometrics or natural science or mathematics. Once such a point of the exhaustion of reason has been reached, any residual conflict which remains is to be considered necessarily irreconcilable and of a sheer normative kind. And such sheer normative opinions, upon which it is not possible to bring to bear any further objective consideration, are to be supposed to express the purely subjective attitudes and feelings of the individual person, opinions which might happen to be shared by others too, but which are certainly closed to further argumentation, whether in public or in the person's own mind. Put a little differently, the theory of knowledge and policy, which we shall see to have been widely accepted by many economists in the twentieth century, has made an assumption that while all

18

questions of analysis and evidence can have objectively true or false answers, only some and not all questions of evaluation and prescription can have objectively right or wrong answers.

**2.** Underlying the consensus among economists has been a more general thesis in the theory of knowledge or epistemology. It is a thesis which may be called 'moral scepticism', and its most brilliant and influential exponent in the modern period has been David Hume (1711–1776). Among those to have advanced influential and persuasive points of view of a similar kind in twentieth-century moral and political philosophy have been C. L. Stevenson, R. M. Hare, A. J. Ayer, and Karl Popper.[2]

In the course of a critique of dogmatic religion and ethics, the young Hume was to attack with a sceptical scalpel what he took to be the illogic of trying to deduce evaluation and prescription from analysis and description: 'In every system of morality, which I have hitherto met with . . . the author proceeds for some time in the ordinary way of reasoning . . . when of a sudden I am surpriz'd to find, that instead of the usual copulations of propositions, *is*, and *is not*, I meet with no proposition that is not connected with an *ought* or an *ought not*. This change is imperceptible; but is, however, of the last consequence. For as this *ought*, or *ought not*, expresses a new relation or affirmation, 'tis necessary that it shou'd be observ'd and explain'd; and at the same time that a reason should be given, for what seems altogether inconceivable, how this new relation can be a deduction from others, which are entirely different from it.'[3] While the precise context and implications of this passage continue to divide philosophers, it will be adequate for our present purpose to follow the sympathetic and influential modern interpretation given by the Oxford moral philosopher R. M. Hare, and obtain for an economic context what may be called *Hume's First Law: No normative conclusion, for example, about what a private economic agent or a government ought to do or not do, can be validly deduced from a set of solely positive premises, i.e., from premises which only describe what is the case. No normative conclusion can be deduced without at least one normative premise having been made.*[4] A dualism of this kind between the 'is' and the 'ought' has been frequently supposed to separate science from ethics, the objective from the subjective, the rational from the irrational, public knowledge from private opinion.

Hume was to reinforce this opinion a decade later in a more recondite form of words: '[A]fter every circumstance and every relation is known, the understanding has no further room to operate, nor any object on which it could employ itself. The approbation or blame which then ensues cannot be the work of the judgement, but of the heart; and is not a speculative proposition or affirmation, but an active feeling or sentiment.'[5] This passage too continues to divide philosophers, but for our present purpose R. M. Hare's recent writing is once more helpful in obtaining a modern interpretation. Hare asks whether, in addition to logical questions and factual questions about how the world is, there can be 'irreducibly evaluative or prescriptive questions' as well; once we have 'done all we can' by way of reasoning and adducing evidence, 'will there remain something to be done which is neither logic nor fact-finding but pure evaluation or prescription?'[6] Hare answers yes it is possible, and in the same vein we may restate the idea to obtain for an economic context what may be called *Hume's Second Law: After every empirical question and every logical and mathematical question has been answered in an economic problem, there is no further scope for common reasoning to work. If an evaluative statement is made at such a point, then it can express no more than a subjective attitude or feeling of the individual economist towards the subject.*

This is a maxim which does grant that a measure of common reasoning and evidence can be brought to bear upon particular normative questions, and so some normative disagreements may come to be objectively resolved. But it also allows for the potential for such reasoning to become exhausted, leaving merely a subjective residue of personal sentiment or feeling which people might or might not happen to share with one another but which would be beyond further question and discussion. In the pages to follow, a position will be referred to as 'humean' if it implicitly or explicitly endorses one or both of Hume's Laws as stated above. The small 'h' is used to suggest that a close examination of Hume's works may show him to have been not entirely clear in his own meaning, as well as to suggest that the question of what Hume himself may have actually or fully meant is not of as direct importance for the present purpose as the question of what he has been taken to mean by contemporary economists.

The remainder of this chapter is given to documenting at fair length the fact that a number of the pioneers of twentieth-century economics have quite unambiguously seemed to endorse a humean point of view in the theory of knowledge. Chapter 3 will be given to placing this fact in an appropriate historical context. This needs to be done not only in order to understand the nature of the consensus as fully as possible, but also to realize how close economists have been to one another on a central question in the theory of knowledge, even while being engaged in any number of deep and well-known and seemingly interminable disputes on substantive matters. The reader who may be impatient with a detailed record of this kind, or who is prepared for the present to take its existence for granted, may wish to move on directly to Chapter 3 without losing the main threads of the argument.

**3.** *Friedman* Following Neville Keynes, Professor Milton Friedman has clearly and emphatically argued the importance of extending the scope of common reasoning in economics: 'Positive economics is in principle independent of any particular ethical position or normative judgments. . . . [It] is, or can be, an "objective" science, in precisely the same sense as any of the physical sciences. . . . Normative economics and the art of economics, on the other hand, cannot be independent of positive economics. . . . differences about economic policy among disinterested citizens derive predominantly from different predictions about the economic consequences of taking action – differences that in principle can be eliminated by the progress of positive economics – rather than from fundamental differences in basic values, differences about which men can ultimately only fight.'[7] It is well known that in this and other works, Friedman has argued for the extension of common reasoning and evidence, or positive economics, as the surest means to resolving normative disputations. Yet from the passage quoted, it is clear that Friedman has also accepted something like Hume's Second Law, to the effect that while common reasoning can have some and indeed much scope, a point of ultimate and sheer normative disagreement can still be reached, distant though it might be, where reasoning must be considered to have become exhausted and 'men can ultimately only fight'. In the same essay, Friedman added that it was the practical importance of economics which impeded objectivity and promoted confusion between 'scientific analysis and normative judgment', suggesting an endorsement of Hume's First Law as well.

*Myrdal* Gunnar Myrdal argued for many years that a number of economic concepts purporting to be analytical or descriptive in character in fact had evaluative or prescriptive overtones. Myrdal and his editor and translator, Professor Paul Streeten, argued that a view that there is no place for normative judgements in economic science has been a guise for the advocacy of a specifically liberal political economy, a thesis which might well be endorsed by many marxian and keynesian economists. While postponing an assessment of this claim to a later chapter, we may note that Myrdal also happened to endorse the extension of the scope of positive economics, with as much emphasis as Friedman would do after him: 'By subjecting to impartial criticism those arguments in political controversies which concern the facts and the causal relations between them, economic science can make an important contribution to the political sphere. As often as not, conflicting political opinions spring not so much from divergent valuations about the best possible future state of society and the proper policy for securing it, as from subjectively coloured and therefore distorted beliefs regarding actual social conditions.' Myrdal went on to endorse Hume's First Law in recommending that the economist leave the supply of evaluative premises to the politician. While the economist can provide descriptions, explanations and conditional predictions, 'the scientist must not venture beyond this. If he wishes to go further he needs another set of premises, which is not available to science: an evaluation to guide him in his choice of the effects which are politically desirable and the means permissible for achieving them.'[8] Finally, Myrdal reached the humean conclusion that the normative differences between economists are ultimately beyond objective resolution: '[E]conomic reasoning is often obscured by the fact that normative principles are not introduced explicitly, but in the shape of general "concepts". The discussion is thus shifted from the normative to the logical plane. On the former there is either harmony or conflict; conflict can only be stated, not solved by discussion. On the logical plane we should define our concepts clearly and then operate with them in a logically correct manner. What is "correct" and what "false" can be discussed with the methods of logic, whereas conflicting interests can be recognized, never solved scientifically.'[9]

*Robbins*  In his influential writings over many years, Lionel Robbins made a distinction between 'economic science', having to do with such questions as how best to allocate scarce resources between alternative ends, and 'political economy' or normative theories of economic policy, prescribing the ends themselves and the weights to be attached to them. In his well-known methodological work we read as clear a statement of Hume's First Law as might be found in economics: 'Propositions involving "ought" are on an entirely different plane from propositions involving "is". . . . Economics is neutral as between ends. Economics cannot pronounce on the validity of ultimate judgements of value. . . . Economics deals with ascertainable facts; ethics with values and obligations. The two fields of inquiry are not on the same plane of discourse. Between the generalizations of positive and normative studies there is a logical gulf fixed which no ingenuity can disguise and no juxtaposition in space or time can bridge over.' Robbins's endorsement of the Second Law was equally emphatic. While positive economics extends the scope of common reasoning, it is still possible to find normative differences which are rationally irresolvable: 'If we disagree about ends it is a case of thy blood or mine – or live and let live according to the importance of the difference or the relative strength of our opponents. But if we disagree on means, then scientific analysis can often help us to resolve our differences. If we disagree about the morality of the taking of interest (and we understand what we are talking about), then there is no room for argument.'[10]

*Samuelson*  Professor Paul Samuelson has seemed to feel a tension in the humean position, but also that its logic compelled him to follow closely in Robbins's path: 'It is fashionable for the modern economist to insist that ethical value judgments have no place in scientific analysis. Professor Robbins in particular has insisted upon this point, and today it is customary to make a distinction between the pure analysis of Robbins *qua* economist and his propaganda, condemnations and policy recommendations *qua* citizen. In practice, if pushed to extremes, this somewhat schizophrenic rule becomes difficult to adhere to, and it leads to rather tedious circumlocutions. But in essence Robbins is undoubtedly correct. Wishful thinking is a powerful deterrent of good analysis and description, and ethical conclusions cannot be verified in the same way that scientific hypotheses are inferred or verified.'[11]

*Hicks* Like Samuelson, Professor Sir John Hicks has seemed to feel a tension in the humean position, yet he too must be considered as having endorsed at least an important version of it. On the one hand, Hicks has seemed critical of mid-century positivism and emotivism, and claimed the main rationale of the 'new welfare economics' to be that it allowed a route of escape from them. 'During the nineteenth century, it was generally considered to be the business of an economist, not only to explain the economic world as it is and as it has been, not only to make prognostications (so far as he was able) about the future course of economic events, but also to lay down principles of economic policy, to say what policies are likely to be conducive to social welfare, and what policies are likely to lead to waste and impoverishment.' Since then positivism had declared that explanation and only explanation may be part of scientific economics, and any move to prescribe 'must depend upon the scale of social values held by the particular investigator. Such conclusions can possess no validity for anyone who lives outside the circle in which these values find acceptance. Positive economics can be, and ought to be, the same for all men; one's welfare economics will inevitably be different according as one is a liberal or a socialist, a nationalist or an internationalist, a christian or a pagan.'[12] But such a position is 'rather a dreadful thing to have to accept', one which might 'become an excuse for the shirking of live issues, very conducive to the euthanasia of our science.' Fortunately we are not compelled to accept it, since the new welfare economics advanced by Kaldor, Hotelling and Hicks himself was a viable alternative, not open to the objections the positivists had raised to the utilitarianism of Pigou and others.[13]

Yet we may ask, what had the new welfare economics been about? And did it in fact make a break with the positivism which seemed to be troubling Hicks, or had it not been prompted precisely by humean doubts? As is well known, the new welfare economics had to do with questions such as whether the potential gainers from a change in policy could possibly compensate the potential losers from the change by enough so as to get them to go along with it, or conversely for the losers from a change to compensate the gainers from the change by enough so as to get them to go along without it, and so on. As Hicks himself makes clear, it was a discussion very much motivated by the belief that while the Pareto criterion was not a wholly adequate substitute for the utilitarianism of Pigou, any emendation of the paretian theory must leave untouched its basic positivistic premise, *viz.*, that interpersonal comparisons cannot be conceived of as anything but purely subjective judgements, outside the scope of objective reasoning.[14] Hicks claimed it was because the new welfare economics avoided making interpersonal comparisons that it should be considered a positive advance, a scientific advance. And Hicks has emphasized that he, like Robbins, has not wanted any truck with interpersonal comparisons. The old welfare economics of Pigou required one 'to admit the possibility of comparing the satisfactions derived from their wealth by different individuals. This is where Professor Robbins parts company; for my part, I go with him.'[15] More recently: 'A single individual . . . shows by his choices that he prefers one thing to another; we may put this, if we like, in the form of saying that he derives (or thinks he derives) greater satisfaction from the one than from the other. But there is no similar way in which we can *see* that the satisfaction derived by one individual from one good is greater than the satisfaction derived by another individual from another good; these satisfactions are not compared in any actual choice, so that for the comparison between them there is not the same evidence.'[16]

While we shall be returning to these questions in Chapter 10, what we may note here is that since interpersonal comparisons certainly amount to being a particular species of evaluative judgement, Hicks's scepticism with respect to the possibility of making them objectively must be considered to amount to an endorsement of at least a species of moral scepticism. If so, it would seem to sit uncomfortably with Hicks's opinion that he had not cared much for the positivist dichotomy between explanatory science and subjective prescriptions, which was said to have prompted the search for the new welfare economics in the first place.

*Robinson*  Writing on the theory of employment, Joan Robinson was to give a superbly clear account of the humean position at its best, which requires no commentary: '[All economic] controversies should be capable of resolution. The rules of logic and the laws of evidence are the same for everyone, and in the nature of the case there can be nothing to dispute about. Controversies arise for five main reasons. First, they occur when the two parties fail to understand each other. Here patience and toleration should provide a cure. Second, controversies occur in which one (or both) of the parties have made an error of logic. Here the spectators at least should be able to decide on which side reason lies. Third, two parties may be making, unwittingly, different assumptions, and each maintaining something which is correct on the appropriate assumptions. . . . Here the remedy is to discover the assumptions and to set each argument out in a manner which makes clear that it is not inconsistent with the other. Fourth, there may not be sufficient evidence to settle a question of fact conclusively one way or the other. Here the remedy is for each party to preserve an open mind and to assist in the search for further evidence. Fifth, there may be differences of opinion as to what is a desirable state of affairs. Here no resolution is possible, since judgements of ultimate values cannot be settled by any purely intellectual process . . . argument in the nature of the case can make no difference to ultimate judgements based on interest or moral feeling. The ideal is to set out all the arguments fairly on their merits, and agree to differ about ultimate values. On questions of policy, the differences can never be resolved.'[17]

*Hayek*  Professor F. A. Hayek has stated an unambiguous commitment to Hume's First Law, as when he wrote recently: 'Our starting point must be the logical truism that from premises containing only statements about cause and effect, we can derive no conclusions about what ought to be.'[18] In his earlier discussion of the economics of socialism, Hayek had hinted at the Second

Law as well, saying that 'problems of ethics, or rather of individual judgements of value . . . [are] . . . ones on which different people might agree or disagree, but on which no reasoned arguments would be possible.' If the questions about socialist planning are ethical by this definition then 'no scientist, least of all the economist' would have anything to say about them.[19] Positive argument presumes there to be some common values between the participants: 'Meaningful discussion about public affairs is clearly possible only with persons with whom we share at least some values. I doubt if we could even fully understand what someone says if we had no values whatever in common with him. This means, however, that in practically any discussion it will be in principle possible to show that some of the policies one person advocates are inconsistent or irreconcilable with some other beliefs he holds.'[20] In particular, the argument over socialist planning should be seen to be one on positive grounds: '[E]veryone desires, of course, that we should handle our common problems as rationally as possible and that, in so doing, we should use as much foresight as we can command. In this sense, everybody who is not a complete fatalist is a planner, every political act is (or ought to be) an act of planning, and there can be differences only between good and bad, between wise and foresighted and foolish and shortsighted planning. An economist, whose whole task is to study how men actually do and how they might plan their affairs is the last person who could object to planning in this general sense.'[21] The dispute between socialists and their critics is 'not a dispute about whether planning is to be done or not. It is a dispute as to whether planning is to be done centrally, by one authority for the whole economic system, or is to be divided among many individuals.'[22]

*Lange* Oskar Lange, the famous adversary of Hayek and Robbins on the question of socialist planning, was agreed with them that the only task within the scope of scientific economics was the determination of the best means, with economic ends having been decided politically. He gave this infelicitous analogy to the economist's role: 'The situation may be compared with that of two physicians treating a patient. There is no necessity of interpersonal agreement about the objective of the treatment. One physician may want to heal the patient, the other may want

27

to kill him (e.g., the patient may be a Jew in a Nazi concentration camp; one physician may be a fellow prisoner who wants to help him, the other may be a Nazi acting under orders to exterminate Jews). But once the objective is set for the purposes under discussion (either of the two physicians may, of course, refuse to act upon it), their statements as to whether a given treatment is conducive to the end under consideration have interpersonal validity. Any disagreement between them can be settled by appeal to fact and to the rules of scientific procedure.'[23]

*Schumpeter*  In discussing the *wertfrei* controversy between Carl Menger and the German historical school, Joseph Schumpeter was to suggest that the epistemological matters involved were neither difficult nor interesting and could be disposed of shortly. The distinction between 'is' and 'ought' had been correctly and adequately drawn already, so it only needed to be accepted that an 'ought' statement, 'that is to say, a precept or advice, can for our purpose be reduced to a statement about preference or "desirability".' Schumpeter went on to endorse Hume's First Law, saying that an acceptance of one value judgement always requires the acceptance of others. This 'is of little moment when the "ultimate" value judgments to which we are led up as we go on asking why an individual evaluates as he does, are common to all normal men in our cultural environment.' Unlike Lange, Schumpeter gave the physician as a negative analogy: '[T]here is no harm in the physician's contention that the advice he gives follows from scientific premises, because the – strictly speaking extra-scientific – value judgment involved is common to all normal men in our cultural environment. We all mean pretty much the same thing when we speak of health and find it desirable to enjoy good health. But we do not mean the same thing when we speak of the Common Good, simply because we hopelessly differ in those cultural visions with reference to which the common good has to be defined in any particular case.'[24] I.e., common reasoning can proceed in normative discussion but only so long as we find common values among 'all normal men in our cultural environment', which is to suggest reasoning may be helpless with abnormal men or those who are outside our cultural environment. Further, siding with Menger, Schumpeter suggested that the bitterness of the *wertfrei* controversy could be explained because it had been not so much a logical dispute as one between those who were practising and those who were protesting a kind of scholarly deceit, *viz.*, the propagation of personal dogmas within an ostensible pursuit of objective knowledge: 'Those who profess to be engaged in the task of widening, deepening, and "tooling" humanity's stock of knowledge and who claim the privilege that civilized societies are in the habit of granting to the votaries of this particular pursuit, fail to fulfil their contract if, in the sheltering garb of the scientist, they devote themselves to what really is a kind of political propaganda.'[25]

*Arrow* In opening his famous paper on the theory of social choice, Professor Kenneth J. Arrow was to refer explicitly to the ancient ontological dualism between Nominalism and Realism. To take aggregate rankings of 'social states' as independent of individual rankings "is to assume, with traditional social philosophy of the Platonic realist variety, that there exists an objective social good defined independently of individual desires. This social good, it was frequently held, could be best apprehended by the methods of philosophic inquiry. Such a philosophy could be and was used to justify government by elite, secular or religious, although the connection is not a necessary one. To the nominalist temperament of the modern period the assumption of the existence of the social ideal in some Platonic realm of being was meaningless.' Nineteenth-century utilitarianism had 'sought instead to ground the social good on the good of individuals', which, when combined with a hedonistic psychology, implied 'each individual's good was identical with his desires' and 'the social good was in some sense to be a composite of the desires of individuals.' Such a view 'serves as a justification of both political democracy and laissez-faire economics, or at least an economic system involving free choice of goods by consumers and of occupations by workers.'[26]

While Arrow found it necessary to remark that a connection between elitist rule and a Realist ontology was 'not a necessary one', he did not also remark upon whether he took a connection between democratic rule and a Nominalist ontology to be logically necessary. If not, then we might of course entertain other cases equally well, such as Nominalism being associated with elitist rule, or Realism with democratic rule, or perhaps more subtle cases which may arise from a denial of the dualism altogether – matters to which we shall return more explicitly in Part II. In any case, it would seem evident that Arrow's sympathy has been with the humean thesis, which he endorses strongly in suggesting, like Schumpeter, that no distinction can be made between a personal preference and a judgement of value: 'One might want to reserve the term "values" for a specially elevated or noble set of choices. Perhaps choices in general might be referred to as "tastes". We do not ordinarily think of the preference for additional bread over additional beer as being a value worthy of philosophical inquiry. I believe, though, that the distinction cannot be made logically, and certainly not in dealing with the single isolated individual. If there is any distinction between values and tastes it must lie in the realm of interpersonal relations.'[27] That Arrow believes normative questions to be only personally and subjectively answerable is further suggested by his remarks that '[t]he only rational defense of what may be termed a liberal position . . . is that it is itself a value judgment'; that his own values are such he is willing 'to go very far indeed in the direction of respect for the means by which others choose to derive their satisfactions'; that he personally shares 'a strongly affirmed egalitarianism, to be departed from only when it is in the interest of all to do so'; that he is personally 'in favor of very wide toleration'; and so on.[28] In Chapters 9 and 10, we shall return to examine certain aspects of the theories of general equilibrium and social choice which Professor Arrow has helped pioneer.

*Blaug*   In his influential writings in the history and methodology of economics, Professor Mark Blaug has appealed directly to Hume, declaring that the 'orthodox Weberian position on *wertfrei* social science is essentially a matter of logic: as David Hume taught us, "you can't deduce ought from is".' Blaug grants that scientific practice does continually call for the exercise of judgement, but he wishes to distinguish 'methodological' judge-ments, having to do with such questions as 'the levels of statistical significance, selection of data, assessment of their reliability, and adherence to the canons of formal logic', from 'normative' or 'appraising' judgements, which 'refer to evaluative assertions about states of the world, including the desirability of certain kinds of behavior and the social outcomes that are produced by that behavior; thus all statements of the "good society" are appraising value judgments.' It is judgements of this latter sort which are 'incapable of being eliminated in positive science'. In support of such a dualism Blaug claims 'there are long established, well tried methods for reconciling different methodological judgments' but none 'for reconciling different normative value judgments – other than political elections and shooting it out at the barricades.' Blaug's acceptance of Hume's Second Law is as explicit as may be found in contemporary economics. There sometimes can be rational discussion over normative differences 'and that is all to the good because there is a firmer tradition for settling disputes about facts than for settling disputes about values. It is only when we distil a pure value judgment . . . that we have exhausted the possibilities of rational analysis and discussion.' Echoing Robbins, Blaug suggests that at such a terminal point we are left with 'factual statements and pure value judgments between which there is indeed an irreconcilable gulf on anyone's interpretation.'[29] Like Arrow, Blaug also makes reference to an ontological division between Realism (or 'essentialism') and Nominalism, and hints at a necessary link between a Realist ontology and dogmatism and tyranny. From Plato and Aristotle up through the nineteenth century, Western thought had been under the malign and mistaken impression that 'it is the aim of science to discover the true nature or essence of things'. Such a view 'raises its ugly head' even today, and Blaug charges the authors of a recent marxian thesis as being one such recent manifestation: 'Adherents of essentialism are inclined to settle substantive questions by reaching for a dictionary of their own making, and Hollis and Nell exemplify this tendency to perfection: reproduction is *the* "essence" of economic systems because *we* tell you so!'[30]

*Hahn* Professor Frank Hahn reports that contemporary economists 'in keeping with the Positivist perspective' make 'a thorough distinction of "is" from "ought" (positive from normative).'[31] While Hahn has been mostly guarded in his own opinion as to the precise relationship between positive and normative, he has suggested recently that while normative questions are subject to reasonable argument, and economic theory is intended to widen this scope of common reasoning, 'the intention is to take a small step in distilling what are genuinely questions of values.'[32] Such a remark would seem to place Hahn among the moderate humeans like Joan Robinson and Milton Friedman – which in turn would make it an interesting fact that while Hahn has had long and well-known disputes on substantive matters with both Friedman and Robinson, he would appear closely agreed with them on a point in the theory of knowledge, *viz.*, that while there is much room for objective discussion to take place, it is possible for sheer differences of a normative kind to exist and come to be identified.

*A few others*   To take some final examples, Mr Robert Sugden affirms 'Hume's Law reflects a liberal view of the universe'; Professor William Baumol and Professor Allan Blinder write in their textbook that the economist defines rational decisions as those 'that are most effective in helping the decision maker achieve his own objectives, whatever they may be'; Professor James Quirk writes in his textbook that 'normative economics is based on a system of axioms, but these axioms concern ethics' and because these and any propositions derived from them are not 'verifiable through empirical observation', a person is 'free to accept or reject the conclusions of normative economics as he wishes, simply by accepting or rejecting the axiom system – there are no scientific issues involved.' And Professor Jack Hirschleifer wrote in his textbook that 'if one economist prefers Maoism and another capitalism, or if one prefers to exterminate and the other to tolerate an inconvenient minority group, the fundamental sources of contention are almost surely divergences in ethical values . . . [which] will not be eliminated by advances in scientific economics.'[33]

# 3

# *Understanding the Consensus*

The great German philosopher and mathematician Gottlob Frege suggested at one place that we should not 'ask for the meaning of a word in isolation, but only in the context of a proposition.'[1] In the same vein, it may be said that the meaning of a proposition or a hypothesis should not be asked for except in relation to the particular context in which it has been advanced. And we can maintain this without requiring the description of such a context to be fully explicit or even one which can be easily expressed in words. A proposition needs to be understood in relation to the fullest possible description of its implicit and explicit context – which may be a good sense, too, in which to understand the reference by Wittgenstein to the concept of a 'language-game'.[2]

In the previous chapter, we have marshalled considerable evidence for our initial thesis that there has been a broad measure of consensus among many of the pioneers of modern economics about the appropriate relationship of the positive to the normative. Irrespective of their many and well-known substantive differences, they have seemed all to share an affinity with a humean thesis of moral scepticism, whether in a radical way like Schumpeter and Professor Arrow when they say there can be no difference in kind between personal preferences and value judgements, or in a more moderate way like Joan Robinson and Professor Friedman and Professor Hahn, when they say there can be a great amount of room for objective argumentation to take place about normative questions before a naked and irreconcilable difference will be found to appear. The first question that needs now to be addressed is how this consensus should be understood, and this will require as full a description as can be attempted in this work of the context in which it has occurred. The second question would be whether or not the consensus is correct and justified – whether or not there are firm and adequate grounds for us to think we should join it, and so take the is-ought dualism to be a barrier which it is neither possible nor necessary to surmount. The reader will have known from Chapter 1 that it is a main purpose of this study to make the argument that such grounds are not in fact available, that a humean position is ultimately untenable and misleading, and deserves to give way to a theory of economic knowledge and policy which treated objectivity and freedom as compatible concepts deserving of equal respect. Nevertheless we are first obliged to identify the strengths and motivations of a humean point of view, if only so that we may explain how it has come to command the kind of assent it has done among many of the most eminent of twentieth-century economists as well as the many more who have followed them. When expressed as thoroughly as it has been by some, a humean point of view is certainly a respectable and recondite one to hold in the theory of knowledge; there seems nothing obvious that is wrong with it; to the contrary, it may seem foolhardy to try to refute it or even place its merits under scrutiny. In other words, a well thought-out moral scepticism deserves the respect of its critics, and any difficulties with it may be expected to be of a relatively subtle and not self-evident kind.

The purpose of this chapter will be then to give as full a description as possible of the historical and political context – of the 'language-game' or the *civilization* – within which it is possible for the humean consensus in modern economics to be understood. The economists quoted in Chapter 2 do not appear to have attempted such descriptions themselves, and may even have assumed a humean point of view on the positive and normative to be self-evidently justified, for little thought seems to have been given as to why we should want to endorse it. Thus it will be fair to caution the reader that while a possible justification and explanation of a humean point of view will be given here, it will be one which has been constructed by a critic. Furthermore, the discussion will refer first to a more distant and then a more proximate context, and the discussion of the former will have to be speculative and greatly simplified – a mere thumbnail sketch of an actual drama of indefinite proportions.[3]

**2.** The adoption of moral scepticism in twentieth-century economics may be most briefly explained as having been motivated by a genuine desire to shield against dogmatism and tyranny, whether in political, economic, scientific, or religious contexts. As scientist and scholar, the economist has been naturally concerned to extend the scope of common reasoning, as well as to protect the objectivity of the findings of his science from the imposition of personal or political dogma. Equally, it has been felt that the choices of the individual agent who is studied by economists, whether as consumer or voter, deserve to be treated with the fullest respect. A humean scepticism may have been adopted because it has been believed to be necessary and possibly sufficient for this kind of respect to be shown to the results of popular choice, whether in parliament, the market place, or in private life. This is summarized in, for instance, Sugden's remark 'Hume's Law reflects a liberal view of the universe', as well as in Schumpeter's suggestion that the *wertfrei* controversy had been merely one between those who practised and those who protested a kind of scholarly deceit, namely, the propagation of personal dogma in the guise of a pursuit of knowledge. In other words, someone might become a moral sceptic because he wishes to defend, and wishes perhaps to be seen as defending, the freedom of the individual person to form and hold his or her own normative beliefs, as well as the objectivity of science from being compromised by the forced imposition of the beliefs of any one or a few people. In particular, the modern humean economist is likely to wish to contrast his theory as sharply as possible with the famous theory given by Plato, both directly with the political philosophy which is to be found in Plato's writings, as well as indirectly, with the medieval scholasticism which came to be deeply influenced by the rediscovered works of Plato and Aristotle and to which the origins of modern economic and political thought can be traced.

Now the question of whether there *is* any objective knowledge in a field of inquiry is open to be understood either as asking whether there *possibly* can be any knowledge in the field, or as asking *who* should be thought of as possessing such knowledge and how they may have been identified. The first of these senses can be thought of as epistemological and the second as political in character. In *Republic*, Plato offered answers to both questions with respect to the knowledge of the statesman, and the answers he gave were yes – not only is it logically possible for there to be objective knowledge of use to the statesman, but it is practically possible to identify certain men and women in society as actually possessing or being considered fit to possess such knowledge. It is these special people who are the only true lovers of wisdom in society, and since we surely should want the policies of a state in which we lived to be the wisest and most prudent possible, informed by the best available knowledge, it appears to follow at once that what needs to be done is unite knowledge with authority and make these special people our guardians and rulers.

Plato's ideal city-state is a place where individual freedom is conspicuous by its absence. Its rulers are to be imagined as being about as perfect rulers as there can be: the single and genuine source of all true wisdom and justice, and deserving therefore to be granted absolute authority on all significant questions of private and political conduct, including the right to suppress dissent, since any dissent would be misguided by definition. This is not to say the philosopher-kings would be entitled to a life of luxury or even ordinary comforts. To the contrary, since those who deserve to be philosopher-kings may well be disinclined to seek power and privilege for themselves in the normal course of politics, they may have to be first discovered and then forcibly drafted to take the office which rightfully should be theirs. In preparation for the serious business of piloting the ship of state, they will be placed in seclusion and rigorously educated in such disciplines as aesthetics and gymnastics and mathematics and music, their lives certainly without any of the signs of corruption that we would frequently associate with the exercise of power. At the end of the tenure of one generation of such rulers, they will be retired and replaced by a new generation, bred and educated through a similar and careful programme of eugenics and training in the arts and sciences of statesmanship. Finding actual examples of such extraordinary beings may be quite impossible; perhaps some appropriate mixture of the Dalai Lama, Gandhi, Atatürk and Mozart's Sarastro might help our modern imagination.[4]

A number of modern political thinkers have roundly condemned Plato for having written a theory hostile to democratic political institutions, and even for having provided the blueprints for the tyrannies of modern history. Yet while there is no question that Plato was no friend of democracy, or at least of the kind of democracy which had brought about the judicial murder of his friend and teacher Socrates, a fair-minded reader of *Republic* is unlikely to find in it any justification of tyranny at all. If we were to define tyranny in the way Plato and his contemporaries would have done as the rule of the ignorant and capricious, it would be a state of affairs Plato found abhorrent, the complete antithesis of his own ideal of a full union between knowledge and authority, of rule by the genuinely wise and the genuinely good; even the faulted system of democracy would be preferable to it. Moreover, Plato was to discuss at length the dynamics of how even his ideal city-state would be likely to degenerate into a tyranny; and besides, his single attempt to put theory into practice ended in pathetic failure, when he accepted an invitation to train a fatuous prince, who was incapable of and soon became bored with the rigorous education Plato had in mind for him, and who eventually became the worst of tyrants, much to Plato's disgust.[5] In fact Kant, the modern lover of freedom, was led to come to the defence of Plato, the ancient authoritarian, precisely because the logical possibility of a utopia is suggested to the reader of *Republic* – a state of affairs in which everyone is a genuine lover of wisdom, everyone a philosopher-king, and therefore all external government made redundant.[6] *Republic* is a masterpiece of philosophy and mathematics and literature and political economy as well, and it would be a mistake to suppose its author to have been so inexperienced of human nature and society as to provide it as a textbook for grand or petty tyrannies, whether of his own time or of ours.

What is true, however, is that the theological culture of medieval Europe would come to be deeply influenced by the rediscovered works of Plato and Aristotle, with which a synthesis of medieval Christianity was sought to be made. And it may also be fair to say that regardless of Plato's intentions, *Republic* came to provide something of a model for the tyrannies to be experienced in subsequent European history.

37

Social and economic life in medieval Europe is marked by a four-fold division of society into the nobility, the clergy, free artisans and tradesmen self-governed within a system of guilds and corporations, and the peasantry. The medieval church is seen as an eternal institution representing divine will on earth, deserving to be endowed with final and absolute authority on all significant questions of right conduct, somewhat perhaps in the manner of Plato's philosopher-kings. Specific duties and rights belong to the members of different occupations, and it is within one's calling that one is expected to lead one's life in accordance with the divine law as interpreted by the church and the natural law as discovered by the temporal authorities. In particular, there is a notion that economic activities may be licit or illicit in nature, and since the general moral question of what ought to be done is closely identified with whether there is the sanction of the church for it to be done, whether a particular economic activity is to be approved of or not comes to depend on whether or not it has such a sanction. There is an idea too of economic goods having a 'true' or 'intrinsic' or 'natural' value endowed in them by God – an idea which will become perhaps a precursor of the labour theory of value of classical economics in the eighteenth and nineteenth centuries. Determining this intrinsic value establishes the 'just' price of a good or service, i.e., the price at which it ought to be traded, even if the actual market price as determined by the subjective estimates and actions of traders happens to differ from this contingently. There is a related concept of 'equivalence' in transactions, with a suggestion that one party to a trade can gain from it only at the expense of the other. Merchants and middlemen thus come to be treated with some disdain, since it does not seem apparent they are adding anything to the intrinsic values of goods, making the just price of their services seem hard to determine. Indeed the unabashed pursuit of wealth by anyone is probably the object of some considerable social and religious disapproval. Similar thinking may underlie the condemnation of usury, since, given a premise of money having no intrinsic worth, what is perceived to be the lending out of money should seem to have a just price of nought.

The common medieval culture and economy was to be transformed drastically though differently across Europe between the fourteenth and eighteenth centuries. The sea routes are discovered, nation-states emerge competing with one another in trade and war, the age of modern science begins, a long and rapid succession of scientific discoveries and technological inventions takes place, there is a vast expansion of commerce and population and the settlement of European colonies in other continents. Accompanying these transformations in some places are intellectual rebellions against the medieval church, and almost everywhere in Europe a decline in the influence of formal faith. The assertion of individual will and conscience as the principal guides of human conduct is a challenge directed at church doctrine and dogma; but given that the medieval concept of reasoning is one of reason ultimately bounded by the doctrines and dogmas of faith, the assertion of a subjective individual will may have been assumed to amount to being a challenge to the full possibilities of objective reasoning itself.

In this new mercantilist age, the pursuit of material gain must come to be freed of the sanction of the church, and once more, since right and wrong are closely identified with such sanction and prohibition, a declaration of the independence of economic activity from the sanction of the church amounts virtually to a declaration of its independence from ethics as well. In particular, the medieval notion of 'equivalence' in the intrinsic value of goods in a transaction is transformed with the aid of mechanistic analogies at hand into a concept of 'equilibrium' in trade, such that each party to a trade is conceived of as gaining from it as an individual and continuing to transact until the prospect of such gain has come to be exhausted. It is understandable perhaps that England and Holland will be in the vanguard of the mercantilist revolution, given their theological distance from Rome as well as their growing commercial interests and naval power. Nor does it seem obviously foolish, at least in the early mercantilist years, for the wealth of a nation to be identified with its ability to export and its holdings of precious metals, when the circumstances of the time make it a first priority of the business of government to have liquid payment available for navies and armies. In France there comes to be the liberal protest of the physiocrats against the iniquities upon the peasantry, a protest which serves to rehabilitate a more secular version of the natural law of the scholastics. But the calls of men like Quesnay and Turgot for reform are too late, and the system of physiocracy is itself swept away with the onset of the French Revolution.

Adam Smith however has admired and learned from the physiocrats, while observing at first hand the dismal effects of a British mercantilism grown stale. This he rises to condemn in *The Wealth of Nations*, thereby starting an intellectual revolution of his own, ringing in a new century of free enterprise and imperial expansion, and establishing the concern of the economist with the workings of individual interest and the market economy which continues to this day. Forty years later it is David Ricardo who introduces to political economy the practice of an abstract hypothetical method, by which it is a body of abstract and general principles that the economist's speculations and ratiocinations are intended to discover, detached from the rush of concrete economic realities. And Ricardo and his immediate followers exemplify the application of the new method to a main subject of Smith's preoccupation, namely, the workings of individual self-interest and the market economy.

In the musty passageways of Victorian thought, the new methods of abstraction in political economy must have been felt to be as invigorating as fresh air. Jevons, Walras, Menger and the other original neoclassicals firmly insist upon making the plain and simple observation that in the case of many and perhaps most goods, the prime determinant of relative value is not how much labour went into the different production processes, nor how much intrinsic value God might have placed in the goods, but rather the subjective estimations of economic agents in the market place. The victory seems complete. Out of the medieval notion of the scope of reasoning being limited by the dictates of doctrine and dogma, is eventually born the neoclassicals' notion of the concept of value as fully and exactly synonymous with the concept of *scarcity* or market value, or *rareté* in Walras's term. Economists are seemingly freed to speak of 'a theory of value' when meaning to refer more specifically to a theory of scarcity-determined relative prices, determined by conditions of supply and demand in the marketplace. From an idea that something is or is not a good only and merely because the church happens to say so, the wheel comes full circle to an idea that something is or is not a good only and merely because of the price it happens to command in the marketplace. The moral absolutism of the platonist and the scholastic gives way to the moral scepticism of the humean, and we reach the threshold of the modern period of economics in the later nineteenth and early twentieth centuries.[7]

**3.** Briefly, then, the development of the kind of sceptical and subjectivist point of view represented by Hume and the humean economists may be seen as the democratic reaction which occurs to medieval and platonist authoritarianism. And in parallel with these democratic developments occurring in the marketplace and economic thought, there occurs between the medieval and the modern period an emancipation of the political mind as well. No more will it be for clergy and aristocracy to dictate divine and temporal laws respectively. Men are born *equal* – which is to say there are not grounds *ex ante* why one human being should be supposed to deserve more or less authority or dignity than another merely in virtue of his or her humanity. The political process must reflect this new emancipation, and displace the hierarchies of the past with the equalitarian notion that every man's vote should count the same, and the most popular choice be established to rule.

The modern institutional context of a parliamentary democracy, bound by formal or informal constitutional principles and precedents, may be roughly sketched somewhat as follows. From among the body of citizens, some will choose to run for elected office. While reasonable restrictions may be placed on who can so choose (e.g., they must be adult nationals) any citizen normally will be free to be a candidate. Before a vote is conducted, a reasonable time will be allowed for candidates to put their respective cases to the public. There will be some constitutional rule, like first-past-the-post or proportional representation, agreed upon more or less unanimously in advance of the vote, which will map how the actual balloting will induce particular outcomes as to the composition of the parliament. The individual voter casts his or her ballot, reflecting some private mixture of interest, prejudice, caprice or good sense about the common welfare. The rule is applied, and the largest coalition of winning candidates comes to constitute the new government, with smaller coalitions constituting the loyal opposition. Once elected, a government will be expected *prima facie* to carry out the agenda it had proposed to the public before the election and not something different. What it actually does will be the subject of

41

constant scrutiny and criticism by the opposition, the press, and the public at large, but the laws finally enacted will have jurisdiction over all. After a certain maximum time, elections must be held again and the process repeated, with an incoming government either maintaining or changing the policies of its predecessor in large or small measure. The system may be considered indirectly democratic insofar as that at any given time citizens shall have given themselves, via their elected representatives, the policies and laws under which they are themselves to live.

While a government would be expected to implement the agenda chosen indirectly in this way by the public, it will be expected also to elicit expert advice upon the best means to be employed towards achieving the chosen ends. Yet the expert must be appropriately humbled, brought down from the high altar where Plato had placed him to being the modest and self-effacing servant of the popular will. The scientist in government is to take as given the ends of his political masters, under a presumption that these reflect the democratic choice and any interference or criticism would be impertinent. More generally, the competence of the expert in a democratic society is not to extend to questioning the uses to which his expertise may be put. Thus Popper was to write: 'No amount of physics will tell a scientist that it is the right thing for him to construct a plough, or an aeroplane, or an atomic bomb. Ends must be adopted by him, or given to him; and what he does *qua* scientist is only to construct means by which these ends can be realized.'[8] Or as Myrdal put it in the passage quoted in the previous chapter, the expert must not go beyond advising on the means, for he would otherwise require premises of a normative kind which have not been given to science, but which are to be presumed available instead to the elected politician. And Robbins wrote of how economists ought not to judge the ends to which economics is put, indeed that ultimately 'there is no room for argument' about ends, but rather how the quintessence of economics is the study of the optimal allocation of scarce resources between competing ends. It is only the question of the best or optimal means towards such an allocation that is within the scope of rational inquiry, and therefore within the competence of the economist *qua* scientist; it is not for the economist to question the ends given to him by the representatives of the public.

Now the widespread view since that there is a unique and quintessential economic problem, and that in particular it is the problem of the allocation of scarce resources between competing ends, is of course one initially advanced in the course of the neoclassical revolution. As Marshall put it: 'if a person has a thing which he can put to several uses, he will distribute it among these uses in such a way that it has the same marginal utility in all. For if it had a greater marginal utility in one use than another, he would gain by taking some of it from the second use, and applying it to the first.'[9] The housewife must decide how much yarn should be put to making socks and how much to making vests so 'as to contribute as much as possible to family well-being'; she will have allocated the yarn efficiently if the marginal increase in family well-being is the same whether she puts the last ball of yarn to making an extra pair of socks or to making an extra vest. In modern terms, the problem is one of constrained maximization in which a concave objective function is to be maximized subject to a number of linear or non-linear constraints. We might imagine, for example, a hospital administrator who must allocate fixed quantities of various resources at his disposal like medical staff, beds, dressings, and so on, between a number of alternative outputs which have to be produced in different hospital wards, with the aim of maximizing an objective function containing these outputs as concave arguments. The objective function itself, that is, the relative weights which should be given to the various outputs, is not ultimately for the administrator to decide, but rather to be taken by him as a parameter from an appropriate authority. If the necessary conditions for a maximum are met, an optimal allocation would be one in which (a) the ratio of marginal increases in the objective function from marginal increases in the output of any two goods equalled the implicit shadow prices of their technologies, and (b) the marginal increase in the objective function from increased use of a resource in any two production activities would be the same and equalled the shadow price of the particular resource. Thus the marginal hour of a nurse's skills would be equally well applied whether in assisting mothers in

43

labour or in providing aid in the Emergency Room. Similarly, a humean view of the expertise of economists would be one in which the economist did not question the social objective function but rather took as his or her task the statement and solution of the formal problem of the allocation of scarce resources between the defined ends.

With the necessary change of detail, the same has been required in the influential theory of macroeconomic policy advanced by Professor Jan Tinbergen and his principal expounder, Professor Henri Theil.[10] In this theory, normative premises are seen as being given to the expert economist by a representative of the political process, for instance 'the Minister of Finance or Economic Affairs, who is interested in the employment level of his country and its balance of payments'.[11] Such a person is assumed to know the set of variables relevant to determining the present state of the economy, which are divided into those whose values can be changed ('instruments') and those whose values cannot be changed ('targets'), with a change in the value of an instrument being defined as a 'policy measure'. The expert economist is called upon to specify as well as possible the structural relations between targets, instruments, and exogenous disturbances, and predict as well as possible the future course of the targets under alternative assumptions about the instruments. As Theil put it, the policy-maker is to receive from his forecasters 'conditional expectations about the time-patterns of non-controlled variables, the conditions being alternative measures to be taken by himself in the present and the future.' Alternative futures of the economic model are then to be evaluated one against the other by means of a social utility function decided upon by the policy-maker. Its arguments could be a pair of macroeconomic ills such as inflation and unemployment implying that the function should be minimized, or a pair of microeconomic goods like efficiency and equity implying that the function should be maximized subject to the relevant constraints, with the relative weights given to the ends presumed to be reflecting the democratic mandate.[12] An optimal vector of targets is determined which yields the least possible social disutility or the highest possible social utility; the values of the instruments which would result in this optimal vector are calculated, and changes from the present values of these instruments to these optimal values define the optimal set of policy measures to be taken.

Such, briefly, was the kind of theory of economic policy Tinbergen put forward in the early years after the Second World War. It was soon to have much influence among macroeconomists, especially in the United States.[13] Fairly or not to both Keynes and Tinbergen, the models themselves came to be called 'Keynesian', yet their influence has been significant enough that contemporary critics of both Keynes and Tinbergen have described their method and purpose in similar terms.[14] For keynesians and their critics, the macroeconomist principally has a positive role, extending the scope of reasoning and discussion on logical and empirical grounds as far as he is able to. He assumes a constitutional democracy, and takes for granted that the normative premises of the policy-maker reflect the popular will.

**4.** Drawing together, then, the main threads of this highly simplified and summary discussion, it may be possible to explain the adoption by twentieth-century economists of a humean theory of knowledge by the widespread belief that such a theory provides a necessary and even a sufficient defence against dogmatism and tyranny. It is part of the democratic reaction to medieval authoritarianism. The modern civilization which has adopted the moral scepticism of Hume is one born out of the great medieval civilizations which had been influenced by the authoritarianism of Plato. And just as Plato's theory was affected by his disgust with the doings of the democracy of his time, so it may be the theory of knowledge which has come to be adopted by as eminent and diverse economists as Robbins, Friedman, Samuelson, Hicks, Robinson, Myrdal, Arrow, Hayek, Lange, Tinbergen, Hahn, and Schumpeter, and the many others who have followed them, has been conditioned in part by their disgust with the tyrannies and ideologies of twentieth-century history, and their desire to protect from these both the objectivity of economic science as well as the individual in his or her capacity of consumer and voter.

The question arises, however, whether, in making their escape from Plato, the pioneers of twentieth-century economic thought have not become entranced by Hume.

# 4

# *Difficulties with Moral Scepticism*

We have now a description of some of the main features of the theory of economic knowledge most widely accepted in the twentieth century, and we have seen also how its plausibility and influence may be explained by placing it in appropriate historical and political context. In this chapter we shall examine some of the main difficulties and paradoxes which happen to arise with this theory. These have been serious in their implications, and the more general problems from which they derive have been well known to many contemporary philosophers, yet they do not appear to have been given adequate notice by modern economists.[1]

Briefly, the difficulties are two-fold.

First, if the justification of adopting a humean theory of knowledge by contemporary economists is to be what we have taken it to be, *viz.*, that such a theory and only such a theory can provide an adequate bulwark for science and the individual against tyranny and dogmatism, then we clearly have the makings of an internal contradiction on our hands – since what is patently a moral purpose would have been advanced within a theory of knowledge whose ostensible aim was to deny the possibility of moral knowledge! In a theory in which all moral propositions are taken ultimately to be statements of mere personal opinion, the defence of the freedom of the individual or of the integrity of science must also be taken ultimately to be matters of mere personal opinion, and the declared or undeclared purpose of protecting freedom by adopting moral scepticism would have been internally defeated by that very scepticism itself.

46

Second, we shall find that sceptical attacks just as powerful as Hume's attack on the possibility of moral knowledge can be made upon the possibility of knowledge in a number of non-moral contexts as well. Hume himself is responsible for one such attack when he raised his famous doubts about the possibility of induction, and analogous attacks can be made in diverse other contexts such as those of science, history, mathematics, or psychology. The result of recognizing these new possibilities for scepticism is to make evident that an acceptance of moral scepticism on its own may force a choice between either sliding into *total* scepticism, the position of believing there is ultimately *nothing* whatsoever that can be objectively known, or forsaking parity of reasoning, and denying that what may be sauce for the goose is also sauce for the gander. Either the possibilities of mathematical knowledge and scientific knowledge and historical knowledge *all* come to be denied ultimately because we wish in a consistent way to deny the possibility of moral knowledge, or one sort of knowledge is accepted and another sort rejected when there are reasons to think they must stand or fall together. Either all of positive economics is attacked with just as much scepticism as anything in normative economics, or we accept one and reject the other when instead there are reasons to think they share the same ultimate grounds and must be accepted or rejected together.

Such will be the main hazards we shall find on the humean course taken in the theory of knowledge by the economists quoted in Chapter 2. Their precise locations however are subtle and quite well hidden, so if we are to avoid them we must move here as carefully and precisely as possible.

2.   Let us recall at the outset Hume's First Law to the effect that a normative conclusion cannot be validly deduced from solely positive premises; that a normative conclusion cannot be deduced without at least one normative premise being made. Faced with a normative proposition, then, a moral sceptic will ask to see the set of prior positive and normative premises from which it is to derive. To take a simple example, if you were to say 'I think the government should reduce the rate of growth of the money supply $\dot{m}$ from 6 per cent to 3 per cent', a moral sceptic may ask 'Could you say why you think so, since your proposition is plainly

normative and cannot have derived from a set of solely positive premises?' (We can suppose this not to be meant rhetorically, that some opinion like 'What a stupid idea!' is not being surreptitiously introduced in the guise of asking a question, but rather that a genuine inquiry is being made to be told the grounds that may go to support the proposal.) If you were to reply 'Well, the government should try to reduce the rate of inflation $\dot{p}$, it is necessary and/or sufficient to reduce $\dot{m}$ in order to reduce $\dot{p}$, that is why I think the government should reduce $\dot{m}$,' it would remain open for the sceptic to respond 'Certainly I can agree that *if* your premises are true *then* your conclusion follows. But your premises once more are not solely positive ones, including as they do one that is plainly normative. Could you now say why you think the government should try to reduce $\dot{p}$ in the first place?'

It is not difficult to imagine a fair reply being given to this as well, such as, perhaps, 'Well, inflation has been rampant and the election was fought and won on a promise inflation would be curbed, election promises should be attempted to be kept, that is why the government should make a determined attempt to reduce $\dot{p}$.' But in practice the economist would typically and rightly allow such discussion to fade into the background – since an important and difficult task would already have been defined for him, which is to ask whether it is likely a reduction in $\dot{m}$ by the stated amount will succeed in reducing $\dot{p}$, assuming that the government should be trying to do this in the first place. Trying to answer it will require abiding by the practices of language and logic and scientific method; but the question itself is a positive and not a normative one insofar as it asks what is the case, or what has been the case or is likely to be the case, and the desire to keep it distinct for analytical convenience from the explicitly normative may be understandable. The modern economist is one of many kinds of expert in civil society, and as such is expected to have some special theoretical or practical knowledge not possessed by the non-economist. And economists everywhere are in fact being called upon to evaluate whether or not a dam or a highway should be built, a budget balanced or unbalanced, a bond released or redeemed, a tax or a tariff levied or lifted; to judge whether the argument of a government or a colleague or a student or a critic is valid, substantiated, compelling, sound, cogent. In any such investigation, it may well be useful for purposes of clarity and analytical convenience to work with a dualism between the 'is' and the 'ought', the descriptive and the prescriptive – just as it is commonly useful to work with a dualism between an analytical sense of 'is' as in 'two plus two is four', and a descriptive sense of 'is' as in 'the cat is on the mat'.[2]

Yet from saying it may be useful to make *working* dualisms between what is possible and what is actual or between what is the case and what ought to be done, it does not follow that there are any absolute or ineradicable lines to be drawn. Taking a set of normative premises as given and from there proceeding to extend the scope of positive reasoning would not imply the normative premises are *un*questionable – only that they are not *now* in question, not *presently* in question. It is as if they have been temporarily taken out of the game while we attempted to see how far we may proceed without them. They can still be brought back and others taken out – indeed, in the game of inquiry, we might even wonder if there needs to be *any* proposition which must be so privileged as never to be benched, so indispensable that we must fear the whole project will collapse without it.

**3.** We may recall next Hume's Second Law to the effect that while it may be possible to bring to bear objective reasoning in some normative discussions, a point of sheer and unadulterated difference over 'basic' or 'ultimate' values can nevertheless come to be reached. The moderate humean may allow for much room for common reasoning to take place, but takes the further step of supposing such reasoning to have a limit, a *finite* limit. In any normative discussion, it is eventually possible for the scope of objective reasoning to become exhausted and a difference of a sheer normative kind to come to be identified. While it is clear that the economists quoted in Chapter 2 have meant to refer to a limit of this sort being reached, it is strictly speaking not clear if they have meant to refer to such a limit being reached just as a contingent matter of fact – in actual arguments and discussions – or whether they have meant to refer to such a limit being possible in principle as well. In other words, whether it is merely intended to be an empirical possibility that a disagreement will come to end without resolution, or whether it is also intended for this to be the logically necessary outcome. If a residue of disagreement remains after the processes of common reasoning have been allowed to work, is this residue to consist of differences which just happen to be closed to further discussion in a particular case, say because the discussants lack patience or good humour or tolerance or perseverance or whatever, or is it supposed to consist of sheer and naked differences over 'basic' values which must be thought of as necessarily beyond the scope of further discussion?

If it is the first interpretation alone which has been intended, then only a fairly small claim would have been made, which may need to be clarified and fully set out but which would not need to be disputed by someone wishing to attribute a greater scope to reason than does the moral sceptic. For it is quite evident that actual arguments and discussions frequently do come to end without full resolution – those between physicists, mathematicians, biologists, doctors, or engineers no less perhaps than those between politicans, economists, writers, historians, spouses, or nation-states. Yet an observation of this sort of the frequency or intensity of disagreement would not be directly relevant to the theory of knowledge, insofar as the *fact* that an argument happens to stop where it does, does not bear upon whether a question in dispute is *capable* of having a true or a right answer. It is possible for the true or right answer to a question not to be available to those who happen to be discussing it, or even to others in their generation or those in later generations; that there *can* be an objectively true or right answer to a question is a different question from whether it has been found or will be found today or tomorrow or next year. What the answers happen to be to the questions raised by Darwin or Freud or Keynes is a different question from what they themselves might have thought the answers to be, or what their contemporary state of opinion happened to think the answers to be, or what the state of opinion in our own time or in some future time happens to think the answers to be. It is of course natural to want to know the true or right answer to a question, to know whether the answer which we think is true or right *is* true or right, and certainly we should be surprised and find it incongruent if someone said he or she believed something even while knowing it was not true, or approved of something even while knowing it was not right – we normally want to know what is true and what is right and make our beliefs congruent with it. In other words, we may distinguish the actual and contingent *history* of inquiry and conflict from the *logic* of inquiry and conflict.

Moreover, some concepts and propositions will be found to form a context or a background in any disagreement, being understood by both sides and being unnecessary to be made explicit. If we were discussing the monetary history of the United States in the 1980s for example, we would take for granted such facts as that the United States was not at war or civil war or in the throes of any major social convulsion during this time; assumptions which may not have formed the implicit background if we were instead discussing the monetary history of the 1960s or the 1860s. Not every feature of a description may be relevant to a particular question at hand nor must it be made explicit. And an observation of this kind may be made of any dispute in economics, once it has been carefully and thoroughly characterized, whether on method or theory or evidence or policy, in microeconomics or macroeconomics, whether between mathematical economist and applied economist, or keynesian and quantity theorist, or marxian and mainstream. Some aspects of any description will be implicitly understood or taken for granted by the participants in a discussion.

More strictly, it has been argued by the Cambridge philosopher Renford Bambrough that it is *necessary* for the participants in a discussion to be in at least some agreement before they can be even said to be in any disagreement at all: 'You and I cannot be known to be in conflict unless it is possible to identify a proposition that I assert with a proposition that you deny; no such proposition can be identified unless there is some expression that you and I use in the same way; if we use an expression in the same way then we regard the same steps as relevant to determining the truth or falsehood of what is expressed by it; for a disagreement about what *is* relevant is or involves a disagreement about what the dispute is that we are engaged in, and when such a case of cross-purposes is resolved it resolves itself either into agreement or into a disagreement to which all these conditions again apply.'[3] In other words, it must be *either* that the participants in a dispute are giving different answers to the same question *or* that they are giving answers to different questions. If the first, we have identified a genuine case of disagreement; if the second, we have what is strictly speaking not a genuine disagreement at all but a case of cross-purposes, where each is giving a different answer to the question as to what the question they are disagreeing over happens to be. The English literary critic F. R. Leavis suggested at one place that critical inquiry proceeds as if one person declares to another 'This is so, isn't it?', and the other replies 'Yes, but . . .'.[4] When A declares 'This is so, isn't it?' he has invited both the challenge and collaboration of others. B's yes in reply would indicate a certain agreement, while his 'but . . .' would indicate that the agreement was not total, that there perhaps is some case or circumstance to which what A has said will be found not to apply. In effect, the 'but . . .' amounts to being a fresh 'This is so, isn't it?', inviting in turn the collaboration and challenge of A, and so on. Applying such a scheme to our example of a simple debate over economic policy, we would obtain an abstract form of the following sort:

$A : n^1$.
$B :$ Why $n^1$?
$A :$ Given $n^2$, $p^1$ implies $n^1$.
$B :$ Granted $(p^1)$, but why $n^2$?
$A :$ Given $n^3$, $p^2$ implies $n^2$.
$B :$ Granted $(p^1, p^2)$, but why $n^3$?
$A :$ Given $n^4$, $p^3$ implies $n^3$.
$B :$ Granted $(p^1, p^2, p^3)$, but why $n^4$?

A can think B to be stupid or stubborn or self-seeking, and B can think the same of A, and neither or one or both of them may be partly or wholly correct in thinking so, and all these may be facts which go to explaining *how* their dispute actually happens to proceed or fail to proceed over time – yet the correct answer, the most reasonable and justifiable answer, to the question to which different answers may be given at any stage will be independent of all this. We should want to distinguish, in short, questions of the logic of thought from questions in the history of thought.

Thus if someone becomes persuaded to a moderate moral scepticism only through observing that *as a matter of fact* many normative disputations seem heated or interminable, then we need only to demonstrate that such an observation does not and should not be allowed to bear upon the theory of knowledge or epistemology we come to hold. Certainly the scope of objective reasoning may be found to be finite in practice in actual disagreements and disputations between people, because there happens to be a lack of patience or good humour or tolerance or perseverance or whatever. But from that it does not follow at all that there is no further room for discussion, or indeed that reasoning cannot be thought of as being of potentially indefinite scope.

If however, as seems equally likely, the economists who have endorsed a humean theory of knowledge have meant it to be possible not only in practice but also *in principle* for the scope of objective reasoning to become exhausted, then a much more serious claim would have been made, which deserves appropriately more rigorous scrutiny. It would then have been claimed that it is logically possible for A and B to be in total and justifiable agreement about *all* the empirical evidence and about *every* logical relation, and still for each to declare in favour of a sheer and contradictory 'ultimate' value.

B : Granted $(p^1, p^2, p^3, \ldots, p^{\omega-2})$, but why $n^{\omega-1}$?

A : Given $n^\omega$, $p^{\omega-1}$ implies $n^{\omega-1}$.

B : Granted $(p^1, p^2, p^3, \ldots, p^{\omega-2}, p^{\omega-1})$; but why $n^\omega$?

A : $n^\omega$ that's why! (Go jump in the lake if you don't accept it too.)

B : I deny $n^\omega$ that's all! (And it's you who can jump in the lake.)

Not only in practice but also in principle the scope of common reasoning would be supposed to have a finite limit. Not only is it a handicap we have to live with that many disputes between economists or scientists or citizens or spouses or nation-states *do* come to a halt without full and justifiable resolution, through lack of patience or tolerance or good humour or whatever, but it is *inevitable* that common reasoning will become exhausted and only sheer and unadulterated differences remain over 'basic' or 'ultimate' values over which only the irrational holds sway. Hume and Hare among philosophers certainly may be interpreted to have taken such a view, and, on the basis of the writings quoted in Chapter 2, it would not be unfair to interpret at least some of the economists to have meant the same. However no proof or example of the existence of a sheer dispute over 'basic' or 'ultimate' values between people who are in justifiable agreement over everything else, has ever been offered by Hume or any philosopher or economist after him. It seems merely to have been asserted or taken for granted that a point can come where the scope of reason must have become exhausted and nothing further could remain to be said or done.[5]

**4.** We are in position to have a clear sighting at last of the first major hazard which is present on the humean course: It is possible that the declared purpose of the humean economist of extending objectivity and thwarting dogmatism will be contradicted by an ultimate adoption of irrationality and personal dogmatism. Huge and invaluable edifices of inquiry and argument can crumble to the ground because the scope of reasoning must sooner or later become exhausted, and mere personal prejudice take its place. The presence of a single 'ought' would signal the presence of another, and then another, and another . . . until some set of private moral primes or absolutes or supreme principles are supposed to be reached, which others might or might not share but which are in any event beyond further question. According to the received theory of knowledge, the economist is ultimately able only to persuade or coax or cajole or perhaps bribe others into accepting the absolutes he may himself wish to endorse, but common reasoning is of no further avail. Sooner or later the advice of the expert economist *cannot but* express the personal dogmas and prejudices of the adviser (or those of his employer).

It was a tension of this kind in the humean doctrine that Professor Samuelson may have felt when he called it a 'somewhat schizophrenic rule' even as he endorsed it in the passage quoted in Chapter 2. Yet while Samuelson was not afraid to describe the role of the economist in society that follows from the humean thesis, he did not see the paradox to which it leads. Following Robbins and in keeping with the modern theory of economic policy, Samuelson said that we should keep distinct the economist *qua* scientist from the economist *qua* citizen. The former expresses objective knowledge ('pure analysis'), the latter expresses subjective opinions ('propaganda, condemnations and policy recommendations'). Thus when Professor Samuelson himself writes from his offices at the Massachusetts Institute of Technology, we must take him to be doing so *qua* rational, objective, scientific economist, while if the very same person writes from his home *qua* citizen of the United States, we must take him to be expressing a subjective and possibly irrational personal point of view. Or must Samuelson expect himself to sign and stamp everything he writes *either* as being a claim to objective knowledge made by the eminent economist which he is and deserving the world's attention, *or* as being a subjective and possibly irrational opinion expressed by the ordinary citizen and human being which he also is, and perhaps not deserving nearly as much of the world's attention? What would happen if the same human being came to say the same thing in both scientific and civic capacities? Clearly we would be in a quandary of having to decide whether it should be considered objective or subjective, public knowledge or private opinion, rational or irrational, economic science or personal prejudice. In the previous chapter we have seen that the humean economist is likely to want to sharply contrast his theory of the role of economic expertise with the famous theory given by Plato in *Republic*. Now we are able to see that there seems to be a less well known similarity too between the moral scepticism of the humean and the moral absolutism of the platonist. For just as in Plato's theory so in the modern humean theory, there is evidently no way of telling from within the theory *who* is supposed to be the expert. Either the humean has to join the platonist whom he takes to be his enemy and declare there to be some arbitrary and unspecified way of distinguishing expert from layman, philosopher from commoner. Or the humean has to part company with Plato and the scholastics, and say that there is ultimately no objective distinction possible between knowledge and opinion, expert and layman, science and prejudice. What appears to be at stake when the merits of the humean epistemology are brought under critical scrutiny in this way, therefore, is nothing less than whether there ultimately *can* be objective knowledge in economics; and so, whether or not the economist *can* rightly consider himself to be a seeker after such knowledge – or whether we are all involved merely in some highly evolved and sophisticated branch of rhetoric, having 'the semblance of wisdom without the reality' whose teacher and practitioner is just 'one who makes money from an apparent but unreal wisdom.'[6]

**5.** The problem we are observing here with the received theory of economic knowledge can be placed in relief by comparing the moderate moral sceptic with his more radical cousin, the emotivist. For the emotivist is one who flatly denies there to be any scope at all for common reasoning to occur upon normative questions, maintaining instead that normative propositions amount only to being the expressions of personal feeling or emotive attitude. Thus a statement like 'the government should reduce ṁ from 6 per cent to 3 per cent' would be taken by the emotivist to express merely the personal feelings or preferences of the individual, its full meaning and implications being equally well described if the speaker had said 'I wish the government would reduce ṁ from 6 per cent to 3 per cent', just as someone might say 'I wish to have my coffee black' or 'I don't like boiled vegetables' or 'I like to wear colourful shirts'.

Now the feelings and emotions and attitudes of a speaker or author may be naturally and normally involved in the making of evaluative or prescriptive statements, in a way they may not be in the making of logical or empirical statements. When I propose something should be done I must *mean* what I say, or I would not be being sincere: what I outwardly expressed would be incongruent with what I inwardly felt, I would be engaged in a kind of self-contradiction or inner dissonance. Yet this sort of involvement of matters of personal sincerity and authenticity in the making of normative judgements does not imply that these are all that is involved, or even the most important of what is involved, or that common reasoning cannot make headway in normative discussion. The emotivist correctly observes the involvement of the emotions in normative discussion but exaggerates its significance, perhaps by the confounding of simple and literal uses of concepts like 'taste' and 'preference' as in 'I have a taste for ice-cream' or 'I prefer my vegetables lightly cooked' with looser and more metaphorical and so more complex uses of the same concepts like 'I prefer Truman to Dewey' or 'I have no taste for public executions'.[7] Where the moderate moral sceptic supposes a residue of irrational difference to remain *after* every relevant empirical and logical question has been answered, the emotivist wants to call a halt the instant a normative proposition is sighted. The difference is one of degree and not of kind. If a moderate moral sceptic like R. M. Hare or Milton Friedman or Joan

Robinson remonstrated with the emotivist saying 'Look, you really should try to bring to bear as much logic and evidence as you possibly can in a normative dispute', the emotivist has only to coolly reply 'Sorry, but what you have just said is patently normative. Since, as you know, I take *all* normative propositions to amount to being expressions of personal taste or emotive attitude, I cannot take what you have said to be anything more than that either. That does not mean I cannot share the same emotive attitude as you, but that is no reason to think we can construct an objective justification for it.' The humean can bang his head in frustration at the emotivist's behaviour, but he may not without circularity argue against it.

A more dramatic illustration of this sort of difficulty with the humean doctrine may be found in the writings of Hare and Popper, suggesting that even the most tough-minded and critical of moral sceptics may have allowed themselves to admit an ultimate irrationalism. Hare considers a fanatic who so fervently believes some group of innocent people should be put to death that he is prepared to be made such a victim himself if his own ancestors transpired to be of the same group. And the fanatic is closed to all further discussion of the matter. This, Hare takes it, would be a case of an ultimate value judgement, impervious both in practice and in principle to further question. Hare says that 'fortunately' there are few fanatics who would be found to hold such an 'extreme' position, leaving unsaid that if they were found then they should be just as entitled to their opinion as anyone else – not merely in the sense of having a legal right to hold such an opinion but in the more significant sense that such an opinion ultimately must be considered to be just as good, just as reasonable, just as cogent, just as sound, as its contrary.[8] We could try to persuade or cajole or bribe our fanatic to give up his opinion and to hold ours, but there is no way for us to say he is simply wrong in his belief. If it turned out there were more fanatics than there were of us, it could of course become their turn to persuade or cajole or bribe us away from our opinions, yet none of their acts could be condemned, since, in the last analysis, there cannot be any such thing as moral knowledge.

Popper has written frankly that he knows of no rational grounds for recommending a rational temperament: 'It is impossible to determine ends scientifically. There is no scientific way of choosing between two ends. Some people, for example, love and venerate violence. For them a life without violence would be shallow and trivial. Many others, of whom I am one, hate violence. This is a quarrel about ends. It cannot be decided by science. . . . you cannot, by means of argument, convert those who suspect all argument, and who prefer violent decisions to rational decisions. You cannot prove to them that they are wrong. . . .' 'I frankly confess that I choose rationalism because I hate violence, and I do not deceive myself into believing that this hatred has any rational grounds. Or to put it another way, my rationalism is not self-contained, but rests on an irrational faith in the attitude of reasonableness. I do not see that we can go beyond this.'[9] But if Popper is entitled to have an irrational faith in being reasonable, then the fanatic is surely entitled as well to have an irrational faith in being unreasonable. Thus Professor Max Black responds on behalf of the fanatic who engages Popper thus: 'Bravo! You hate violence, but I hate argument (a sneaking use of force by other means). You call me irrational, but I glory in that title. Like you, I hold that there are no ultimate *reasons* for my irrationality (for that would detract from the purity of my position). The difference between us is like that between a Protestant and a Catholic: your faith is my heresy; my faith is your heresy. That's all there is to say.'[10] (Yet Black himself does not say why differences between Protestant and Catholic must be supposed beyond discussion!)

**6.** This kind of internal contradiction we are observing here to be associated with moral scepticism can be seen in a slightly more positive light as well. For we may ask, what does the moral sceptic's recognition that dogma and tyranny should not be imposed upon science or the individual amount to except a manifest example of a *moral* recognition? Or a proposal that the integrity of science as well as the freedom of the individual as consumer and voter should be preserved, except a manifest example of a *moral* proposal? All the economists quoted in Chapter 2 have recommended and practised the extension of the scope of common reasoning in economic science; what sort of recommendation would that be except a patently *moral* recommendation? When the theory of economic policy requires the economist to respect the ends of the elected politician, what sort of a premise does that rest upon except a *moral* premise that the institutions of constitutional democracy should be respected and not abused? It would presuppose in turn such things as that parliamentary elections do take place periodically and are in fact genuine and not fraudulent elections, that citizens will be judicious and well enough informed in their voting so that a good indication of what things are conducive to the common welfare will come to be determined as closely as possible given the size and diversity of the electorate, that the policies of a resulting administration are sincere attempts to reflect the ends chosen by the voters, that candidates for elected office and private citizens and scientists and scholars and others are not subject to being shot or jailed or persecuted for saying publicly what they think these ends should or should not be, and so on.[11] It is implicitly or explicitly *within* the context of a free and open society, and one which probably has working democratic institutions, that the modern theory of economic policy makes sense at all, that positive questions like 'Does the evidence support the hypothesis that reducing $\dot{m}$ from 6 per cent to 3 per cent is necessary and/or sufficient to reduce $\dot{p}$?' are supposed to be discussed in the first place. Regardless of what the humean economist happens to say or suppose himself to be doing or not doing by adopting the theory of knowledge which he does, we are entitled to conclude that he is in fact far from asserting there cannot be any such thing as objective moral knowledge – since he himself may have advanced his moral scepticism precisely upon substantive moral grounds. Put differently, it does not seem possible without contradiction to start with a set of moral premises and arrive at a conclusion that there cannot be moral knowledge.

Equally, if the received theory of economic policy must presuppose a context of a free and open society and working democratic institutions, then it would seem it must be silent where such a context cannot be presumed. When we consider that most societies most of the time probably have not been very open or very democratic (and in such a count we must consider societies not only on the scale of nation-states but also families and clubs and corporations and university departments and armies and religions, and so on) this would at once make the received theory one of quite special and contingent application. Indeed it is a theory which must be silent about the appropriate role of the expert not only under conditions of tyranny (Solzhenitsyn: 'The prison doctor was the interrogator's and executioner's right-hand man. The beaten prisoner would come to on the floor only to hear the doctor's voice: "You can continue, the pulse is normal"'[12]), but also where the duly elected government of an open and democratic society proceeded to do things patently wrong or tyrannical (the imprisonment of the Japanese Americans). Hence Popper's 'paradox of democracy' and 'tyranny of the majority'.[13] It is ironic that the economist who may have adopted a humean epistemology as a reaction to dogmatism and tyranny in the first place, will come to be prevented by his own moral scepticism from condemning an act of tyranny whether it is committed in the name of the popular will or by an outright despotism. A theory of economic policy which both assumes a free and open society and bases itself upon a moral scepticism cannot have anything to say ultimately about the objective reasons *why* a free and open society may be preferred to an unfree or closed society, or about the good or bad outcomes that may be produced by the working of democratic processes.

A parallel difficulty arises for the humean economist with respect to market institutions and their possible outcomes. Ultimately, the received theory of economic knowledge cannot allow that there may be *objective* reasons why market institutions may be preferable (or not preferable) to non-market ones, whether one is speaking roughly and generally in a theory of political economy or more precisely and specifically about some actual set of concrete circumstances. Just as the medieval scholastics might have said that a good was a good only because the church said it was a good, so the modern humeans may have to say that a good is a good only because market forces have made it a good – i.e., because it happens to have a positive price in an equilibrium of supply and demand. And just as the church may have said a lot of things were goods which were indeed good, so market forces may make a lot of things goods which indeed *are* good – for instance, food, clothing and shelter, because they are conducive to some valuable human purpose. But also, just as there could have been things which the church said were good but were not, and things which were good but which the church said were not, so it is not at all hard for any of us to find in experience things which the market may have put a high value on but which were not in fact valuable, as well as things which the market did not value but which were indeed valuable.

**7.** Drawing these simple threads together then, a first set of reasons why the modern economist may think himself poorly served by a subjectivist theory of knowledge has to do with the fact that it is a theory which falters and fails even in its own declared or understated purpose of being an adequate shield against dogmatism and tyranny. In a theory in which nothing, ultimately, can be considered objectively right, it cannot be objectively right to extend the scope of reasoning in economics, or to preserve the integrity of science, or to protect the individual from dogmatism or tyranny. In a theory in which nothing, ultimately, can be considered objectively wrong, it cannot be wrong to block or subvert reason or to force dogma and tyranny upon science or the individual. If all moral propositions are ultimately taken to be matters of mere personal opinion, then the defence of individual freedom or the integrity of science also must be taken ultimately to be matters of mere personal opinion. Professor Arrow remarks: 'The only rational defense of a liberal position . . . is that it is itself a value judgment.'[14] Combine with this the idea that judgements are subjective, and you would have the result that no objective justification can be given ultimately for a liberal position, or for any other position either for that matter. When all has been said and done, protecting individual freedom is no better or worse than attacking it, preserving the integrity of science is no better or worse than destroying it. 'Nothing is good or bad, but thinking makes it so.' Such fragile things as the preservation of human freedom and the integrity of science would seem to have been left exposed by the accepted epistemology in twentieth-century economics to the shifting whims of popular opinion. The purposes that many eminent economists may have had in adopting the humean thesis, and these may have been invaluable purposes, would seem to be able to be fulfilled only in a theory which denies the humean thesis that nothing can be right or wrong but thinking makes it so.

**8.** We have now sketched the first important set of dangers that are present on the humean course which has been adopted by modern economists. There happens also to be a second set with equally serious implications, calling for us to continue to move as carefully and precisely as possible. The reader who may have been unconvinced by the argument so far will therefore have a fresh set of challenges to consider, while the author will have to ask for the patience of the reader who may have agreed that there does happen to be something wrong at the foundations of the received theory of economic knowledge.

In short, there is the problem that an adoption of moral scepticism on its own may lead by parity of reasoning to *total* scepticism, to the 'pyrrhonism' which Hume himself had drawn back from.[15] For what will come to be noticed by the truly serious and tough-minded sceptic is that the general logic employed in Hume's First Law is in fact extremely powerful, more powerful than Hume or the modern humean economist may wish or intend it to be. For the tough-minded sceptic will look at Hume's First Law and say: Why stop at ethics? Why so half-hearted? That it is not legitimate to deduce one kind of statement from another kind of statement is surely an argument of more general application. Just as a sceptical attack can be launched upon the possibility of ethics, so why not launch sceptical attacks everywhere: on the possibilities of science and history and induction and deduction and *everything*? In particular, the tough-minded sceptic will say to the humean economist: 'Why do you stop with normative economics? – Surely you can and you must destroy all of positive economics as well!'

It was shown some years ago by the English philosopher John Wisdom how sceptical attacks analogous to Hume's attack on ethics in fact can be made in a number of other contexts as well. Let us consider an example similar to one given by Wisdom to show how easily it may be possible to proceed to be sceptical of something so obvious as our knowledge of the past.[16] A sceptic says 'Do we really know anything about what has happened in the past? Can we be certain about anything that has happened at all before this very instant?' You say to him 'What do you mean? Surely you don't mean that while we know some things for certain such as that we are now having this conversation, we don't know for certain other things such as that we did get up from bed this morning or that Nazi Germany did invade Poland on 1 September 1939?' The sceptic says 'Yes, that's the kind of thing I mean.' You reply 'Well, that's crazy. I for one am just as confident of knowing that here I am talking with you now, as I am that I got up this morning, as indeed I am that Nazi Germany invaded Poland on 1 September 1939.' The sceptic says 'Please tell me how you can be so certain you got up this morning.' Staring at him in disbelief, you reply 'Look, I usually get up to the alarm clock at 7 a.m.; this morning was no different; I remember the clock going at 7 a.m. as usual, and I got up. That's all there is to it.' The sceptic makes a flanking movement. 'If you remember something taking place you would of course imply the event did take place?' You are now perhaps quite irritated by this odd fellow – 'Obviously; I could not have remembered the alarm clock going off if it had not in fact gone off.' But in fact the sceptic has got you exactly in his sights and can move in for the kill. 'In that case it appears to me you have missed the point of my original question completely. I wished to know how we can know anything about the past. You gave me an example that you knew you had gotten up this morning, and that you knew this for certain because the alarm clock had gone off as usual and that you remembered getting up when it did. I can agree of course that *if* you knew this premise to be true *then* you are entitled to deduce that you know you did get up this morning. But you will have to grant that this is a premise which *itself* refers to the past. So all you would have done in supporting one statement about the past is to have given me another statement about the past, when the point of my question was to ask how we can know *anything* at all about the past for certain.'

Just as the fact that we cannot deduce a normative conclusion without a normative premise having been made might lead someone to a moral scepticism, so the fact we cannot deduce a conclusion about the past without a premise about the past being made might lead someone to a historical scepticism. That Nazi Germany did invade Poland on 1 September 1939 cannot be deduced except by reference to other historical premises – films and photographs of the dive-bombers going in against the Polish Cavalry, government documents, the testimony of eye-witnesses, reports in the newspapers of 2 September 1939, etc. The sceptic agrees that *if* the premises were known to be true *then* the conclusion would be true as well, but he says that that would be to miss his point. Like the moral sceptic, he is challenging the possibility of our knowledge of *all* propositions of a particular kind, and it is no use giving him for his scepticism what amounts to merely another proposition of the same kind. Bambrough has put the matter clearly thus: 'So long as the premises used in support of a proposition include any propositions of the same type as itself, a philosophical sceptic, or any other enquirer who is determined to seek the ultimate grounds, is properly dissatisfied, since his question is about how propositions of that whole type are to be validated, and he cannot consistently permit any such proposition to be unproblematic when it occurs among the premises of an argument whose conclusion is of the same type . . . . the grounds offered for a proposition of kind *k* will necessarily be either of kind *k* or not of kind *k*; if they are of kind *k* they may be logically sufficient for the proposition that they are intended to support, but a further question will arise about the validation of the premises themselves; if on the other hand they are not of kind *k* then they necessarily cannot be logically sufficient for the truth of the proposition that they are intended to support.'[17]

Yet once this box has been opened, we are obliged to examine all its contents, and there are quite a number. For one thing we may now join with the sceptic of the senses and cast doubt on all the knowledge the natural sciences purport to provide of the physical world; since, surely, no conclusion about the physical world can be deduced without a premise about the physical world having been made. Next we might join with the solipsist and question the possibility of knowledge in psychology, doubting whether one can ever know what someone else thinks or feels; since, surely, no conclusion about a mind other than one's own can be deduced without a premise of the same sort having been made. It is this species of scepticism which forms the basis of the widespread belief in modern economics of the impossibility of interpersonal comparisons of utility, which we observed in discussing the views of Professor Hicks in Chapter 2 and to which we shall be returning in Chapter 10. Then of course there is Hume himself being just as famous for his sceptical attack on the possibility of induction as he is for his attack on the possibility of ethics: 'there can be no demonstrative arguments to prove, that those instances of which we have had no experience resemble those of which we have had experience.' 'Nay, I will go farther, and assert, that [reason alone] could not so much as prove by any probable arguments, that the future must be conformable to the past. All probable arguments are built on the supposition, that there is this conformity betwixt the future and the past, and therefore can never prove it. This conformity is a matter of fact, and if it must be proved, will admit of no proof but from experience. But our experience of the past can be a proof of nothing for the future, but upon a supposition, that there is a resemblance betwixt them. This therefore is a point, which can admit of no proof at all, and which we can take for granted without any proof.'[18] In short, no conclusion about the future can be deduced without at least one premise about the future having been made.

And then again, the full force of the sceptical onslaught can be felt when we direct its method against that of which we might seem most certain of all: the procedure of deduction itself in logic and mathematics. Adapting an example given by Wisdom and Bambrough, we can see how it may not be possible without circularity to use deductive reasoning to justify deduction itself.

For consider the propositions *All firms maximize profits* and *GM is a firm*. We would be normally inclined to think *GM maximizes profits* is something which follows from these. But the serious sceptic can once more ask how we may justify such a conclusion. We might be inclined to take such a challenge lightly, and try to dismiss it by stating a general rule of the form: 'If all *S* is *P*, and *x* is *S*, then *x* is *P*.' But that would be a mistake and we would have fallen directly for the trap set for us, since the sceptic would need only to make the following decisive response: 'A rule of this sort must necessarily either exclude or include the particular case at hand. If it is intended to exclude this particular case but is intended to apply to every other case, then clearly I need not accept in this case that the conclusion *GM maximizes profits* follows from the premises *All firms maximize profits* and *GM is a firm*. On the other hand, if the rule is intended to include this case as well, then you are asking me to reason as follows: "In all syllogisms, deduction proceeds like this; this is a syllogism; therefore, deduction proceeds like this here as well." All you would have done in trying to justify the deduction at hand is to have given me yet another deduction against which all my arguments would apply with equal force once more. You may not mind arguing in a circle but I am not going to join you.' If making an is-ought dualism is sufficient ground for us to doubt the possibility of moral knowledge, then we seem now to have just as good grounds to doubt we can know anything at all.

The upshot of these kinds of sceptical attacks on the practice of modern economics may be seen quite readily. For consider the fact that it would be difficult to overestimate the significance to the practice of modern economic science of (i) the elementary mathematical concept of a function, mapping all the values taken by one variable $X$ upon a range of values taken by another variable $Y$, and (ii) the formal and informal procedures of statistical inference. Yet at their foundations, all procedures of statistical inference must rest upon the possibility of a rational induction. Suppose there was some economic variable $Y$ which has been found to take a particular value in each of the last 100 or 200 or 300 or 500 periods. Or suppose it is found in each of a large number of observations that $Y$ happens to be systematically related by some identifiable functional form to another economic variable $X$. It will be seldom if ever that we shall be obliged with such neat data, but it will be readily agreed that the study of such relationships whether in economic theory or in economic history or in applied economics or in econometrics constitutes the very stuff of the modern science. The variable $Y$ might be the quantity traded of a good where $X$ is the market price, or $Y$ the long-term interest rate and $X$ the state of expectations, or $Y$ the change in the price and $X$ the difference between quantity demanded and quantity supplied, or $Y$ the rate of inflation and $X$ the money supply, and so on indefinitely in hundreds of different contexts. If we are genuinely serious about adopting a humean scepticism – that is, adopting it consistently, without contradiction – then we must lead ourselves to conclude that even with 1000 observations of $Y$ taking a certain value (or a value in a certain interval) after $X$ had taken a certain value (or a value in a certain interval), we would still have no grounds, no *deductive* grounds, for predicting the value of $Y$ given the 1001st observation of $X$. From *no* amount of past evidence can *any* proposition about the present or the future be deduced. Equally, if we were to prevent ourselves out of a debilitating scepticism of this kind from employing the *modus ponens* of deductive reasoning – if all $S$ is $P$, and $x$ is $S$, then $x$ is $P$ – then all reasoning in economic theory would immediately come to a standstill. Without induction and deduction, we cannot proceed in economics or elsewhere: it would be not only normative economics but *all* of economics which would come to be lost in the whirlpools of scepticism.[19]

The point the sceptic wishes to make is that we cannot *deduce* one kind of proposition from an altogether different kind of proposition – the is-ought dualism may be a useful reminder that we cannot *deduce* a normative conclusion from any number of positive premises. Every normative conclusion must have had at least one normative premise, and it is the attempt to justify one normative proposition by offering another as a premise that allows the moral sceptic to keep repeating the challenge indefinitely. But that does not prevent us from asking whether the sceptic has not skewed the rules of the game in such a way that he must always win, and if he has done so, we can certainly decline to play. For what the sceptic seems to require is that the grounds for any kind of justification specifically be deductive grounds. We are to *deduce* every proposition as the descendant of other higher or more primitive propositions, which might explain how the sceptic is able to raise the threat of an infinite regress in every field in which he attacks. 'Everything we offer and everything we could conceivably offer is either too little or too much. . . . Nothing will ever do to meet the sceptic's requirement. But that is different from saying nothing will ever do.'[20] Perhaps it is not necessary to meet the sceptic's requirement. Perhaps it is not even possible to do so. Perhaps we do not *have* to have a deductive proof to justify that we can and we do know *some* things in science, in history, in ethics, in psychology, in economics, or that we can and do frequently and reliably use inductive reasoning in these and a hundred other contexts. In Part II we shall be making an argument on these lines more fully to show how scepticism can be avoided even as we steer well clear of the opposite dangers of dogmatism. What is important here is only to notice the slide into total scepticism that may be entailed by adopting moral scepticism on its own. The economist who accepts an is-ought dualism as an adequate reason for adopting a subjectivist theory of knowledge comes to face an unhappy choice between *either* becoming, in the interest of consistency, a sceptic of *all* of economics – theory, history, econometrics, everything, not to mention everything else outside economics as well like natural science and mathematics and history; *or* denying the parity of reasoning, and not having adequate grounds for believing objectivity is possible in one context but not another. Either accept the propositions of positive economics and natural science and mathematics and history etc. to be, in the final analysis, *just as* subjective as normative propositions. The infinite regress threatens everywhere, what is sauce for the goose is sauce for the gander, so there cannot be objective knowledge of any kind anywhere. The economist slides into a scepticism about *everything* – into the pyrrhonism which Hume himself had rejected. Or become a partial and prejudiced sceptic like the positivist – led to the inconsistency of threatening only normative propositions with infinite regress when analogous sceptical attacks can be made with equal force in any number of non-normative contexts as well, and therefore not having adequate reason to maintain objective knowledge to be possible in contexts other than ethics. When asked 'Can there be objective knowledge in economics?' if we answer 'No, truth is defined merely by agreement of opinions; we know a proposition in economics to be true only insofar as economists happened to agree it to be true; if such agreement fails to hold in the future the proposition would no longer be true', we next may be asked 'Can there be objective knowledge in physics?', to which we can only reply yes or no. If yes, we shall have said that there is merely rhetoric in economics, perhaps a highly evolved and sophisticated rhetoric but mere rhetoric nevertheless, certainly not objective knowledge. We would justify the cynic and the cartoonist who mock economists as the most querulous of breeds, for every one who says this there is another who says that, how it is entirely a matter of caprice or fashion or pecuniary interest which side one happens to take, whose 'paradigm' one happens to accept. We should have to admit frankly to the scholarly community that since there is nothing which may be properly called objective knowledge in economics, the Department of Economics in every university should be closed down, or that there might just as well be a Department of Astrology on campus too, teaching and researching the reading of palms, the writing of horoscopes, and so on. On the other hand, if we denied there to be objective knowledge possible of the physical world as well, if we said we cannot be certain of such things as that there is a table in this room or that the window is open and there is a tree outside it, then we would have to do battle not only with every scientist in history but also with the man on the street, whose commonsense like our own tells us the opposite.

It is said that Hume thought himself leaving his scepticism behind when he left his study. Yet '[his] scepticism is at odds with his actions even when he is at his most deliberately and consciously philosophical. His pen goes confidently to the ink-pot, he turns the pages of Sextus Empiricus with the well grounded expectation that Book II will be found between Books I and III . . . . it is shown by his *life* that he believes what he is trying to doubt.'[21] Just as surely as the scholastics fell under the Spell of Plato, so modern economists may have fallen under the Spell of Hume. The time has come at last to see how both spells may be broken.

# PART II

# 5

# *Objectivity and Freedom*

Suppose there was a philosopher who addressed modern economists in a strange way as follows:

> Consider the entities that we call 'firms'. I mean banks, manufacturers, airlines, law partnerships, farms, grocery-stores, and so on. What is common to them all? – Don't say: 'There *must* be something in common, or they would not be called "firms" ' – but *look and see* whether there is anything in common to all. – For if you look at them you will not see something that is common to *all*, but similarities, relationships, and a whole series of them at that. To repeat: don't think, but look! – Look for example at banks with their multifarious relationships. Now pass to savings and loans associations; here you find many correspondences with the first group, but many common features drop out, and others appear. When we pass next to manufacturers and transporters, much that is common is retained, but much is lost. – Are they all 'profit-maximizing'? Compare the taxi company with the electricity company. Or is there always a separation of ownership from management? Think of the tailor's shop at the corner. With corporations there is the buying and selling of shares; but when a farmer is offered a price for his homestead this feature too may have disappeared. Look at the part played by entrepreneurship; and at the difference between the entrepreneurship of a mom-and-pop shop and the entrepreneurship of a firm of lobbyists. Think now of firms like

73

General Motors; here is the element of giant size, but how many other characteristic features have disappeared! And we can go through the many, many other groups of firms in the same way; can see how similarities crop up and disappear.

What should we think of such a strange philosopher? And what answer is to be made to him by the economist?

The philosopher is Ludwig Wittgenstein, and the passage which has been paraphrased here, odd though it may seem, is among the most famous in twentieth-century philosophy, from his posthumous work *Philosophical Investigations*.[1] The problem that can be found to be raised in it is the ancient problem of universals, the problem of the One and the Many, of Unity and Diversity: Must all instances of a general term or concept have anything in common, over and above the fact they are all instances of the same concept? Must all firms have anything in common, over and above the fact they are all firms? Must all red things have anything in common, over and above the fact they are all red things? Certainly we know there to be individual red things like red poppies and red roses and red corpuscles and redheads and Red Square, and we know there to be individual firms like General Motors and Mitsubishi and Kodak and the corner grocery-store. But how is each individual red thing related to the general concept 'Red'? How are General Motors, Mitsubishi, the corner-store etc. each related to the general concept 'Firm'? Should we think of red poppies and red corpuscles and redheads as each sharing or partaking of some transcendental property – a universal – called 'Redness'? Should we think of General Motors and Mitsubishi and the corner-store as each sharing or partaking of some universal called 'Firmhood'? Would it be because they do that we call a red thing red or a firm a firm?

Interpreting Wittgenstein's passage in this way, one response that might be made to it would be this: 'What you seem to be doing is to test whether there is any property common to all firms. However, as your example suggests, individual firms are actually indefinitely varied – in their goals, constraints, size, type of ownership, operating characteristics, and so on. (Even if they were not indefinitely varied as a matter of fact, we can certainly imagine them being indefinitely varied in principle.) Indeed so

74

much do individual firms vary that, in my opinion, we should not think there to be anything at all in common to all of them, besides of course our arbitrary decision to call them all "firms".' Let us call such a reply the reply of the *Nominalist*.

But another response to the same passage could go like this: 'I agree that what you are trying to suggest is that there is no common property between all the things we call firms. But surely in applying the concept "firm" we must have an objective justification. For instance, while we do and we may apply the concept to General Motors and to Mitsubishi and to the corner-store, we do not and may not apply it just arbitrarily to any old thing at all – such as to my umbrella or to the number sixteen or to Harry Truman or to the characters in a Dickens novel. Even when people refer to modern Japan as "Japan Inc.", what they mean is that some analogy can be drawn between the way a firm works and the way political and economic arrangements in Japan seem to work, not that Japan is *literally* a firm, for that would be absurd since Japan is not a firm but a sovereign nation-state, a parliamentary democracy, a former Axis power, etc., and to call her a firm would be an objective misuse of language. It is likely that a property common to all individual firms does exist, and indeed it seems to me it is precisely because it does exist, whether or not we have been able to identify it, that we are entitled to call all firms "firms", and so distinguish what *are* firms, such as General Motors and Mitsubishi and the corner-store, from what are *not* firms, such as Harry Truman or my umbrella or the nation-state of Japan.' Let us call such a reply the reply of the *Realist*.

The Nominalist stresses the Many – he is the lover of Freedom and Diversity, and the enemy of all Dogmatism and Conformity. He looks and insists that we look at the vast *differences* there are or can be – between firms, in the uses of words and concepts, across ways of life and culture, in the histories of nations, in the circumstances and personalities of individuals. The Realist worries about the indiscipline and caprice that can result from the exaggeration or corruption of freedom. He recognizes and insists that we recognize the vast areas of *commonality* there are or can be. We use words and language only because there are objective or 'intersubjective' (Popper) ways of speaking and understanding. No matter how diverse individual personalities or circumstances or ways of life may be, the fact is we belong to one species (or one genus etc.), which implies something different from if we had not. The Realist stresses the One; he is the lover of Objectivity and Reason, and the enemy of all Scepticism.

A similar division may be made to obtain with any of a number of other concepts in economics as well – 'capital', 'money', 'utility', 'competitive market', 'unemployment', 'development', 'mixed economy', 'socialist economy', or any of a hundred others. In each case, the plea of the Nominalist would be that we observe the differences between the individual instances, the plea of the Realist that we respect the similarities. Indeed what should be supposed to be in common between individual economists themselves? From Aaron, Abramovitz and Ackley, through Bagehot, Baran and Bauer, and Cantillon, Cassell and Cournot, all the way to Zeckhauser, Zellner and Zeuthen, what is there in common except that each happens to be listed in a recent bibliographic dictionary of economists? The Nominalist would say 'Nothing. Ultimately there is nothing in common to all economists except that we have chosen to call them all economists. That these people happen to be in the dictionary and other people like Picasso or Jesse Owens or Greta Garbo are not is, ultimately, just a matter of arbitrary choice.' The Realist would say 'Surely there must be *something* in common to all economists, otherwise we would not call them economists. We wouldn't in our right minds consider Picasso, Jesse Owens, or Greta Garbo to be economists, just as we wouldn't consider Wicksell, Keynes, or Milton Friedman to be famous artists, athletes, or cinema stars. There must be an objective justification to calling someone an economist – it must be that economists are economists because they all believe in $Q$'; where $Q$ would refer to some criterion like the practice of mathematical modelling, or an attribution of utility-maximization, or an attendance to statistical data, or a concern with the distribution of wealth and income. If someone did not believe in $Q$, did not fall under a specific definition of this kind, the Realist would be inclined to say such a person was not really an economist at all but something of an imposter or a charlatan who did not rightfully belong in the dictionary. And of course if one man chooses one $Q$ and another chooses another then we may begin to explain how each might think himself to fall under his own definition of economist while it was the other fellow who was the charlatan.

A similar division can be made to obtain upon the larger concept of science itself. The Nominalist would observe the rich and indefinite variety there is in the methods and subject-matter of the individual sciences, and indeed that there can be *within* any of the individual sciences as well – certainly within physics, chemistry, biology, and engineering but also within mathematics, law, medicine, economics, history, and philosophy itself. Dazzled by all the different colours and the different shades of different colours, the Nominalist would tend to conclude there to be no unifying characteristic between the sciences, nothing except that we have chosen to name them all sciences. The Realist for his part would observe and be impressed by the many points of comparison there are between and within the individual sciences. And being especially concerned to protect the concept of science from being hijacked and employed arbitrarily to just anything at all, the Realist will be in search of the common ingredient which he thinks must be present in each individual science to warrant our calling it a science at all. The Realist will be inclined to say that all scientific statements have *this* in common – where his *this* would now refer to something like 'hypothetico-deductive methodology', or the use of mathematics or deductive proof, or the empirical testability or falsifiability of propositions, or knowing the means of verification. The Realist searches for the criterion or set of criteria which he believes to be necessary to *demarcate* science from non-science (Popper), public knowledge from private opinion. And again, if one man chooses one criterion to demarcate science from non-science and another chooses another and contrary criterion, we can imagine the merry possibility of how each might think himself to fall under his own definition of scientist while really it is the other fellow who is the charlatan and the fraud.

Parallel to this kind of a division between Nominalism and Realism in the theory of existence occurs the division between Scepticism and Dogmatism in the theory of knowledge which we have met with in previous chapters. A Nominalist in ontology is likely also to be a Sceptic in epistemology, and a Realist in ontology is likely also to be a Dogmatist in epistemology and vice versa. C. S. Peirce had remarked that two points of contrast between scholastic and modern thought lay in the modern opinions that thought 'must begin with universal doubt, whereas scholasticism had never questioned fundamentals' and that 'the ultimate test of certainty is to be found in the individual consciousness; whereas scholasticism had relied on the testimony of sages and of the Catholic Church.'[2] The Dogmatist finds there are at least some things which are certainly known. Therefore, he concludes, it must be that we cannot question *every*thing, it must be that there are at least some propositions which should be supposed to be closed to further inquiry and discussion. Thus the medieval schoolmen would have supposed the Christian Scriptures to contain at least some propositions of this sort. Certainly there is scope to reason but it is a scope necessarily limited by the doctrines and dogmas of the faith. It would be precisely against this kind of a barrier being placed on the road of inquiry that the Sceptic protests. And finding there to be no human belief which must be thought of as closed to further question, the Sceptic concludes that it must be we cannot know *any*thing for certain. Each side seems to have a compelling reason in its favour yet to be in direct contradiction of the other. One asks for belief and conviction, the other for doubt and question. The feeling of an antinomy arises because we feel we must choose between them.

It was suggested in Chapter 3 that medieval political thinking was platonistic and absolutist in important respects, and evidence has been given in Chapter 2 that modern economists have adopted the sceptical humean epistemology which may be seen as a reaction to the medieval dogmatism. As Peirce's remarks make clear, this would not be a new thesis, though it is perhaps something which has not been adequately noticed before by modern economists and it has now been plainly set out. It is also a thesis which amounts to being a generalization, and suffers, as all generalizations must, from a lack of truth in its details, especially in not doing nearly enough justice to the depth and diversity of medieval thought.[3] Yet every generation must be concerned with identifying and correcting the errors of its own time, and the purpose of trying to establish even such a generalized thesis as this has been to correct contemporary errors: to argue that the humean foundations of the modern theory of economic knowledge entail serious difficulties, that it is these and not the is-ought dualism which turn out to be insurmountable, that the broad and long-standing consensus on the central question of the relationship between economic knowledge and economic advice, the positive and the normative, cannot be held consistently and deserves to be abandoned.

Nevertheless the reader who may have agreed with the drift of these arguments may wish to ask whether, in an attempt to correct contemporary errors, we shall not be led to commit the errors of an earlier time. Will we become Dogmatists if we renounce Scepticism? Are we forced to choose between Realist and Nominalist, Dogmatist and Sceptic, Plato and Hume? Must we *either* admit objectivity and reality and knowledge and expertise and common reasoning and commonsense, and suppress diversity and individuality and creativity and freedom and question and criticism; *or* embrace diversity and individuality and creativity and freedom and question and criticism, and abandon objectivity and reality and knowledge and expertise and common reasoning and commonsense? Can we lead our thinking lives coherently enough without making a choice, or would we find ourselves inevitably being shuttled between the rival parties, one moment in the Nominalist's camp, the next moment in the Realist's, one moment with the Sceptics, the next moment with the Dogmatists? If we decide to abandon Hume, is there no choice but Plato? If we find Plato's embrace too close and claustrophobic, is there no alternative but to continue to live in doubt with Hume? Are we caught between the Spell of Plato and the Spell of Hume? Is the choice: *Either* Objectivity *or* Freedom?

**2.** The simple answer that may be offered is that it is not. When objectivity and freedom, knowledge and doubt, have been carefully and adequately characterized, there is no conflict which must arise between them, whether in natural science, mathematics, ethics, history, economics, medicine, law, literature, or any other context of inquiry. There may be good reasons to be a Nominalist and also good reasons to be a Realist and yet better reasons to be neither. There may be good reasons to adopt a sceptical theory of knowledge and also good reasons to adopt a dogmatic theory of knowledge and yet better reasons to adopt neither. A course can be found which will allow us to steer clear of the hazards of Dogmatism on the one side while avoiding the whirlpools of Scepticism on the other.

How we may proceed to chart such a course is by airing and

exposing a hidden and questionable assumption which may be being shared by both Nominalist and Realist. Namely, an assumption that for a general term or concept like 'firm' or 'game' or 'science' to be objectively employed, there must also correspond some sort of *object*. Just as alcohol is common to whisky and beer and gin, so some common ingredient must be present in General Motors and Mitsubishi and the corner grocery-store in order to make them all firms. If such an assumption does happen to be at the source of the division between Nominalist and Realist, we might readily explain how it is that each seems plausible in part yet neither seems satisfactory as a whole. The Nominalist finds he cannot distil out any single common ingredient from all the particular instances of firms that there are or can be. But because he may be committed to an assumption that such an ingredient is necessary for the concept 'firm' to be objectively employed, he concludes it cannot be objectively employed. The Realist is certain the concept 'firm' can be objectively employed, and very certain it should not be arbitrarily employed, but because he too may be committed to the same assumption, he concludes there must be a common ingredient, a common 'essence' which every particular firm must share, prompting him to make a search for it or merely declare his faith in it being 'there', somewhere, 'out there'.[4]

Wittgenstein in his later works (as well as others before and after him such as H. A. Price) may be understood to have offered a suggestion that to make this kind of dualism between Nominalism and Realism is ultimately mistaken and misleading. After careful and detailed examination of a variety of the individual entities or institutions or activities which fall under a general concept like 'firm' or 'game' or 'competitive market' or 'mixed economy' or 'economist' or 'science', it may well be that we shall wish to make an entry in our notebooks of the following sort: 'We see a complicated network of similarities overlapping and criss-crossing: sometimes overall similarities, sometimes similarities in detail. I can think of no better expression to characterize these similarities than "family resemblances"; for the various resemblances between members of a family: build, features, colour of eyes, gait, temperament etc. etc. overlap and criss-cross in the same way.'[5] An alternative to a common ingredient model of the structure of concepts would be a *family resemblances* model, and an example constructed by Bambrough may easily illustrate its working. Suppose there to be five objects, A, B, C, D, E, each of which has four out of five possible properties, a, b, c, d, e. A pattern may be produced like

| object | A | B | C | D | E |
| --- | --- | --- | --- | --- | --- |
| properties | bcde | acde | abde | abce | abcd |

in which each object would evidently share 75 per cent of its properties with every other yet there would be no single property or set of properties common to all the objects. 'But if someone wished to say: "There is something in common to all these constructions – namely the disjunction of all their common properties" – I should reply: Now you are playing with words. One might as well say: "Something runs through the whole thread – namely the continuous overlapping of those fibres." '[6]

Many concepts, perhaps even most concepts, may be family resemblance concepts, their instances constituting 'a "family" of diverse things bundled together by virtue of shifting similarities'.[7] While there may be no single or *constant* similarity between all the individual instances of firms or games or economists or sciences or competitive markets or mixed economies, there may be diverse and *shifting* similarities between the different instances. It is these shifting similarities which can provide an adequate justification for supposing the different instances to fall under the same concept; while the recognition that there is no need for them to be anything but shifting in kind would equally justify not making a search for some mysterious essence which must be common to the individual instances. (We might even 'throw away the ladder' after we have climbed with it – for armed with such a model of the structure of concepts, we might even take Nominalism and Realism as family resemblance concepts themselves!)

A parallel observation is suggested about the division between Sceptic and Dogmatist, and a parallel resolution may be offered as well. Perhaps there too the problem occurs because the Sceptic and the Dogmatist have been united in sharing a hidden and questionable assumption, *viz.*, that if knowledge is to be considered *objective*, it must also be considered *absolute*, not admitting any error or exception. The Sceptic correctly sees error to be possible, indeed to be ubiquitous, and so an absolute or exceptionless knowledge to be impossible; from which he mistakenly concludes objective knowledge to be impossible. The Dogmatist correctly sees many things indeed to be known, but mistakes the character of what is known or at least some of what is known as incorrigible and unexceptionable, and goes on to deny error and exception to be possible. An equal and opposite error would be to confound the notion of something being personal or subjective with respect to an individual and the notion of something being *relative* to a given individual case or context or circumstance. That something can be true or right in a given case, context, or circumstance does not imply it must be true or right in all cases or contexts or circumstances. Nor does it have to mean that such knowledge must have been derived by applying an absolute and unexceptionable law or theory to a particular case. What may be true or right simply may be true or right relative to the particular case or context or circumstance, while the fact that it *is* relative to the case or circumstance would not imply that it is a matter of subjective choice *whether* it is true or right.

An example can illustrate. If a child asked us whether Chicago is to the left or the right of New York, we might say that this is an incomplete question with no definite answer. Relative to someone looking north in Washington, Chicago is certainly to the left of New York, while relative to someone looking south in Montreal, it is to the right of New York. In each case, there *is* an objectively right answer to the question *relative* to the situation of the observer. And the significant fact would be the *situation* of the observer, not what his subjective beliefs might happen to be. If a man in Montreal said Chicago was to the left of New York he would be making an objective mistake in the sense that *anyone* in his situation should be reasonably expected to conclude the opposite. Or consider that while the West is due West and the East is due East of Istanbul, the West is due East and the East is due West – of Honolulu. The Sceptic would take the fact that different and conflicting answers are possible to the same question as evidence for the conclusion that it is ultimately arbitrary what we call West or East, or whether Chicago is to the left or right of New York. The Dogmatist would take one or the other answer and conclude it must hold absolutely true everywhere, without possibility of exception or error. The division has been expressed clearly by Bambrough like this: 'Both the sceptic and his dogmatist opponent assume that the absoluteness of logical space is necessary for the objectivity of enquiry; that in seeking knowledge and understanding we orient ourselves, if at all, by fixed landmarks whose own positions neither can be nor need to be the subject of investigation. Sceptics become sceptical because they recognise that what they believe to be necessary is nevertheless not possible. Dogmatists become dogmatic because they rebel against the paradoxes of scepticism but still agree with the sceptic on what is necessary for the validity of our knowledge. One party denies the possibility of knowledge because it sees that logical space is relative and the other denies that logical space is relative because it sees that knowledge is possible.'[8] Both Sceptic and Dogmatist may be seen as united in their belief as to what will be allowed to *count* as knowledge – in what must be supposed to be the appropriate model of the *justification* of knowledge. In answering the question 'How do we know this?' both may be assuming that we have to *deduce* our answer from some previous and more general law, rule, or theory; the answers we seek or arrive at must always be a particular application or exemplification of some more general thesis. (Wittgenstein wrote of a 'craving for generality' and a 'contemptuous attitude towards the particular case'.[9]) The Sceptic becomes sceptical because he finds the process of deduction to be one without end. Deduction cannot be done without a remainder of unproven premises – a conclusion is deduced from a set of premises, each of which is the conclusion of other sets of premises, each member of which is the conclusion of yet other sets of premises, and so on. For every proposition there seems to be a genealogical tree consisting of all the lines from which the proposition deductively descends. The fact that these lines can be indefinitely extended to unknown reaches leads the Sceptic to think the pedigree of every proposition to be questionable, that every argument ultimately must be inconclusive, that there really can be no such thing as certain knowledge. The Dogmatist *shares* the same kind of idea that the only justification of knowledge is a deductive justification, and also observing the same kind of threat of infinite regress in argument, decides to call a halt at some or other point; the precise point where to halt either being determined *ex cathedra* (the medieval schoolmen) or being chosen arbitrarily (the humean economist!). At such a point the Dogmatist is ready to stand and fight, and of course if different people choose different and contrary points, we may expect some mighty rows indeed to develop between rival dogmas. Indeed it is possible that economists who have subscribed to the received theory of knowledge have been both sceptical about the possibility of moral knowledge and dogmatic about the existence of supreme unquestionable normative primes and principles. The widespread adoption of moral scepticism may be itself a relevant fact in explaining how it is that numerous divisions of opinion have been so persistent in modern economics, whether with respect to the methods or the substance of inquiry in the subject. Thus it is possible to find eminent economists being in deep and seemingly irreconcilable conflict with one another on questions of method or theory or evidence or policy, being members or even founders of rival schools of thought, yet being completely agreed that the logical status of economic advice is equivalent ultimately to that of personal bias or prejudice. As Peirce remarked: 'When society is broken into bands, now warring, now allied, now for a time subordinated one to another, man loses his conceptions of truth and of reason. If he sees one man assert what another denies, he will, if he is concerned, choose his side and set to work by all means in his power to silence his adversaries. The truth for him is that for which he fights.'[10]

**3.** It is possible that this parallelism between the Nominalist/Realist divide in the theory of existence and the Sceptic/Dogmatist divide in the theory of knowledge is not accidental. There is a possible connection which goes back to Plato. For it was part of Plato's thinking that the things we find in the world are merely distorted and defective versions of *ideal* entities not actually given to human experience. In mathematics for example, a platonist would say that the dot we make on a piece of paper and call 'a point' is but a defective image of the *ideal* point which has no parts or magnitude; the chalk mark on the blackboard which we call 'a line' is but a defective version of the *ideal* line which has no breadth or width, and so on. It is these kinds of ideal points, lines, planes, etc. which are the *true* objects of mathematics; while they do not have location in the world in which we live that does not mean they are any less real. Rather, mathematical objects should be thought of as inhabiting a kind of transcendental universe, a domain not directly observable yet which is reachable through the reasonings of the mathematician and philosopher, whose task it would be to discover and chart this unobservable terrain much as the geographer and astronomer discover and chart the observable earth and universe in which we live. As the English mathematician G. H. Hardy put it: 'For me, and I suppose for most mathematicians, there is another reality, which I will call "mathematical reality"; and there is no sort of agreement about the nature of mathematical reality among either mathematicians or philosophers. Some hold that it is "mental" and that in some sense we construct it, others that it is outside and independent of us. . . . I believe that mathematical reality lies outside us, that our function is to discover and observe it, and that the theorems which we prove, and which we describe grandiloquently as our "creations", are simply notes of our observations.' Professor Michael Dummett has put it recently like this: '[Platonism is] the thesis that there really do exist such structures of abstract objects, and that we are capable of apprehending them by a faculty of intuition which is to abstract entities as our powers of perception are to physical objects.'[11]

And ideal mathematical objects need not be the only inhabitants of Plato's heaven. So could be ideal men and ideal women, ideal marriages and ideal families, ideal languages and ideal cultures, ideal economic agents trading at ideal prices in ideal markets, ideal societies and ideal polities. In fact there is some evidence to think that modern economic theorists may have subscribed to such a view. For example, Professor Arrow remarked in his Nobel Lecture: 'In my own thinking, the model of general equilibrium under uncertainty is as much *a normative ideal* as an empirical description. It is the way the actual world differs from the criteria of the model which suggests social policy to improve the efficiency with which risk bearing is allocated.' And Professor Hahn in his Political Economy Lecture at Harvard University and elsewhere has argued that the model of general equilibrium 'serves a function similar to that which *an ideal and perfectly healthy body* might serve a clinical diagnostician when he looks at an actual body', that even though the model 'is known to conflict with the facts' and 'is not a description of an actual economy' it nevertheless tells us 'what the world would have to look like' if a neoclassical view of the economy is to be considered plausible.[12] What is it possible to understand Arrow and Hahn to mean by such remarks except to be endorsing a platonist ontology? If so, it would of course sit oddly with their subjectivism elsewhere; we shall return to these matters in Chapters 9 and 10.

The platonist seeks to mentally *grasp* the ideal entities by his 'mind's hand' as it were, to use a phrase of Professor Morton White.[13] And once he believes himself to have done so, the expression of his understanding would amount to being not only an expression of objective knowledge but an expression of absolute knowledge as well – something which is necessarily free of error or exception since it would have been the ideal which had been understood and expressed. The Realist becomes the Dogmatist. The Nominalist for his part wants nothing whatever to do with tales of airy-fairy entities in transcendental heavens. As Professor W. V. O. Quine might have put it, what needs to be done instead is to make a clean shave of Plato's Beard with Occam's Razor.[14] But in rejecting a picture of transcendental entities and the theory of absolute knowledge that goes with it, if the Nominalist cuts too thickly, he ends up rejecting the possibility of objective knowledge as well; the Nominalist becomes the Sceptic.

The theory of knowledge to be found in the writings of Peirce and Wittgenstein independently, suggests a third route. Reject Plato's theory of a transcendental universe, as being unnecessary to the resolution of any question in the theory of knowledge. With it therefore is rejected the idea that to know something certainly and objectively we must have deduced it from some absolute and general law, theory, rule or principle; that when we say we know something we must be in fact expressing the discovery of some ideal transcendental 'form'. Gone at once would be the possibility of an error-free and exceptionless knowledge which forms the basis of the Dogmatist's dogmatism. Error and folly are ubiquitous: Let freedom ring! At the same time, once we unshackle ourselves from the cramped idea that every claim to genuine knowledge must be deduced from some previous and higher claim to knowledge and ultimately from some set of unquestionable supreme principles or axioms, we may reject Hume just as decisively as we reject Plato. The antidote to Hume's debilitating and self-contradictory scepticism is *commonsense*. – We *know* some things are true and other things are false, we *know* some things to be right and other things to be wrong. And we can know these things without having to be haunted by an idea that we do not truly know them unless we have deduced them from some 'higher' or more general proposition. The general rule or principle or theory may serve perfectly well as the unquestioned premise of one argument only to be the questionable conclusion of another. The inductive and the deductive may alternate in the activity of reasoning, as we proceed from one set of particular cases and questions to another set of particular cases and questions via as many general rules, principles, and theories that we need. As John Wisdom put it: 'Examples are the final food of thought. Principles and laws may serve us well. They can help us to bring to bear on what is now in question what is not now in question. They help us to connect one thing with another and another and another. But at the bar of reason, always the final appeal is to cases.'[15]

Furthermore, there may be a third and alternative mode of reasoning too, namely, reasoning by *analogy*. When faced with a question to which we do not have an answer, what may be required of us may involve neither induction nor deduction but *comparison* and *contrast*. The most reasonable way to proceed in a given situation may be to take the question at hand to which we do not presently have an answer and compare and contrast it with questions on either side of it to which we *do* have true or right answers. Here is a question $L$ to which we do not presently have an answer. But we do know the answer to a question $K$ which is close to $L$ on one side, as well as the answer to another question $M$ which is close to $L$ on the other side. Now our question is, is $L$ more like $K$ or more like $M$? The reader may agree that that is how much reasoning does *in fact* proceed – in mathematics as much as in medicine, in science as much as in literature, in engineering as much as in ethics. It may turn out that on a particular question $L$ the present state of our knowledge happens to be so poor that we require an answer not only to $K$ but also to $I, H, G, F, E$, on the one side of it, as well as an answer not only to $M$ but also to $N, O, P, Q, R$, on the other side of it, as well as perhaps to questions above and below and all around it. Will that mean our project is hopeless or that common reasoning can be of no avail in answering *L*? Not at all – it would only mean *there is that much work to be done*. For inquiry to be inchoate does not have to be cause for despair.[16]

This kind of a notion that in the actual process of inquiry we always do start *somewhere*, and indeed that that is the only place *to* start, is to be found being expressed in the writings of Peirce: 'We cannot begin with complete doubt. We must begin with all the prejudices which we actually have when we enter upon the study of philosophy. These prejudices are not to be dispelled by (the Cartesian maxim that philosophy must begin with universal doubt) for they are things which it does not occur to us *can* be questioned. Hence this initial skepticism will be a mere self-deception, and not real doubt; and no one who follows the Cartesian method will ever be satisfied until he has formally recovered all those beliefs which in form he has given up. . . . A person may, it is true, in the course of his studies, find reason to doubt what he began by believing; but in that case he doubts because he has a positive reason for it, and not on account of the Cartesian maxim. Let us not pretend to doubt in philosophy what we do not doubt in our hearts.'[17] Then again: 'Philosophers of very diverse stripes propose that philosophy shall take its start from one or another state of mind in which no man, least of all the beginner in philosophy, actually is. One proposes that you shall begin by doubting everything, and says that there is only one thing that you cannot doubt, as if doubting were "as easy as lying". Another proposes that we should begin by observing "the first impressions of sense", forgetting that our very precepts are the results of cognitive elaboration. But in truth, there is but one state of mind from which you can "set out", namely, the very state of mind in which you actually find yourself at the time you do "set out" – a state in which you are laden with an immense mass of cognition already formed, of which you cannot divest yourself if you would; and who knows whether, if you could, you would not have made all knowledge impossible to yourself? Do you call it *doubting* to write down on a piece of paper that you doubt? If so, doubt has nothing to do with any serious business.'[18] A remarkable resemblance to this line of thought is to be found in the later writing of Wittgenstein: 'If you tried to doubt everything you would not get as far as doubting anything.

The game of doubting itself presupposes certainty.'[19]

No theory of knowledge can compel us to think of the activity of reasoning to be starting all of a sudden out of nothing and nowhere, nor are we obliged to suppose it must have any necessary end. We always start *somewhere* – there are *always* cases to which we do have answers with which to compare and contrast the particular case presently in question. And there are *always* unexamined cases and unasked questions remaining, which we may bring to test the validity and soundness of any general law or theory or definition or principle in which we may have come to believe on the basis of the known and settled cases. Thus reasoning can be thought of as a certain and objective activity without having to be thought of as an exhaustive activity. Argument can be potentially endless, but it is not thereby inconclusive. It is conclusive, but it is not thereby absolute or final. There need not be either any canonical points from which we have to begin our reasonings, or any ultimate destination at which we have to stop. Reasoning can be objective without being thought of as having to have either an absolute beginning or an absolute end. We can be objective without being platonist, we can admit a rich and indefinite variety and diversity without being subjectivist.

In the next chapter this line of argument is continued in more detail and concluded.

# 6

## *Expertise and Democracy*

In this chapter we shall consider in more detail the thesis introduced in the last, with the intent of together providing the main outlines of a theory of economic knowledge with which to replace the received humean theory.

**2.** Our first task is to try to provide a more formal refutation of scepticism, i.e. to formally prove the existence of knowledge, a task which is in fact quite readily accomplished.

We have noted in previous chapters the important difference between the question of whether it is possible for an objective answer to be given to a question, and the question of whether someone should be thought of as possessing such an answer and how we are supposed to identify him or her. The question of whether there *can be* any expertise about a given matter is independent of (and prior to) the question of *who* if anyone should be thought of as an expert about it. Scepticism, considered technically as a thesis in the theory of knowledge, needs to be concerned with the former question alone; the consistent and universal sceptic being someone who takes each and every concept like 'scientific knowledge', 'historical knowledge', 'moral knowledge', 'mathematical knowledge', 'probable knowledge', 'economic knowledge', etc., and argues it to be empty, devoid of content, ultimately extending to no instances, in the way concepts like 'unicorn' or 'reigning Czar of Russia' would be said to have no instances. Equally a refutation of scepticism may proceed as a logical exercise as well, amounting to showing the *existence* of just one instance of knowledge. And to argue the possible existence of knowledge in this way would not be to commit oneself to any claim of knowing who should be thought of as an expert or indeed to any claim of knowledge for oneself. The heated political problem of who is supposed to be an expert and how we are supposed to identify him or her deserves to be kept separate from the cooler logical problem of whether there can be any knowledge on a question in the first place.

It is in such a light that we may view the proof of the existence of an external world given by the English philosopher G. E. Moore. Moore raised his hands one at a time before the British Academy and declared to the effect 'Here is one hand and here is another. Therefore we know there are at least two objects in the external world.' Or Moore might have taken a pencil from his pocket and said: 'Here is a pen; therefore we know there to be a world outside our minds.' The sceptic who protested that Moore was holding a pencil and not a pen would have *helped* Moore to prove his point, in that an attempt to deny Moore was holding an object in his hand could not be more certain than Moore's claim itself. A single such example may suffice to show the concept 'knowledge of the external world' to be not empty and scepticism of the senses to be false and misleading. Moore wanted to show that we can and we do know *some* things for certain, and that we know them neither by induction or deduction necessarily, nor by fiat or dogma or mysticism, but simply by commonsense. Furthermore, if a theory of knowledge came to imply we did not know such things to be true when we *did* know them to be true then it was likely that it was the theory and not commonsense which was in error. Thus Moore declared that he most definitely knew that there was a living human body which was *his* body; that his body had been born at a certain time in the past and had existed continuously since then though not without changes; that it had come into contact with and been at various distances from many other things also having shape and size in three dimensions; that the earth had existed for many years before he had been born; that his body had been always in contact with or not far from the surface of the earth, and so on. Moore said that not only did *he* know these things to be certainly true, but that *all* of us know such things to be certainly true as well. In short, the problem of proving the existence of knowledge of an external world had a simple and yet rigorous solution.[1]

An analogous proof of the existence of moral knowledge has been given recently by Bambrough by way of the following example: 'We know that this child, who is about to undergo what would otherwise be painful surgery, should be given an anaesthetic before the operation. Therefore, we know at least one moral proposition to be true.'[2] Bambrough claims there can be no argument to refute this proposition which does not accept the logical existence of moral knowledge. For suppose we tried to disagree on whether the child should be given the anaesthetic; there might be any of a number of grounds for doing so – such as the parents forbidding it, or because it went against the religion of the child and the child refused it, or because it was wartime and there was a shortage of anaesthetic and the child needed only a stitch on the hand when there were more serious cases needing the same scarce anaesthetic, or because the child was a premature and underweight newborn and there was danger it would not survive an operation under anaesthetic, and so on. That is, because there were other values besides that of avoiding unnecessary pain which were considered relevant to the problem at hand. We would have entered into a *substantive* moral debate with Bambrough, and *pari passu* we would have implied that whether it was he who was right to say the child should be given the anaesthetic or we who were right to say the child should not be given the anaesthetic, there *was* a right answer to the question whether the child should or should not be given the anaesthetic in the circumstances. A logical thesis of the objectivity of moral knowledge needs to establish only that there is, in principle, a right answer to every question as to what ought to be done. And this can be maintained without having to make any claim of either having the answer oneself, or knowing with whom it lies, or even knowing whether the answer has been in fact found. All substantive normative argumentation might be seen to take place within, as it were, this kind of logical space and would presuppose its existence. Likewise it may be said that there is to every question, once it has been appropriately characterized, a true answer, whether or not we happen to have found it. 'If a question can be framed at all, it is also *possible* to answer it.'[3]

An analogous proof can be and needs to be given of the existence of objective knowledge in economics. And just as

Moore did not refer to relatively complex physical propositions such as whether the universe is or is not expanding, nor Bambrough to relatively complex moral propositions such as whether abortion is or is not justifiable in some cases, so too we do not have to refer to relatively complex propositions in economics such as $\hat{\beta} = (X'X)^{-1} X'y$; or that if $U_h$ is a continuous utility function from a non-empty compact subspace $B_h$ of $X_h$ to the real line then $U_h(X_h)$ has a maximum; or that with identical consumer preferences and production techniques a difference in factor endowments between countries is sufficient to explain the existence and direction of trade, with a country tending to export those goods which used relatively intensively the relatively abundant factor, and factor prices tending to equalize across countries. Just as very simple and uncomplicated propositions are sufficient to prove the existence of objective knowledge in physics or ethics, so only very simple and uncomplicated propositions are sufficient to prove the existence of objective knowledge in economics. For example: 'In any human society which is not tribal or nomadic, there will be households concerned with the terms at which they are able to trade some of what they own for some of what they want, and this may well be true of tribal and nomadic societies as well. Therefore, we know at least one proposition in economics to be certainly true.' This would be a weak substantive claim, which can be made even weaker if in place of a generalization we merely point to *this* particular person who happens to be concerned with the terms of trade and declare: 'Here is a person who happens to be concerned with the terms at which he can trade what he has for what he wants; therefore, we know at least one proposition in economics to be certainly true.' Or perhaps weaker still: 'Here is a London taxi driver who knows how to get his passengers from King's Cross to Knightsbridge; therefore, we know at least one proposition in economics to be certainly true.' The sceptic who tried to deny any of these as examples (albeit *simple* examples) of economic knowledge will have to bring to bear reasoning and evidence; will have to refer to propositions which he would say *are* true of economics – for instance, that this person in particular or people in general are not really concerned with the terms of trade or that the taxi driver does not really know his roads and intersections. Like Moore's sceptic of the senses or Bambrough's moral sceptic, the sceptic of economics would help us to prove our point, namely, that there exists a right answer to the substantive question to which he and we were giving different answers – as well as to every other substantive question, once it has been adequately characterized, which happens to have divided economists, whether or not its answer has been actually found. Once again to maintain that there *can be* objective knowledge in economics – that is, certain and definite answers known to be true about substantive questions in an economic context – would not commit us to any claim of knowing with *whom* such knowledge lies or even to claiming any such knowledge for ourselves. The cool logical question may be answered affirmatively that there is objective knowledge and expertise in economics without commitment to any answer to the heated political question of knowing who should be thought of as an expert on a given economic matter.

What may be indicated by this line of argument is the self-refutation that seems to be inherent in the sceptical position. As Frege remarked: 'If anyone tried to contradict the statement that what is true is true independently of our recognizing it as such, he would by his very assertion contradict what he had asserted; he would be in a similar position to the Cretan who said that all Cretans are liars. To elaborate: if something were true only for him who held it to be true, there would be no contradiction between the opinions of different people. So to be consistent, any person holding this view would have no right whatsoever to contradict the opposite view.'[4] It is also the requirement of Socrates that to be engaged in rational thought or action what one may not do is contradict oneself: 'And yet I think it better . . . . that the majority of mankind should disagree with and oppose me, rather than I, who am but one man, should . . . contradict myself.' I, who am but one man, carry myself within as a partner, so to speak, and my thinking consists of the silent conversation in which we engage. If I find nothing uncomfortable in being inconsistent in my thought, I am at odds with myself and perhaps may not be said to be engaged in thinking at all. Likewise I would not be saying what I meant if my words contradicted my thoughts, and I would not be doing what I said if my actions contradicted my words.[5]

**3.** Now it is the political question of course of *who* should be thought of as having knowledge, who should be thought of as being an expert, which leads everywhere to the most and the merriest discussion. As we have seen in Chapter 3, a moral scepticism may have been found appealing by economists because it has been believed to be a doctrine which protects both the individual and the integrity of science from dogmatic claims that knowledge and expertise derive necessarily and absolutely out of unique or special sources. Plato may be considered responsible for this, if only indirectly through the misunderstandings and corruptions of his philosophy which have occurred from medieval times onwards. Plato was no friend of the democracy of his time, and dreaded the rise to high office of the charlatan who might proceed in caprice and folly to ruin public institutions and bring about civil chaos and misery. In the parable of the ship of state, which is overrun by a mob of sailors who then constantly try to fight one another for its control, the warning is issued of how mob rule can lead inevitably to the adulation of fraud and the condemnation of knowledge and justice. And certainly if we grant it to be possible that power and authority will fail to coincide with competence and virtue and instead coincide with ignorance and vice, we would be agreeing in some measure with this lesson in *Republic*.[6] Plato's solution was to propose the coincidence of competence and virtue with power and authority, either by suitably re-educating those already in office or by replacing them with those already educated in the arts and sciences requisite of statesmanship.[7]

With the first part of such a solution, the modern democrat will have no dispute. In the modern theory of economic policy advanced by Professor Tinbergen and his followers, for example, the maker of economic policy is imagined as someone representing the democratic political process, who, while setting the weights to be given to the variables in the social objective function to reflect the popular choice, also elicits expert advice on the best means to achieve these desired ends. The expert economist is imagined as someone specifying the constraints, doing the calculations and recommending how the intended 'targets' can be most expeditiously reached given the 'instruments' at hand. The modern theory differs from Plato's in saying that the democratic choice deserves respect, and that it is not the place of the expert to gratuitously debate it; but the modern democrat would be fully and rightly in agreement with Plato that the policies of a state deserve to be as well advised and well informed, as judicious and as prudent as they can be made.

Even some of the second part of Plato's solution need not be disputed by the modern democrat. For the notion that an incompetent or corrupt government deserves to be replaced by one expected to do better is after all a principal reason for holding elections in modern democracies ('throw the rascals out'). What *will* be disputed by the democrat is Plato's view that genuine knowledge and wisdom ultimately cannot be the property of any more than a few people, specifically a closed and identifiable set of philosopher-kings. We have seen in the previous chapter a possible connection between Plato's theory of knowledge and his ontology or theory of existence; now we may add that Plato's political philosophy too may be connected to his ontology. For it is only the *genuine* lover of wisdom, the *true* philosopher, who is supposed to have access through his pure reasonings to the transcendental domain of ideal 'forms', and thus come to possess what amounts to not just objective knowledge but absolute and infallible knowledge as well. Hence if knowledge and authority are to be made to coincide in the interest of good statesmanship, it is such a person and only such a person in whom they should be united. We have seen that we can sever Plato's link between the possibility of objective knowledge and his ontological idea of the existence of a transcendental domain; likewise a democratic political theory might sever the link between the existence of political wisdom and Plato's idea that such wisdom must be the ultimate property of only a few. It seems likely that Plato misconstrued the character of knowledge in this respect, and especially the task the scholar and scientist have of elucidating it. Yet it is possible to preserve the merits of his thought even while we reject its mistakes.

For what would there be to prevent us from characterizing the concept of knowledge fully and thoroughly as a family resemblance concept – as a concept of *indefinite* variety of kind and instance? As something which is the ultimate property neither of the one or the few as the platonist tells us, nor of no one at all as the humean tells us, but rather of *everyone* – precisely as the democrat tells us? In the previous chapter it was proposed that the activity of reasoning need not be conceived of so narrowly as to require deduction and induction alone as its methods; it can and often does require and involve a third method as well which is the method of analogy, i.e., the comparison and contrast of a question to which we do not presently have an answer with questions on all sides of it to which we do have answers. The expert answer is merely the correct answer, the most reasonable and most justifiable answer. When Plato has Socrates asking questions like 'Who would you go to for advice in medicine or carpentry or shipbuilding?' the most natural answers are the ones given by Socrates's respondents 'Why, to the doctor and the carpenter and the shipbuilder, of course!' We expect the doctor's answer to a medical question to be better than our own because we expect the doctor to have encountered many similar cases before in his training and practice; in other words, to have had *experience* of a larger stock of similar cases, drawing upon which he is expected to come more quickly and more surely than we would to the right answer to the question at hand. Learning from experience in any context, whether removing an appendix or piloting an aircraft or driving an automobile or tailoring clothes or running a household or a business, involves facing and resolving an indefinite number of similar cases. We call someone an expert about something *relative* to his or her stock of experience, and the novice or apprentice or student may be the expert relative to the complete layman. Understood in this way, everyone may be thought of as in fact having *some* experience, *some* expertise, *some* knowledge. And then, if we are all specialists at some things, we must be laymen at everything else. Knowledge and expertise, as well as the power of reason as the means of their acquisition, may be relative and not absolute quantities, possessed in some measure by all and in complete measure by none. (And it is this perhaps, we might say with Kant, that accords to every individual, to every rational being, a certain *dignity*.[8])

**4.**   A line of argument of this sort may be developed further in two aspects, with more specific reference, first, to knowledge of a public and scientific kind, and second, to the private knowledge of the individual agent.

Not everyone who may want to know the answer to a given question may be able to answer it correctly or have access to the correct answer. 'The ionic addition to unsymmetrical alkenes proceeds in such a way that the more positive part of the reagent attaches itself to the least substituted carbon atom of the double bond' is not something self-evident to everyone, yet it is as a matter of fact something quite elementary to the student of organic chemistry, who refers to it as 'Markofnikoff's Rule' and knows it to be true under particular conditions, predicting for example that hydrochloric acid reacts with ethanol to give ethyl chloride and water. But why should the non-chemist be obliged to accept it? If the chemist tells us we must do so merely because all chemists happen to accept it, we may tell him he is making an *ex cathedra* claim and begging the question, since what we wish to know is from where the community of chemists itself derives its authority. Indeed the distinction we have made between the logical question of the existence of knowledge and the political question of who is supposed to have knowledge, makes it evident that even if every scientist or expert or a whole community itself took something to be true or right, that would not by itself *make* it true or right. For it is clearly possible to imagine a world in which all those who were called scientists or experts about a given matter happened to be inadvertently or deliberately spinning myths and falsehoods; to be engaged in self-deception and deception on a vast scale; e.g. Lysenkoism or Nazi genetics – but there are many less obvious examples too. (At once the claim of Mark Blaug reported in Chapter 2 is seen to be untenable. Blaug says 'methodological' judgements can be and have to be made objectively in science but similar objectivity is not possible about 'ethical views about the desirability of certain kinds of behavior and certain social outcomes.'[9] But let a community unanimously have as its 'ethical view' one which entails deception or self-deception on scientific matters, and Blaug's position becomes helpless.) Rather it is precisely because it *is* possible for even a unanimous group of experts to be wrong that we have a reason, an objective reason, *why freedom deserves to be valued.* As J. S. Mill put it: 'If all mankind minus one were of one opinion and only one person of the contrary opinion, mankind would be no more justified in silencing that one person, than he, if he had the power would be justified in silencing mankind.

Were an opinion a personal possession of no value except to the owner; if to be obstructed in the enjoyment of it were simply a private injury, it would make some difference whether the injury was inflicted on a few persons or on many. But the peculiar evil of silencing an opinion is that it is robbing the human race; posterity as well as the existing generation; those who dissent from the opinion still more than those who hold it. If the opinion is right they are deprived of the opportunity of exchanging error for truth; if wrong, they lose what is almost as great a benefit, the clearer perception and livelier impression of the truth, produced by its collision with error.'[10] Where there is no freedom to ask what is the case, there may be answers but there will not be *justifiable* answers as to what the case is. In other words: *freedom is necessary for objectivity*. Just as Mill was clear that what is important is not only the formal presence of the freedom of dissent and criticism but its active exercise, so Karl Popper in more recent times has urged scientists to actively and continually try to refute their own and others' conjectures about the world.[11] It is only when we engage in conversation, in critical argument and discussion, in inquiry, whether within ourselves or with one another, that we are able to find out whether our beliefs are true or false, right or wrong, justifiable or unjustifiable, sound or unsound. If we are prevented by force or dissimulation from engaging one another in conversation, all we would be left with is the private reasoning in our own minds, as Orwell's hero found in *1984*: 'The Party told you to reject the evidence of your eyes and ears. It was their final, most essential command. His heart sank as he thought of the enormous power arrayed against him, the ease with which any Party intellectual would overthrow him in debate, the subtle arguments which he would not be able to understand, much less answer. And yet he was right! They were wrong and he was right. The obvious, the silly and the true had got to be defended. Truisms are true, hold on to that! The solid world exists, its laws do not change. Stones are hard, water is wet, objects unsupported fall towards the earth's centre. With the feeling that he was speaking to O'Brien, and also that he was setting forth an important axiom, he wrote: 'Freedom is the freedom to say two plus two make four. If that is granted, all else follows.'[12] (Also Solzhenitsyn: 'Fastenko, on the other hand, was the most cheerful person in the cell, even though, in view of his age, he was the only one who could not count on surviving and returning to freedom. Flinging an arm around my shoulders, he would say: To *stand up* for the truth is nothing! For truth you have to *sit* in jail!'[13])

When the authority of a scientific or scholarly or expert community is brought to bear in answering some question, it may be understood merely as a shorthand way of saying the result happens to be the best that common reasoning under conditions of freedom has thus far been able to achieve. If we say Markofnikoff's Rule is true because the community of organic chemists say it is or $\hat{\beta} = (X'X)^{-1} X'y$ is true because the community of econometricians says it is, we would mean that so far as is known by anyone who has inquired into the truth of these propositions, they happen to be true under given conditions. If the layman wishes to challenge them, the route remains open for examination and discussion. If the route comes to be closed by force or dissimulation, the layman correspondingly is not obliged to accept as genuine what is being claimed as expert knowledge, and the writ of the experts cannot be said to run; while if it is open for anyone to examine the gamut of reasoning and evidence from common ground right up to the question at hand then we would have another kind of instance in which knowledge may be thought of as objective and yet relative to the situation of the knower. Just as someone in Washington is expected to conclude Chicago to be to the left and not the right of New York, so someone in the position of the econometrician is reasonably expected to conclude $\hat{\beta} = (X'X)^{-1} X'y$ and someone in the position of the chemist is reasonably expected to conclude Markofnikoff's Rule to be true under given conditions.

With respect to dogmatism directed at the individual, our central notion may continue to be applied that knowledge can be objective and yet its objectivity relative to the situation of the knower. Just as the West is objectively due West relative to Istanbul but objectively due East relative to Honolulu, so it may be said about positive questions that there can be a true answer in every case without it having to be that what is true in one case is also true in another, and likewise about normative questions that there can be a right answer as to what should be done in every case or context or circumstance without it having to be that what is right in one case or even right in most cases is also right in every case. Murder is wrong, yet tyrannicide may be an exception (the July 1944 conspiracy against Hitler); slavery is an evil, yet it may have been the lesser evil when ancient victors offered the vanquished slavery or death; the soldier must obey orders, yet mutiny or desertion may prevent what could be worse such as mass murder, and so on. The social proposals of Jefferson or Marx or Keynes might be found strange and irrelevant by the bushmen of the Kalahari or the tribal people of the Amazon not because either the tribesmen or the philosophers are foolish or dogmatic but because the contexts experienced by the one are not the contexts envisaged by the other. 'Circumstances objectively alter cases.'[14] It is possible to suppose normative questions may be answered objectively in each carefully described context, while stopping well short of the further and fatal step taken by the dogmatist of supposing such answers to be of an absolute or infallible or unexceptionable kind. We have seen that the subjectivist epistemology may have had as its purpose to protect the individual from some or other dogmatic rule when the individual is in fact going to be faced with having to make particular judgements in particular circumstances. Yet this is a purpose which may be better fulfilled, without the inconsistencies of the subjectivist epistemology, within an objectivist theory which nevertheless recognizes the diversity, the indefinite diversity, that there can be in individual experiences and circumstances.

Indeed an argument in support of the traditional liberal thesis of the freedom of the individual has been that individual knowledge and expertise is precisely of this particular and relative kind, and not of a general or absolute kind. An observation common to a number of liberal thinkers has been that the evidence relevant to the making of individual decisions is most likely to be available to the agents whom they most concern, that the individual normally has a certain kind of *privileged access* to the data which most concern him. Professor Hayek especially has placed in the foreground of his thinking what he has called the 'indisputable intellectual fact which nobody can hope to alter' that there is a 'constitutional limitation of man's knowledge and interests, the fact that he cannot know more than a tiny part of the whole of society and that therefore all that can enter into his motives are the immediate effects which his actions will have in the sphere he knows.'[15] Aristotle, though

101

not a liberal in a modern sense, had made a similar observation long before: 'the whole account of matters of conduct must be given in outline and not precisely, as we said at the very beginning that the accounts we demand must be in accordance with the subject matter; matters concerned with conduct and questions of what is good for us have no fixity, any more than matters of health. The general account being of this nature, this account of particular cases is yet more lacking in exactness; for they do not fall under any art or precept but the agents themselves must in each case consider what is appropriate to the occasion, as happens also in the art of medicine or of navigation. . . . We do not deliberate even about all human affairs; for instance, no Spartan deliberates about the best constitution for the Scythians. For none of these things can be brought about by our own efforts. We deliberate about things that are in our power and can be done.'[16]

It is an observation made in modern microeconomics as well. When an assumption of rationality is said to require of the individual economic agent merely 'correct calculations and an orderly personality',[17] it is meant that the agent ranks in a consistent way the alternatives he believes himself to be facing, and that the action taken is the highest ranked alternative given constraints of feasibility. The picture is of someone looking to the particular evidence and deliberating upon it, evaluating the alternatives believed to be faced, and doing what is judged to be the most appropriate in the circumstances. 'Ought' certainly follows from 'is' in such a model of man, in the straightforward sense that action and conduct follow from observation and thought – Aristotle would have claimed no more in arguing the objectivity of moral knowledge. If *this* is believed to be the set of alternatives and *this* the set of constraints and *this* the ranking then *this* is the right action, the 'optimal' action – that which the agent *ought* to do. Change the factual ingredients of the individual case, and the right action may well change with it, suggesting again not that there is no such thing as a right action but that what happens to be the right action in one context or set of circumstances may not be so in another. In the theory of general equilibrium too, an economy would be formally defined by the preferences, resources, technologies, expectations, etc., of different economic agents, and it would be taken for granted that an individual agent has available knowledge only of his own particular data ('informational privacy'). To account for the fact that the individual agent knows only of a small fraction of all the tradeable goods there are, we may have to define the specific partition of goods and skills known to the agent as his particular 'information structure', so all of the agent's other data would come to be defined only within this small and particular subspace. It then would be said that for the agent to be able to make decisions and act upon them it suffices that he knows in addition only of relative prices, i.e., the terms at which he can make his desired trades.[18]

It is from positive observations of this sort that the normative liberal recommendations followed. For example, it has been from an observation that the individual agent has a 'special knowledge of circumstances of the fleeting moment not known to others', a 'knowledge of particular circumstances of time and place', that Hayek concludes 'practically every individual has some advantage over all others because he possesses unique information of which beneficial use might be made, but of which use can be made only if the decisions depending on it are left to him or are made with his active cooperation.'[19] Adam Smith had arrived at a similar conclusion from similar grounds: 'What is the species of domestick industry which his capital can employ, and of which the produce is likely to be of the greatest value, every individual, it is evident, can, in his local situation, judge much better than any statesman or lawgiver can do for him.'[20] A correct answer exists to every question. Smith's question is: Who is likely to know best where an individual's resources will earn their highest reward? The expert answer is just the correct answer. In Smith's view, it is the individual himself who is normally the expert, perhaps the unique expert, because evidently it is he in his local situation who is most likely to know where his resources will come to earn their highest reward. In general, the liberal thesis of Adam Smith and J. S. Mill and Hayek and others gave objectivist grounds as to *why* the individual's exercise of expertise should be valued and considered to be part of his 'protected sphere'; *viz.*, because it is usually the individual himself who knows most about his own ends and means while being ignorant of or indifferent about those of others.[21]

Moreover, that the individual agent normally can be expected

103

to have available to him the particular evidence relevant to his own decisions does not imply that what he actually comes to do is necessarily the right or optimal thing to be done. Nor does this in turn imply that he should be forced to do anything different. We know from ordinary experience that it is possible for our actual behaviour to be capricious, mercurial, myopic, foolhardy, thoughtless, profligate – in short, irrational. A person may even know something ought not to be done or be made a habit of and yet continue out of what Aristotle called *akrasia* or weakness of the will. Dostoevsky has Marameladov tell us how he is fully aware of the wretch he has become, that the more he drinks the more he feels it, that he is in search of not happiness but continued wretchedness. As the addict himself may be prepared to grant, behaving out of *akrasia* may be to be acting no longer out of free and responsible volition. Of course the economist typically must ignore all this actual diversity in human behaviour and restrict his study for the sake of economy and analytical convenience only to what is purposeful in an economic context. Yet a potential error in the use of the concept of rationality in contemporary economic science would be to assume that every human action must be an instance of it, when there is no such necessity and to make such an assumption would be to leave the concept without any force. As Frege said at one place: 'It is only in virtue of the possibility of something not being wise that it makes sense to say "Solon is wise". The content of a concept diminishes as its extension increases; if its extension becomes all-embracing, its content must vanish altogether.'[22] If the concept of rationality is made to be all-embracing, its content must vanish altogether.

Furthermore, whether an individual believes what is mistaken or behaves irrationally is a different question from whether he or she should be forced to believe or do any different. This is a difference which has been blurred in the theory of social choice which will be discussed in Chapter 10, where dictatorship is defined as a situation in which one person alone believes $x$ to be better than $y$ and $x$ and not $y$ comes to be imposed on everyone. Certainly dictatorship may imply, among other things, the forced imposition of something over someone else; but in general whether someone should or should not believe or do something is quite a different question from whether he or she should be forced to believe it or do it. Whether it is only one or a few or a minority or a majority or all who happen to believe one alternative to be better than another, that would not by itself *make* one better than the other nor be a ground for others to be forced to believe the same. Whether a lesser or a greater evil happens to be avoided or a greater or lesser good promoted when a law forces everyone to do or not do something would be a question requiring the fullest possible description of the particular case for its answer; the question of whether something should or should not be done by an individual in a given context or set of circumstances deserves to be kept separate from it.

**5.** Thus the Spell of Plato is broken when we recognize the pursuit of knowledge in any context to be a dynamic enterprise which necessarily requires freedom for its success. While we can know and do know many things, everything that we know or will come to know remains open to further enquiry, examination, discussion, and interpretation – open, that is, to fuller and more mature understanding. According to the received theory of economic knowledge, we are to suppose that while some positive considerations may be brought to bear in a normative discussion, a naked subjective conflict can still remain after there has been full and justifiable agreement over the evidence and the analysis. We have been taught to assume that the processes of common reasoning must have a finite limit. Yet even so, it is only supposed to be after *all* the positive questions have been answered, *every* relevant piece of evidence discovered, *every* piece of evidence tested for its relevance, *every* logical relation established, *every* detail in the vector of positive considerations $(p^1, p^2, \ldots, p^{\omega-2}, p^{\omega-1})$ not only agreed upon but justifiably agreed upon; that Hume's Second Law would declare there to be no further scope for reason, nothing more to be said or done. We have found in our study no grounds for supposing such a limit to be anything but a fiction. Instead we are in position to turn the tables on both sceptic and dogmatist and say to them: Surely there is always *something* further to be said, *some* logical argument to be improved, *some* contrast or comparison yet to be made, *some* relevant piece of evidence yet to be established. Even when two disputants seem entirely agreed upon all the positive considerations $(p^1, p^2, \ldots, p^{\omega-2}, p^{\omega-1})$, and seem to be divided only over a sheer normative proposition like n$^\omega$, surely there still remains p$^\omega$ to be discussed! The Spell of Hume upon modern economists can be finally broken when we see that while normative recommendations in economics or elsewhere may be objectively better or worse depending upon how sound or unsound are the positive arguments given in their support, there are no *unquestionable* normative recommendations – *because there are no unquestionable positive grounds*. A set of actions which are the means towards certain ends can be themselves the ends towards which other prior means have to be taken, as Aristotle said.[23] Similarly the ends of certain actions can be the means towards certain others. The rational agent may be capable of deliberating not only as to the means towards certain ends but also as to the reasonableness of the ends themselves. We can accept the sound advice of the humean economist that it is a useful maxim to do these tasks in stages, without having to accept the dogmatic advice of the humean economist that deliberating about ends must sooner or later become dogmatic.

**6.** If these should seem quite simple and straightforward thoughts, it will be all the more remarkable that in recent years there seem to have been but two economists, Sidney Alexander and Amartya Sen, who have come to similar conclusions in their writing. In a very brief and troubled argument, Sen defined a 'basic value judgment' as one held by a person 'under all conceivable circumstances'. Sen admitted the humean position: only if a person's judgement was 'basic' could it be said to be beyond rational discussion; and then continued: while some judgements could be shown not to be 'basic', no judgement could be shown to be 'basic'; there is 'no sure-fire test' which can tell us whether the point has arrived where the scope of reasoning is allegedly exhausted. But Sen was ambivalent, and ended merely with the statement 'it seems impossible to rule out the possibility of fruitful scientific discussion on value judgments.'[24] Sidney Alexander advanced the argument clearly and vigorously that if the foundations of economics are to be laid on positivist premises they would be necessarily inadequate. The positivist economist had seemed to shy away from normative discussion without in fact having done so. Indeed the positivist economist could not help *not* doing so, and besides *need* not do so, because once the scope of reason in the making of judgements has been properly characterized it is in fact seen to be potentially indefinite.[25]

Many economists who have explicitly subscribed to the received theory of knowledge have nevertheless contradicted it in practice, and thereby stood on firmer epistemological grounds than their own theory would permit them to do. To take just two distinguished examples: when Professor Friedman recommends that a monetary authority *ought* to have a steady and declared *k* per cent money supply growth rule, it is because he believes that it *is* the case that money is neutral outside the short run, that the quantity theory more or less accurately describes the demand for real money balances, that the lags entailed by discretionary policies are likely to thwart the intent of such policies, and so on. And Robbins for many years of his life was closely involved with the making of government policy in Britain, especially having to do with higher education. In such a capacity he would have sought to *justify* his evaluations on grounds of reasoning and evidence, and hardly would have said that only a free-for-all was ultimately possible over value judgements. There are these grounds on one side of the issue, and these on the other, he might have said, let us try to stand on the firmest possible. The same may be confidently expected to hold for every economist who has ever made a recommendation as to what ought to be done or not done by a government or a committee or a colleague or a student. Evaluations are grounded on reasons, and an evaluation is good or bad, judicious or capricious as the arguments and evidence which go to support it are true or false, reasonable or unreasonable, sound or unsound. Whenever two economists come to give different answers to the same normative question – who are therefore in genuine disagreement and not at cross-purposes – we may be confident they shall be found to be giving different answers to some or other positive question at the same time. When we disagree on whether the highway should be built, or whether there should be a balanced budget amendment, or whether the deficit or the money supply should be expanded, we shall also be found to disagree on whether the benefits expected of the highway will be exceeded by its costs, whether an amendment will hobble the legislature or discipline it, whether a deficit or an expanding money supply is likely to be inflationary or recessionary, and so on. In any actual public discussion, it is very unlikely that any serious economist will want to make use of, or be permitted by others to make use of, what he happens to be permitted to by the received theory of economic knowledge, which would be to foreclose all further discussion at any point he wishes saying 'Look, I like it and that's that; if you don't like it as well you can jump in the lake.'

7. There is finally to be considered the position of Gunnar Myrdal and Paul Streeten, which has been widely believed to be opposed to the humean theory. In a representative statement Myrdal wrote: 'There is no way of studying social reality other than from the viewpoint of human ideals. A "disinterested social science" has never existed and, for logical reasons, cannot exist. The value connotation of our main concepts represents our interest in a matter, gives direction to our thought and significance to our inferences. It poses the questions without which there are no answers. The recognition that our very concepts are value-loaded implies that they cannot be defined except in terms of political valuations.'[26] And Streeten writes: 'The strict separation of "ought" from "is", which dominates modern liberal economic theory (and, in different versions, modern philosophy) is not, as it claims to be, morally neutral, nor simply a discovery of philosophical analysis. For no observation or logical analysis can discover that we *ought to* separate values from facts, or ends from means. No amount of description or deduction can show that we can fully analyze actual political and moral choices without introducing values into our analysis. . . . The philosophy which denies the logical connection between facts and values and deduces from this denial its own moral neutrality (suppressing a series of necessary unwarranted premises) suits admirably a liberal philosophy of tolerance, in which different political views have an equal right to exist (though it is not explicit whence it derives this claim).'[27]

A sound epistemological premise may be seen here to be leading to an unsound epistemological conclusion. As Myrdal correctly observes, ethics does indeed help to represent our interest in a matter, give direction to our thoughts, significance to our inferences, to pose the questions without which there are no answers. And Streeten correctly hints at the paradoxes resulting from a cramped understanding of the is-ought dualism which have been brought to light in previous chapters. But both

Myrdal and Streeten appear to take for granted with the humean economist, whom they think to be their enemy, that normative questions are only subjectively answerable, indeed that the answers to them might as well be equated with the personal interests of the respondent. Combine with this the correct observation of the involvement of values within the activity of reasoning, and we would be led with Myrdal and Streeten to conclude that there is no distinction – not even a working distinction – between facts and values, means and ends; that making such a distinction is merely a guise for the covert advocacy of a liberal economics; more generally, that the 'main concepts' used by economists or other students of society must be being driven by the covert political motivations of their users – i.e., by 'ideologies'. From trying to establish that some particular economic concepts may have had particular political overtones, Myrdal and Streeten would seem to slide into a position of saying that political motivations permeate the study of man and society completely. Where the valid and useful line between the positive and the normative is exaggerated by the humean to be one which is impenetrable and ineradicable, Myrdal and Streeten over-react to erase it completely. The humean theory makes itself unable to judge the ends to which economic expertise is to be put, and so has a perverse if unintended consequence of confounding the economist as independent scholar or adviser with the economist as mercenary – disapproved of less because of the ends to which his special knowledge might be put than because he himself is indifferent as to whether these are foreseeably right or wrong, justifiable or unjustifiable, good or evil; where the humean theory provides respectability to the mercenary, the theory of Myrdal and Streeten may come to have an equally perverse if unintended consequence of providing respectability to the ideologue – solely and supremely concerned with the advancement or imposition of his own ideas. ('Thanks to *ideology*, the twentieth century was fated to experience evildoing on a scale calculated in the millions.'[28])

We are entitled to take a view less cramped than that offered by either theory.

First, the objectivity of economic knowledge is independent of the history of our controversies. The fact that there may be widespread or even unanimous agreement among economists on a substantive positive or normative proposition does not by itself make the proposition true or right. Equally, the actual presence of deep and long-standing substantive disputes between economists on the answers to positive or normative questions does not constitute grounds for doubting the objectivity of economic inquiry, just as the presence of deep and long-standing disputes on mathematical or scientific or medical questions does not constitute grounds for doubting the objectivity of mathematical or scientific or medical inquiry. We may hold certain and objective knowledge to be possible in economics even while we hold there to be no logical end to inquiry in the field.

Secondly, as we noted in Chapter 4, it would be a cramped understanding of the is-ought dualism which leads to an absolute separation between the economist *qua* objective, rational expert scientist, and the economist *qua* subjective, irrational, opinionated citizen and propagandist; the former allegedly concerned only with the 'is' questions of science, the latter allegedly with the 'ought' questions of dogma or prejudice. We have seen this to be, in effect, the same kind of absolute distinction as is made in Plato's theory between the special people of true wisdom and the ignorant populace at large, and that it suffers from the same internal weakness as well, of not being able to specify how such special people are supposed to be identified. Instead, we are entitled to take a view that the expertise of the economist – like that of the doctor, scientist, historian, writer or mathematician – is relative and not absolute in character. Its authority derives from and rests upon the weight of reasons in its support; upon the extent to which it can be made to stand, or has been subject to and has withstood rational criticism. Where force or dissimulation happens to prevent the possibility of criticism, we may not claim authority for our pronouncements, while if we are ourselves party to the prevention of criticism by force or dissimulation, then we lose by the same token our credentials as experts with special knowledge of the question at issue.

Thirdly, the expertise of the economist, like that of the scientist or the doctor, does not *ipso facto* exempt him from the constraints of ordinary moral reasoning to which everyone else is subject. The fact that we are trained within a particular department of enquiry is hardly sufficient licence for us to ignore or deny the central moral distinctions between right and wrong, good and evil, which we as rational beings are in general capable of making. Indeed the true/false distinction and the right/wrong distinction may be thought of as running in close parallel within the very activity of reasoning. If something *is* true then it *ought* to be believed (normally). Thus Peirce was to regard 'Logic as the Ethics of the Intellect'.[29] And Frege was to remark 'Logic has a closer affinity with ethics. The property "good" has a significance for the latter analogous to that which the property "true" has for the former.'[30] While Wittgenstein spoke of 'the *hardness* of the logical "must"'. 'A proof shews us what *ought* to come out.' 'What I am saying comes to this, that mathematics is *normative*. But "norm" does not mean the same thing as "ideal".'[31]

In sum, our broad strategy has been to show common knowledge to be a sufficient antidote for scepticism, while freedom to be a necessary antidote for dogmatism. We are justified in relying upon our commonsense beliefs in the objectivity of science, yet the history of the progress of science has been a history of the discovery of errors in our beliefs, requiring us to place as much importance upon the ubiquity of error as upon the possibility of knowledge. In turn this shows there to be perfectly objective grounds for valuing freedom, namely, that it is necessary for the progress of our knowledge and understanding and rationality itself, in all the manifold diversity that these concepts may be understood. We are also justified in relying upon our commonsense beliefs that some things are objectively right and others objectively wrong, without having to deduce how we know what is right or wrong in a particular case from some or other allegedly unquestionable, ultimate, moral prime or principle. What may be right or optimal in one case or context or circumstance simply may not be so in another. Furthermore, what we believe to be right in a given context, just as what we might believe to be true, is itself open to question and discussion. Again it is the active exercise of freedom which should be the antidote to dogmatism. The degree of authority resting in a claim of expertise in a given context depends squarely on the weight of reasons in its support and the degree of rational criticism it would be possible for it to successfully withstand. Where freedom is suppressed, whether deliberately or accidentally, whether in a grand or a petty tyranny, and claims to expertise are prevented from being examined for errors with a fine-tooth comb, there would be no genuine authority to be acknowledged.

111

# PART III

# 7

# *An Example from Microeconomics*

'Examples are the final food of thought', and in this third part of the book we shall examine a diverse set of examples and applications with a view to illustrating the theory of economic knowledge advanced in the previous chapters. If this and the received theory of economic knowledge are to be tested for their relative merits, then we may wish the scope of the testing to extend to all manner of discussions. We begin in this chapter with a brief example in microeconomics; specifically, an actual debate spanning about ten or fifteen minutes which occurred not long ago on public television in the United States. Although the subject was of an economic nature the participants were not economists or academics as such; the debate is offered here as representative of similar non-technical discussions on concrete subjects which make up perhaps the bulk of actual discussion on economic policy in any society, and from which the university economist is sometimes far removed. We shall be returning in later chapters to the more abstract kinds of discussions which are to be found in university economics.

The debate to be considered had to do with a decision of the United States Federal Communications Commission (FCC) in December 1984 to require an increase in the charge of purchasing access to the long-distance network. The rate was to increase by one dollar per month in 1985 and another dollar per month in 1986, in the expectation of revenues increasing by one billion dollars in the first year. One participant represented the FCC and was called upon to explain and justify the decision, the other represented the Consumer Federation of America and was called upon to express and explain his criticism of the decision. The two moderators were Mr Jim Lehrer and Mr Robert MacNeil.[1]

LEHRER: Here to explain why the FCC did what it did is Albert Halprin, chief of the agency's common carrier bureau, which oversees telephone rates among many other things. First, why was this charge necessary?

HALPRIN: Well, the FCC took an important step today designed to preserve the viability of the nation's public telephone network and to prevent the division of society into a set of information haves – the very large companies, high-tech companies – and information have-nots – everybody else who will never have any choice but the public telephone network.

LEHRER: Now, how does the one dollar fit into all of that?

HALPRIN: The one dollar . . . covers the cost of connecting every telephone customer to the entire network . . . [as] part of an attempt to price the public telephone network in a way that will not discourage large companies from using it. The FCC believes that the public network serves almost everybody at the cheapest cost –

LEHRER: What do you mean by 'the public network'?

HALPRIN: Well, we have in place a tremendous public telephone system. It connects every subscriber to almost everybody inside the country and in the world. It makes a lot of sense to have everybody use this big, integrated, switchable network, because it's there. Up until now we've developed a system in which we've charged heavy users of that public telephone network a much, much higher price than it actually costs them to use the network. . . .

LEHRER: You mean business customers, mainly?

HALPRIN: Well, in fact residential customers, who are heavy users of long distance service, have been paying to subsidize businesses that do not use long distance service. The key factor here is the people who make a lot of long distance calls have been asked to pay a price that's much more expensive than it would cost them to go around the public network and go over what are called bypass facilities. . . .

LEHRER: What was the FCC's conclusion as to what would be the consequence of not imposing this dollar fee?

HALPRIN: Well, the FCC has been looking at what has been taking place, and we have found an increasing number of large users bypassing the network, either through building special facilities or through ordering new special-line types of facilities, both of which are taking away from the network that serves you and me at home.

LEHRER: And why is this so awful?

HALPRIN: Well, for two reasons. The first, of course, is that those are the people who are paying subsidies now to keep your rates and my rates below the actual cost. If they drop off the network, that goes away. But even more important than that, if they drop off the telephone network, the telephone wires that are in place serving them now will not only not be used, but will be paid for by you and me, by those people who have no choice and will never have any choice but using the public network.

LEHRER: Thank you. Robin?

MACNEIL: For a very different perspective we turn to Gene Kimmelman, legislative director of the Consumer Federation of America, which represents more than two hundred consumer groups nationwide. Mr Kimmelman, I know you object to this new charge. Can you tell us why?

KIMMELMAN: Well, we don't think the access charge is necessary to keep the public network together, and nor do we think it's equitable. We've found in studies of rate increases this past year that residential customers are now paying $2 billion more for basic telephone service. When you take that additional billion dollars in June 1985 for access charges and add them onto recent rate increases, we think that we are losing affordable phone service for the average American household.

MACNEIL: And are people dropping off?

KIMMELMAN: Yes. We found that in 1984, using a model put together by the Bell Companies, that over two million people will do without phone service by June 1985 because of the rate increases that they experienced in 1984.

MACNEIL: And how many more people do you estimate will do without phone service because of this new, by 1986, $2-a-month charge?

KIMMELMAN: Well, at this point it's difficult to predict, but we think at least a million people, if remedial action is not taken by state commissions or by the FCC to try to provide some special help, particularly to low income people.

MACNEIL: I see. How many more did you say again? I'm sorry. How many more?

KIMMELMAN: At least another million. It's difficult to say.

MACNEIL: So that would be three million altogether who would have dropped off, you mean?

KIMMELMAN: Right. We already have over three million households that do not have phone service, and the number is growing as the rates increase. And this is an unnecessary result of phone company pricing changes, and the FCC seems to be buying into this new scheme. . . .

MACNEIL: Well, what about [Mr Halprin's] point that if you don't provide some incentives for big users, they're going to go and set up their own networks to the detriment of the system that is already in place?

KIMMELMAN: Well, I believe it's a legitimate concern. I do not believe it is occurring quite as much as the FCC believes. And even if it is occurring, I think there are other ways of repricing long distance service that will keep everyone on the network without having to shift those costs onto the average residential customer. . . .

LEHRER: Mr Halprin, let's go through some of Mr Kimmelman's points. First of all, this is going to result – the fee, the access charge itself is going to result in another million people losing their phone service.

HALPRIN: Well, it won't, for two reasons. The first, as Mr Kimmelman mentioned, that rather than tracking and seeing that two million people had dropped off the network as a result of past increases, they used a model which predicted that two million people would drop off. The FCC has –

LEHRER: Wait a minute, wait a minute. You're saying that two million haven't dropped off?

HALPRIN: That's exactly right.

LEHRER (to KIMMELMAN): You're saying two million have?

KIMMELMAN: We're saying from the best numbers that we have available from the industry, conservative estimates are that at least that many people are giving up phone service, yes.

LEHRER: Well, because of the way –

KIMMELMAN: Because of the 1984 rate increases.

HALPRIN: The FCC adopted a report today which was not based

118

upon models, which are things you plug into a computer; [but which was instead] based upon studies and the actual numbers of people who are taking telephone service. It's the *Universal Service Report*. There has not been any type of dropoff like this. In fact, as with most other commodities, each year there have been increases in telephone service. . . .

LEHRER: I don't think we can resolve this specific point, but this is awfully confusing. I mean, one of you is saying very clearly one thing and the other the other. I mean, this is a matter of fact, is it not? People either have phones or they don't have phones.

KIMMELMAN: Yes, it is a matter of fact. The important thing to remember is the FCC is moving ahead in imposing these charges and now deciding just to start studying it. No, we do not have precise, absolute figures of the names of the people who have given up phone service, but we have the phone companies' own model that projects what will happen. I seriously doubt that it's an exaggeration of what has happened. I would be happy if the FCC would prove us wrong, because we want everyone to have a phone.

LEHRER (to HALPRIN): Why don't you do that? Why don't you go out and find out how many –

HALPRIN: We have. The FCC adopted a report today which is not based upon computer models but upon an actual survey of what's taken place, and there has not been a loss of universal service. . . .

LEHRER: What do you say to Mr Kimmelman's other point in his conversation with Robin that there are other ways, if you really wanted to ensure the integrity of the national system, there are other ways to do it?

HALPRIN: I don't believe that's correct. I've taken a brief glance at Mr Kimmelman's report, and his answer is to –

LEHRER: You have a report too, Mr Kimmelman?

KIMMELMAN: Yes we do.

LEHRER: Okay.

HALPRIN: It uses a lot of computer models and very few facts. But it basically says that they agree that it's necessary to keep the large customers on the network by reducing their rates, and what they propose is to jack up the price of long distance service for you and me and the people who only make one or two calls. We don't think that can be done. We don't think it's feasible. We don't think it's fair.

LEHRER (to KIMMELMAN): Is that your solution? Has he accurately characterized your solution?

KIMMELMAN: I cannot say he has accurately characterized it. What I can say is we spread the costs of the public telephone network, I believe more equitably, among everyone who uses it. We do not believe the bulk of those costs should be on the local ratepayer. They should be spread equitably among everyone who benefits from the existence of the public network. That means keeping more costs on the long distance users, spreading them slightly differently than is currently done. . . .

LEHRER (humorously): Gentlemen, I'm sure glad we cleared all this up tonight. Thank you very much.

The reader may agree that the first thing that may be said about this debate is that it is one of good quality. It succeeds remarkably well in its purpose of advising and informing the observer of the matter at hand, not of course in any final or absolute way with every possible consideration having been brought up, but adequately enough for at least a number of the pertinent facts and issues to have been raised in the span of a few minutes. The purpose of the discussion is a limited one, and its fulfilment must be judged accordingly. Moreover, it is all four participants who contribute to this quality, protagonists and moderators jointly. The protagonists are willing and able to address the same questions and so come to define what correctly may be called disagreement, in which contrary answers are given to the same questions, rather than be at cross-purposes resulting from one participant answering a different question from the other. There is also little or no stone-walling or prevaricating or obfuscating on either side; and of course it is the moderators who contribute here by asking the precise questions that they do, with a view to creating as much *common* ground as possible upon which the argument may take place. This conversation, brief and mundane as it was, is quite sufficient to show how the process of critical inquiry is a common and not a personal enterprise, reflecting the fact of language as a social institution and not a private possession.

Turning to the substantive questions raised, we find there to be much that may interest the economist. Halprin opens his defence of the FCC's decision by arguing that the *ex ante* situation is not one of equilibrium, and he hints that it has been neither efficient nor conducive to the general welfare. The price charged to long-distance users has greatly exceeded the marginal cost of production, while the opposite has been true for local users. Given current innovations in technology, an implicit tax of this sort on long-distance users may make it possible and profitable for them to substitute away from the public network itself, threatening in the longer term to drastically raise marginal costs for those who remain. Better therefore to take a slightly bitter pill now than a more bitter pill later. Kimmelman's opening round makes the suggestion that the demand curve for telephone service (long-distance and local together) over all households in the economy is quite elastic, and the rise in price is likely to lead to a relatively large fall in demand, especially among poorer households for whom telephones might not be an absolute necessity. Implicit in the positions of both protagonists is a moderate kind of utilitarianism, specifically one according to which households should receive somewhat greater weight in the social utility function than businesses (notice Halprin's quick denial of the suggestion that the FCC's decision was intended to assist businesses at the expense of households), and poorer households receive more weight than other households. Kimmelman especially is concerned to make this last point, perhaps hinting that the availability of telephone service in a home is a good which deserves to be distributed in something of an egalitarian way, that it would be an avoidable injustice if poorer households were unable to call for things like emergency services in the way that others were able to, that the broad principle of equality in the consumption of public goods would suffer in some measure with the proposed charge. Halprin responds not at all by disagreeing with Kimmelman's normative premises about the importance of preserving universal service but rather by disagreeing on the positive question of the nature of the demand curve; suggesting either or both that the demand curve is less elastic than Kimmelman claims, and so there will not be the kind of fall in demand that Kimmelman predicts, and also that the demand curve for this good as for other goods has been gradually shifting out over time with the growth in real income (this latter point being something of a red herring in the context).

Next the discussion takes an interesting turn with Halprin

raising sceptical doubts about the use of a predictive model by Kimmelman in obtaining his results. The model provides only an indirect means, Halprin suggests, and therefore should be contrasted unfavourably with the direct and allegedly plain results of an actual survey. Halprin claims that to be what the FCC has done, hinting perhaps that the observer's prize for a solid, feet-on-the-ground approach deserves to go here rather than to any fancy modelling exercise the ordinary man is likely neither to understand nor want to understand. Kimmelman replies no, of course he does not have the names of the actual households who have dropped off the network, hinting perhaps at the practical impossibility of such an exercise, and suggesting that the use of the kind of model he had relied on is the best anyone can hope to do in the circumstances. Besides, Kimmelman says, the model he used would hardly have loaded the dice in his favour, since it was the very same model formulated and used by the telephone companies themselves, and they surely would not act against their own interests to bias their model in favour of consumers, would they?

*And so on*. Interpreted in this way, the large and potentially indefinite scope which remains for further discussion of the subject becomes readily clear: on the substitution and income effects of the one-dollar increase, on the structure and contestability of the market for long-distance telephone service, on the choice and formulation of the empirical model, on the collection and interpretation of the data, on the political forces and constraints that may be at work, etc. Certainly it is the case that neither Halprin nor Kimmelman is a disinterested observer. To the contrary, each is and may even be expected to be representing as best he can the particular facts and points of view which are relevant to his own constituents. Then again, it is possible that Halprin is a Republican and Kimmelman a Democrat, or vice versa, that one is a conservative and the other a liberal, that they happen to agree or disagree with one another on any number of other substantive matters from the infallibility of the Pope to the fallibility of the local football team. But none of this would be in the slightest way relevant in the given discussion to the *soundness* of their respective arguments – to the truth and plausibility of their premises and reasoning. Nor would it make any difference that their emotions might have become involved in the process. Certainly they could have raised their voices in anger or shouted at one other in trying to make their points – say if the subject had not been the relatively simple and unexciting one of the pricing of telephone service but something more complex and volatile like foreign aid or abortion or the situation in South Africa or the Middle East. Or, it is possible the participants in this or any other debate will deliberately not be fully sincere in what they were saying, in the interests of tact and diplomacy in a public forum, keeping their fingers crossed under the table to remind themselves they did not completely believe what they heard their voices to be saying. But again the truth and plausibility of *what* was being said – whether one million or three million or nobody at all was likely to drop off the telephone network in consequence of a one dollar increase, whether this model is better than the other or not, and so on – would remain entirely unaffected and open to further inquiry and critical discussion by themselves or others.

In sum, we have a simple and straightforward illustration of how it may be possible for inquiry and discussion to continue freely and yet objectively – conclusively yet without necessary or final end – upon a normative question of microeconomic policy. This example of a direct and actual debate upon a concrete question may now be compared and contrasted with the more indirect and abstract divisions to be found in university economics.

# 8

# *A Dialogue in Macroeconomics*

Our next example is of quite a different sort, namely, the academic debate which has occurred in macroeconomics and monetary theory since Keynes's *General Theory of Employment, Interest and Money*. This has of course received a great amount of attention, with innumerable commentaries having been written by many scores of protagonists and moderators around the world. Only a brief and highly simplified summary of these many conversations can be attempted here, within our limited objective of illustrating once more how it may be possible for critical discussion to be seen to proceed freely and yet objectively in economics. In the previous chapter we were fortunate to have had an actual conversation to consider; here our method shall have to be one of constructing a model of a conversation. In honour of Plato, we might name our conversants Athenian and Stranger.

ATHENIAN: Tell me, have you perhaps been following the discussions among macroeconomists? I shall be interested to know what you take their present state to be.
STRANGER: Indeed I have, though of course it is not possible or worthwhile to follow all of what has been said. But yes, I have followed some of it, and certainly we can make it a topic of conversation.
ATHENIAN: Please begin.
STRANGER: Very well. Shall we do so in '36 with the publication of Keynes's book? Rightly or wrongly, this must be considered a

124

watershed in the history of modern economics, if only because most economists since have had to either admit its arguments in some measure or define and explain their disagreement. You'll remember at one time it was said by many that Keynes had fathered a revolution in economic science.

ATHENIAN: Except Chicago and the Austrians.

STRANGER: Quite so. Now more recently a renewal of neoclassical thought has been under way, and many doubts have been raised about the keynesian consensus, so much so that some of the main questions of the thirties seem in modern form to continue to be at issue today.

ATHENIAN: The more things change, the more they stay the same! But when you say Keynes has been a central figure, I take it you mean only that he has been among the most influential and most discussed and nothing more. It is not to preclude judgement on the merits of his book, which is itself of very uneven clarity. Besides there has been too much idolatry and hagiography.

STRANGER: Yes, there is so often a rush to belief and worship. There might have been less if Keynes had survived longer. Yet I should say the broad aim of the work is not hard to see. Keynes himself clearly believes that he is starting a revolution – going so far as to suggest a comparison with contemporary physics. The first chapter says the book aims to provide a 'general' theory, which will explain the traditional model as a 'limiting' case. The second chapter says the theory of value has been hitherto concerned with the allocation of given resources between competing ends; Keynes is going to explain how the *actual* level of employment comes to be what it is.

ATHENIAN: And so begs the question?

STRANGER: Or does traditional theory? That seems to be at the heart of it.

ATHENIAN: Go on.

STRANGER: The theory will be of the short run in Marshall's sense of taking capital as a fixed factor. Traditional theory is said to postulate about the labour market (i) that the real wage equals the marginal product of labour, so there is an assumption of profit maximization by competitive producers giving rise to a short-run demand curve for labour; and (ii) that the utility of the wage at a given level of employment equals the marginal disutility of that amount of employment; i.e., the real wage is just sufficient to induce the volume of labour which is actually forthcoming. So it can account for unemployment due to temporary miscalculations, or intermittent demand, or the refusal or inability of labour to accept a job at a given wage due to legislation or social practices or collective bargaining or obstinacy, or merely a rational choice of leisure – i.e., it can account for frictional and voluntary unemployment but not for what Keynes wants to call involuntary unemployment. What it can suggest is either such things as improvements in foresight, information, organization and productivity, or a lowering of the real wage. But Keynes's critique will not have to do with such causes of the contemporary unemployment; instead the population is said to be seldom 'doing as much work as it would like to do on the basis of the current wage. . . . More labour would, as a rule, be forthcoming at the existing money wage if it were demanded.' But it is not being demanded, and it is not being demanded because there has been a shortfall of 'effective demand'. That is why there is as much unemployment as there is.

ATHENIAN: Or so Keynes claims. And he would take it the neoclassical view would be that it must be the real wage is too high; it is only because the real wage has not fallen by enough that unemployment continues.

STRANGER: Right. To which there are two observations. The first has to do with the actual attitude of workers towards the money wage and the real wage respectively. The traditional supply function of labour is a function of the latter; Keynes claims that at least within a certain range it must be workers are concerned more with the former.

ATHENIAN: How so?

STRANGER: By the interesting and perhaps plausible claim that workers are found to withdraw labour if the money wage falls but do not seem to do the same if the price level rises. A real wage reduction caused by a fall in the money wage and the same real wage reduction caused by an increase in prices seem to have different effects on labour supply. 'Whether logical or illogical, experience shows that this is how labour in fact behaves.' And he cites US data for '32 to say labour did not refuse reductions in the money wage nor did the physical productivity of labour fall yet the real wage fell and unemployment continued. 'Labour is not more truculent in the depression than in the boom – far from it.'

A Dialogue in Macroeconomics

ATHENIAN: And the second observation?

STRANGER: This may be of more interest. 'Classical theory assumes that it is always open to labour to reduce its real wage by accepting a reduction in its money wage . . . [it] presumes that labour itself is in a position to decide the real wage for which it works. . . .' Keynes does not find a traditional explanation why prices tend to follow wages, and suggests it could be because the price level is being supposed to be determined by the money supply according to the quantity theory. Keynes wants to dispute the proposition 'that the general level of real wages is directly determined by the character of the wage bargain. . . . For there may be *no* method available to labour as a whole whereby . . . [it] can reduce its *real* wage to a given figure by making revised *money* bargains with the entrepreneurs.' Hence he arrives at his central definition of involuntary unemployment: if the real wage falls marginally as a consequence of the price level rising with the money wage constant, and there is greater employment demanded and supplied in consequence, the initial state was one of involuntary unemployment.

ATHENIAN: You are saying, then, that Keynes's intent is to establish the existence of involuntary unemployment?

STRANGER: At least a major part of the intent, yes. To make the concept meaningful, to argue that it refers to a logical possibility, and also that much of the actual unemployment of the time may be falling under it, and is a result of lack of 'effective demand'.

ATHENIAN: The neoclassicals have been said to be cavalier about fluctuations in economic activity, when in fact Wicksell and Marshall and Thornton, let alone Hawtrey or Hayek as Keynes's own critics, certainly had profound enough theories of the cycle. Before we go further, I think we should remind ourselves of what they actually said.

STRANGER: Very well.

ATHENIAN: Would you agree that it can be summarized, then as now, as the quantity theory of money married to the theory of general equilibrium?

STRANGER: It may be better to speak of divorce perhaps rather than marriage, in view of the dichotomy.

ATHENIAN: From Smith to Mill, political economists broadly agree that the role of government should extend and be restricted to such activities as defence, civil protection, the rule of law, the provision of public goods, education, the encouragement of competition, and so on. The traditional agenda does not as a rule include direct activity to restrain or otherwise change the natural course of trade, production, or consumption, and certainly no theory of what today is called macroeconomic policy. Underlying it is a broad belief that the competitive pursuit of private welfare within the necessary and minimal framework of the institutions of government will result in tolerable social outcomes, and any further activity may be counterproductive. The State is after all endogenous to the economy, without any resources to its own name.

STRANGER: The minimal state, though not so minimal perhaps as we sometimes think.

ATHENIAN: The main function of money is seen to be that of facilitating real transactions. Hence the main component of the demand for money is the transactions demand, and the broad objective of monetary policy is the maintenance of the stability of the price of money. But this is recognized to be something elusive in practice, and fluctuations in economic activity are expected to occur in spite of the best intentions of the monetary authorities.

STRANGER: How so?

ATHENIAN: Well, we might imagine two or three distinct but related markets: one for real investment and savings determined by intertemporal preferences, resources, and technologies; one a market for investment and savings defined in terms of money; one a short-term credit market. The market for real investment and savings is, as it were, unobservable to the naked eye. Yet it drives the second and third markets for nominal savings and investment in which we actually participate. Monetary equilibrium requires the observable money rates of interest to equal the unobservable real rate of return in the market for physical capital. In particular, the real or natural rate of interest determined in the equilibrium of the first market is not, and perhaps ultimately cannot be, affected by nominal or monetary disturbances in the second or third markets.

STRANGER: Why call it 'natural'?

ATHENIAN: In the sense that it is a function of the real data of intertemporal preferences, resources, and technologies being what they are. If these data changed it should be expected to change too. But given these data, it would be the rate at which intertemporal constrained optimizations by individual agents resulted in planned present consumption equalling planned present production at the same time as planned future consumption equalled planned future production.

STRANGER: In other words, real planned savings equal real planned investment.

ATHENIAN: Exactly. It is the real interest rate, or rather the whole structure of own-rates and cross-rates at various terms, which is the key price signal for macroeconomic equilibrium.

STRANGER: 'Natural' seems to me to carry a physiocratic connotation. A better nomenclature would replace it with something else – perhaps 'equilibrium real rate' or just 'walrasian' rate.

ATHENIAN: Very well, though I for one don't bias myself against the physiocrats! Now consider how a simple business cycle might occur on wicksellian lines. From a position of full real and monetary equilibrium, an expansion of credit has its first effect on the banks, increasing reserves and inducing more lending for reserve/deposit ratios to be restored, and so lowering the loan rate. But customers are only able to perceive a lowering of this nominal rate of interest and cannot know that the equilibrium real rate has not changed. As far as households know, the relative price of present consumption has fallen and there is an incentive for greater consumption and lesser savings. As far as businesses know, the relative price of the future good has risen, and there is an incentive for greater investment. Inventories are run down, and markets for both consumer goods and capital goods are stimulated and show signs of excess demand. But if there was a walrasian equilibrium initially, then the economy will now show signs of inflation; with a gold standard, there would be increased demand for imports and an external drain of reserves, and even perhaps an internal drain if there was a panic and a run on the banks. The loan rate will have to rise once more to rein in reserves, but if the rate is now raised too high relative to the still unchanged real rate, there would be the makings of a recession.

STRANGER: Your point being that economists before Keynes had recognized that the decentralized economy may be fluctuating continually.

ATHENIAN: Surely they had done so quite fully. A first set of causes such as wars, disasters, discoveries and migrations would change the real data of the economy, while a second set would be monetary disturbances like the failure of the authorities to adequately follow the dictates of the real data of the economy, i.e. failure to observe the equilibrium real rate of interest. It may even be intrinsic to the problem that they *must* fail in the attempt to observe, let aside compute, the equilibrium real rate warranted at a given time by the structure of the real data.

STRANGER: Hence the conclusion that they cannot hope to do better than establish a climate of monetary and fiscal stability, such as by declaring a long-term policy and staying with it.

ATHENIAN: Exactly. Private economic agents already face endemic uncertainty with respect to changes in the real data, and must be assumed not to want more added by government policy. You appear to have seen my point nicely.

STRANGER: Very well. But you have jumped ahead as this kind of a conclusion sounds very modern to me. You made me stop all the way back at Keynes's notion of effective demand!

ATHENIAN: As I said, the more things change, the more they stay the same.

STRANGER: Let us go back a little. I think we may be able to rejoin our initial route at a point which may bring us close to where we seem to have come by the route you have taken. Specifically, suppose we go back to the question of the money wage and the real wage, and of the real wage being 'too high'.

ATHENIAN: That has been interpreted a number of ways, has it not?

STRANGER: Yes it has. One would be to say Keynes was merely simple-minded and assumed money illusion on the part of workers. Another would be to say Keynes assumed a short-run context of fixed prices, so it would not make a difference whether labour happened to be concerned with changes in the real or the money wage. Yet a third would be to say Keynes, whether he realized it or not, had come upon a recondite truth about the sort of complex monetary economy in which we live – namely, that when transactions are quoted and made in a monetary economy, it may become difficult *ipso facto* for the walrasian equilibrium to be achieved. Even workers might fully recognize the real wage to be too high and be prepared to work more at a lower wage, but be unable to signal this willingness to potential employers.

A Dialogue in Macroeconomics

ATHENIAN: So involuntary unemployment becomes another sort of equilibrium outcome.

STRANGER: Exactly. Not only of labour but of machines too, along with the unintended holding of inventories. It's as if firms would have sold what they had planned to if only workers had the income to buy it, which they would have done if only they had been able to sell as much labour they had planned to, which they would have done if only there had been an effective demand for it, which there would have been if firms had not cut back on production because they found themselves unable to sell what they had planned to sell. A kind of vicious circle, due to pessimistic and self-fulfilling expectations all around.

ATHENIAN: An unhappy solution to a non-cooperative game you might say.

STRANGER: Quite so. Keynes does not deny that there may be a monetary route out of the impasse. A wage deflation would eventually lead to price deflation, raising the real value of money holdings, so via liquidity preference lead to an increased demand for bonds, raising their price and lowering money interest rates, which through the investment function would lead eventually to increased effective demand. But the fiscal route may be more direct and quicker in its effect on expectations. Trying to deflate across the board in the face of what seem to be excess supplies of goods and labour might be counterproductive, causing unexpected transfers from debtors to creditors and precipitating bankruptcies. Instead: 'Government investment will break the vicious circle. If you can do that for a couple of years, it will have the effect, if my diagnosis is right, of restoring business profits more nearly to normal, and if that can be achieved then private enterprise will be revived. I believe you have first of all to do something to restore profits and then rely on private enterprise to carry the thing along. . . .'

ATHENIAN: A shot in the arm for enterprise in the hope of breaking the pessimism. But Keynes was hardly alone in such thinking.

STRANGER: Quite true.

ATHENIAN: And he certainly seemed to treat the opinions of others without due respect, which is to say he may have exaggerated the significance of his own. Hinting that he was the Einstein of economics set an especially bad example. Only the

131

other day one eminence was comparing himself to Newton, and another was calling his friend Shakespeare. It will be Joyce and Pasternak next!

STRANGER: Flattery and nepotism are common weaknesses, my friend. Like the rush to belief and worship.

ATHENIAN: Besides, you would have to assume the government to be outside the game, and only so being able to see the problem which private agents could not from inside the game. That may be too large an assumption, don't you think?

STRANGER: Yes, it may. Yet it seems to me that pump-priming was a possible solution being offered to a temporary problem. Many of the controversies may have come about because it became institutionalized, because discretionary fiscal policy became a permanent part of the government agenda.

ATHENIAN: And a more direct route out was available too, was it not? With wealth placed in the consumption function directly, a deflation would increase the real value and affect effective demand directly. We would not have to wait for the roundabout effects through so-called liquidity preference.

STRANGER: Which in a way brings us back to a central pillar of traditional theory: with given real data and given velocity of circulation, desired holding of real money balances will be roughly constant. In particular, the demand for real money balances should not be seen as a function of the interest rate.

ATHENIAN: The real rate or the monetary rate?

STRANGER: For neoclassicals certainly the real; Keynes does not seem clear.

ATHENIAN: There may lie a problem.

STRANGER: The title of the book says 'Employment, Interest, and Money'. No question employment is real and money is money – interest is the bridge. If you ask me to bet I would say Keynes's agents make real responses to signals expressed as they must be in a large economy in monetary terms.

ATHENIAN: Perhaps we ought to move on. Tell me, if you think Keynes's book rightly or wrongly ranks as the most influential document of the last fifty years, would you agree it is Friedman's address on the role of monetary policy which must rank second to it if not on a par with it?

STRANGER: Certainly there can be few competitors.

ATHENIAN: Well then, it appears to me the net effect of

Friedman's critique has been a restoration of the wicksellian theory and a banishment of the keynesian theory.

STRANGER: Friedman of course makes his approach via a critique of the Phillips Curve.

ATHENIAN: Yes, but it is Wicksell whom he acknowledges in advancing the notion of a natural rate of unemployment, one which has been 'ground out by the Walrasian system of general equilibrium equations' – in other words, one which happens to be consistent with the structure of the real data of the economy at a particular time.

STRANGER: Though again we may as well speak of walrasian instead of natural.

ATHENIAN: A monetary policy which tried to peg unemployment at lower than such a rate (if such a rate could be determined, which it cannot) is likely to be counterproductive. The initial effect of an expansionary policy on a walrasian equilibrium may be to increase real output. Workers assume the increase to reflect an increase in the unobservable real demand for their services, and hence they expect a higher real wage. Businesses see the same and assume it to reflect an increase in the unobservable real demand for their goods. But given that there was no real excess demand in the first place for either labour or goods, the effect outside anything but the short run will be a return to the initial structure of real wages, and the temporary decline in unemployment is reversed to the walrasian rate at higher prices. If the government tries to maintain unemployment at less than the walrasian rate, it will have to concede – indeed it will have caused – accelerating inflation without any real fall in unemployment.

STRANGER: And vice versa perhaps, so there would be a kind of knife-edge.

ATHENIAN: Now your remark about Friedman making his approach via the Phillips Curve seems to me interesting. We may have been too hasty to make a comparison with the debate in the thirties. For the world suffers a very real and severe shock between Keynes's book and the keynesian consensus, which is the Second World War itself.

STRANGER: I am not sure I follow.

ATHENIAN: Well, think of the consensus afterwards on the need for macroeconomic policy – it is actually Tinbergen's notion of a 'policy-maker' which is married to what seems to be Phillips's finding of a trade-off between inflation and unemployment. It becomes the role of the macroeconomist to advise the politician on how to minimize social disutility from inflation and unemployment subject to the Phillips Curve. Macroeconomics becomes a so-called 'policy science'. Give your expert economist your social utility function, and he will tell you where to slide to on your Phillips Curve.

STRANGER: The available instruments being money supply and tax rates. That is what I meant in saying Keynes's idea became institutionalized.

ATHENIAN: It seems to me this consensus is born out of the War.

STRANGER: How so?

ATHENIAN: Well, just think of the structural problems of the time: demobilization of large armies, reconstruction, all the displaced peoples, and so on. What are democratic governments to do? Say to their voters, right, thank you very much, now could you please go home quietly? What could have been expected *except* an Employment Act? Governments were going to help their returning citizens find work, or at least it would have seemed irresponsible if they had not said they were going to.

STRANGER: You are saying then that Friedman may have been arguing against a new orthodoxy, grown out of what might have been a sensible idea.

ATHENIAN: Exactly. The world is a very different place now than in 1945, in '45 than in '33, in '33 than in 1914. Real shocks every time. It may be a grave mistake for us to look for a unique and universal theory which is supposed to explain all particular circumstances, all of history.

STRANGER: Reminds me of the historical school.

ATHENIAN: Why not? Again I hold no prejudice against them! Anyhow, consider that Lucas and others have followed Friedman to argue it is a mistake to formulate the problem as Tinbergen had done, with unemployment as a target in a social utility function along with inflation. If it ought to be assumed that people will not continually make the same mistakes in predicting policy, then a systematic employment policy is going to be discovered quickly enough and rendered either ineffective or counterproductive. This idea too has its origins in Wicksell. Examining an opinion that inflation might stimulate enterprise and free debtors, Wicksell says: 'It need only be said that if this fall in the value of money is the result of our own deliberate policy, or indeed can be anticipated and foreseen, then these supposed beneficial effects will never occur, since the approaching rise in prices will be taken into account in all transactions by reasonably intelligent people.'

STRANGER: Wicksell said that?

ATHENIAN: Precisely that.

STRANGER: It does sound very modern.

ATHENIAN: Now Lucas speaks of how the advice that economists give should be limited only to 'the well understood and empirically substantiated propositions of monetary economics, discouragingly modest as these may be.' What can we take him to mean? It seems to me he is sharing Friedman's scepticism of the possibilities which had been claimed for macroeconomics by the keynesian consensus. And that surely has been a healthy scepticism, befitting good economists.

STRANGER: As I said, there is so often a rush to belief.

ATHENIAN: Which is really disastrous when combined with the craving for power.

STRANGER: But the question remains, does it not, as to *which* propositions of monetary economics are to be considered 'well understood and empirically substantiated'. I cannot help but think that the propositions taken to be well understood and empirically substantiated in Chicago may be very different from those taken to be well understood and empirically substantiated in Cambridge, or for that matter, those in the US from those in Europe.

ATHENIAN: I don't see any difficulty in this. For first, it would have been granted there *are* propositions in economics which *can* be well understood and empirically substantiated. And *that* must be counted as progress! For something cannot be well understood if it cannot be understood at all, and where there is the possibility of understanding there must be the possibility of objective knowledge as well. And second, why should we not say that the most appropriate task of economic theory or analytical economics is simply one of clarification and elucidation of the conceptual basis of economic thinking and expression? All theory ultimately is, or ought to be, 'Critique of Language'. When we are faced with a particular and concrete problematic situation, the theorist is whom we turn to for conceptual guidance and criticism. If instead you take the role of the theorist to be one of searching the universe for grand and general and absolute and abstract truths, which need to be discovered before we can say anything about some concrete set of particulars, then it seems to me you will either be struck dumb by a total and debilitating scepticism or become very shrill in your dogmatism or alternate wildly between the two.

STRANGER: It seems again I will not disagree. But you have sketched the critique of Friedman and Lucas and indeed the ghost of Wicksell addressed to the dogmas of the keynesian orthodoxy. And I have agreed with you this has been a healthy criticism of the sort we should expect economists to provide. But there has been serious question too of the framework used by Friedman and Lucas, hasn't there? I am thinking especially of Tobin and Hahn.

ATHENIAN: Indeed. Tobin has done much to add clear and reasonable thinking about Keynes; his suggestion that, in actual economies, a certain amount of inflation may be the only way to bring down real wages towards their walrasian rates is especially interesting; it shows how wide the common ground can be upon which the debate may occur. But you will have to tell me what Hahn's criticisms have been. I have always found them too abstract and too caustic.

STRANGER: That they tend to be, but don't let that deter you. As I see it, Hahn argues somewhat as follows. We should grant Friedman and Lucas two important points: first, the government is itself a large economic agent whose actions and announced plans enter the calculations of private agents; secondly, erratic changes in monetary policy away from a steady $k$ per cent rule may have perverse effects 'by confusing signals of relative scarcity with those that arose from the monetary policy'. Also, we may accept that the assumptions sufficient for a full walrasian equilibrium with rational expectations suffice for the absence of any persistent involuntary unemployment by Keynes's definition. But Hahn would say this may not be the relevant empirical description.

ATHENIAN: In what way?

STRANGER: Well, for one thing the pricing axiom or the recontracting assumption of stability theory remains unexplained. It is possible that traders will face quantity constraints, and this often seems so in markets for labour and credit. We may simply find prices not moving in the direction of excess demand even when a quantity constraint happens to be binding. The structure of wages may be 'neither fixed, nor arbitrary, nor inflexible; it is what it is because given conjectures, no agent finds it advantageous to change it.' Moreover, it may not be plausible to suppose there will be convergence after arbitrary displacements back towards a stable equilibrium, because the conditions for stability are very stringent and uniqueness of equilibrium may also need to be postulated. Furthermore, it may be quite unsatisfactory to treat money in models which are isomorphic to the Arrow-Debreu model, because in such a world there is no logical use for money, so there must be some essential features of reality which have failed to be features of the model.

ATHENIAN: You don't think Patinkin's integration was adequate?

STRANGER: For many practical purposes perhaps, but certainly not to full logical satisfaction. If you put real money balances into the utility function and treat money just about like any other good, you have to be prepared to accept a possible equilibrium in which the price of money is zero. Lastly, if there are internal debts denominated in money as there are in fact, you may not assume that equiproportional changes in all prices will not have real effects, unless you are prepared to assume away redistributions between creditors and debtors, which you can do only under another assumption that all households have parallel and linear Engel curves through the origin. Hahn's line of argument is admittedly abstract, but you will have to admit it raises some quite fundamental questions, which have yet to be addressed.

ATHENIAN: Another example, we might say, of the healthy scepticism of the theorist. It seems to be my turn to agree with you. But we can imagine replies too, can we not?

STRANGER: What do you have in mind?

ATHENIAN: Well, to argue that there can be unemployment which is involuntary is not to have argued that an employment policy can be expected to remove it. These seem to be a premise and conclusion too frequently confounded by both keynesians and their critics, with disastrous consequences. Then, Buchanan would argue that a more thorough characterization needs to be given of the making of government policy, especially when it is proposed to supplant the market outcome. Policies are after all proposed, and enacted, and put into effect by actual people – all of whom may need to be assumed to be pursuing private rewards as well in the course of their public duties. The relevant description for the economist needs to be one including this further fact that actual proposals of public policy can embody the private interests of the proposers too.

STRANGER: Making it that much more difficult to determine what *is* in the public interest in a given case.

ATHENIAN: Exactly. And so reinforcing the case for predictability and an orderliness in the framework of government.

STRANGER: But we have been talking now for quite long enough, my friend. I seem to feel a fear too that we have not gained anything at all in our discussions.

ATHENIAN: Don't be so pessimistic! Surely the point of reconstructing such conversations as we have done is not to hold absolutely to the matters raised in them. After all, we have been making summary and highly simplified and unauthorized interpretations. I take the point of it to have been to clarify our thoughts, and perhaps to show ourselves how discussion can proceed between economists of different schools of thought. Arguments might come to a halt for any of a number of reasons, but they needn't be supposed to have any logical or necessary end. Too often we let people retreat into different dogmatic positions, fostering the belief that each is starting from some set of absolute axioms ultimately irreconcilable with those of the other. We may need to keep insisting instead that the pursuit of knowledge and understanding is an open-ended activity with potentially indefinite limits. It yields conclusive results but has no absolute end. You or I might call a halt and retire from it, but that will not mean it cannot or will not continue without us.

STRANGER: Perhaps so. But you are younger than I, and I have become tired by all these thrusts and parries. Besides, there has been the enjoyment of conversation itself.[1]

# 9

# *Mathematical Economics and Reality*

In this chapter we shall examine the appropriate relationship of mathematics to the subjects of economic study. Few divisions on substantive questions in economic science have been as bitter as the dispute which has occurred on this question of choice of methods, with charges of sophistry and humbug being periodically traded in private and in print between the more and the less mathematical among economists. The weapons of 'intemperate discussion, namely invective, sarcasm, personality and the like' have not been spared, not only by those in a minority at some university department to whom they might bring 'the praise of honest zeal and righteous indignation',[1] but also by those in comfortable if temporary majorities.

At first, it was the pioneers of mathematical economics who had faced inert and intransigent opinions against the use of any mathematics at all in economic study. Cournot attributed the prejudice of his contemporaries to their ignorance of mathematics even when they were 'otherwise judicious and well versed in the subject of Political Economy', though he added that they may have been put off algebra by the errors in earlier attempts at applying it. For his own part, Cournot did not wish 'to make a complete and dogmatic treatise on Political Economy' and would be putting aside 'questions to which mathematical analysis cannot apply, and those which seem . . . entirely cleared up already.' Jevons declared that economics, 'if it is to be a science at all, must be a mathematical science', and counselled against despair even though 'the popular opinions on the extension of mathema-

139

tical theory tend to deter any man from attempting tasks which, however difficult, ought some day to be achieved.' Walras inveighed against 'those economists who do not know any mathematics, who do not even know what is meant by mathematics and yet have taken the stand that mathematics cannot possibly serve to elucidate economic principles'; and at the same time against the narrow division of education in his native France into two compartments, 'one turning out calculators with no knowledge of sociology, philosophy, history or economics; and the other cultivating men of letters devoid of any notion of mathematics.'[2]

In recent times the majorities have changed, and it is mathematical economists who now command much more the directions of economic study at many universities. Yet the controversy has continued, and a few examples can give a taste of its bitterness. Professor L. R. Klein has denounced non-mathematical writings in economics as 'fat, sloppy and vague', while Professor Samuelson has considered 'the laborious literary working over of essentially simple mathematical concepts such as is characteristic of much of modern economic theory' to call for 'mental gymnastics of a peculiarly depraved type'[3]. From the other side, Professor N. Georgescu-Roegen quotes Frank Knight as saying 'there are many members of the economics profession who are mathematicians first and economists afterwards' and claims 'the situation since Knight's time has become much worse. There are endeavours that now pass for the most desirable kind of economic contributions although they are just plain mathematical exercises, not only without any economic substance but also without mathematical value. Their authors are not something first and something else afterwards; they are neither mathematicians nor economists.'[4] Keynes had provided similar ammunition: 'Too large a proportion of recent "mathematical economics" are mere concoctions, as imprecise as the initial assumptions they rest on, which allow the author to lose sight of the complexities and interdependencies of the real world in a maze of pretentious and unhelpful symbols.'[5] On the other hand, Samuelson reports with approval Professor Gerard Debreu's remark that 'the discipline which most fully uses in its daily work the frontier refinements of mathematical analysis is modern economic theory.'[6] And Debreu himself justifies axiomatic economic theory as follows: 'Among the many consequences of transformation in methodology that the field of economic theory underwent in the recent past, the clarity of expression that it made possible is perhaps one of the greatest gains that it has yielded. The very definition of an economic concept is usually subject to a substantial margin of ambiguity. An axiomatized theory substitutes for an ambiguous economic concept a mathematical object that is subject to entirely definite rules of reasoning. No doubt the economic interpretation of the primitive mathematical objects of the theory is free, and this is indeed one of the sources of the power of the axiomatic method. . . . [W]hile a primitive concept of an axiomatic theory admits different interpretations a theorist who has chosen one of them succeeds in communicating his intended meaning with little ambiguity because of the completely specified formal context in which he operates. . . . [T]he complete specification of assumptions, the exact statement of conclusions, and the rigor of the deductions of an axiomatized study provide a secure foundation on which the construction of economic theory can proceed. . . . Thus axiomatization facilitates the detection of logical errors within the model, and perhaps more importantly it facilitates the detection of conceptual errors in the formulation of the theory and in its interpretations.'[7] On the other hand we find Professor Lord Bauer: 'The adoption of mathematical methods as the standard form in economics has had serious untoward effects. The use of these methods has even come to serve as a barrier to criticism of a wide range of transgressions. . . . Apart from the shielding of specific lapses, emphasis on the use of mathematical methods has contributed more pervasively to inappropriate practices and habits of mind. Possibly the most important of these inappropriate or even misleading practices is the tendency to elevate technique above substance, form above content. Others include preoccupation with economic phenomena and factors which can genuinely or spuriously be quantified, and consequent neglect of those which cannot be so treated but frequently are much more germane. . . .'[8] As well as Kaldor: 'There is, I am sure, a vague sense of dissatisfaction, open or suppressed, with the current state of economics among most members of the economics profession. . . . On the one hand it is increasingly recognised that abstract mathematical models lead nowhere. On the other hand it is also recognized that "econometrics" leads nowhere – the careful accumulation and sifting of statistics and the development of refined methods of statistical inference cannot make up for the lack of any basic understanding of how the actual economy works.'[9] Professor Werner Hildenbrand writes in defence of Debreu: 'To a traditionally educated economist, who does not have a training in modern mathematics, Debreu's contributions might appear, at first glance, incomprehensibly "abstract". There is then a great temptation to dismiss the work as "too abstract" (with the implication of "unrealistic" whatever this term may mean) rather than to invest the required intellectual effort. In this respect Debreu has never compromised just as he has never followed fashions in economic research. I have often heard him say that every economic problem requires its own mathematical treatment. The economic problem determines the mathematical tool that is applied to obtain a precise formulation of the problem and to analyze it; one does not take a mathematical tool and then look for applications. . . . Debreu presents his scientific contributions in the most honest way possible by explicitly stating all underlying assumptions and refraining at any stage of the analysis from flowery interpretations that might divert attention from the restrictiveness of the assumptions and lead the reader to draw false conclusions.' Hildenbrand quotes Russell, as Professor Hahn had done in an earlier defence: 'Many people have a passionate hatred of abstraction, chiefly, I think, because of its intellectual difficulty; but as they do not wish to give this reason they invent all sorts of others that sound grand. They say that all abstraction is falsification, and that as soon as you have left out any aspect of something actual you have exposed yourself to the risk of fallacy in arguing from its remaining aspects alone. Those who argue in this way are in fact concerned with matters quite other than those that concern science.'[10] But in reply there is Professor Wassily Leontief: 'Not having been subjected from the outset to the harsh discipline of systematic fact-finding, traditionally imposed on and accepted by their colleagues in the natural and historical sciences, economists developed a nearly irresistible predilection for deductive reasoning. As a matter of fact, many entered the field after specialization in pure or applied mathematics. Page after page of professional economics journals are filled with mathematical formulae leading the reader from sets of more or less plausible but entirely arbitrary assumptions to precisely stated but irrelevant theoretical conclusions. . . . Year after year economic theorists continue to produce scores of mathematical models and to explore in greater detail their formal properties; and the econometricians fit algebraic functions of all possible shapes to essentially the same sets of data without being able to advance, in any perceptible way, a systematic understanding of the structure and the operations of a real economic system.'[11] There is also the reflection of Professor Salim Rashid in the course of a reply to Georgescu-Roegen: 'No assistant professor at any reasonably good university can hope to keep his job unless he publishes at least one article a year in a recognized journal. In order for a paper to be published, it must contain something new. How can several thousand junior faculty find topics simultaneously novel and worthwhile? . . . One of the inimitable merits of mathematics is that it mechanizes the process of grinding out articles. If a theorem has been proven with twice continuously differentiable utility and production functions, then the next step is to prove them true for once differentiable functions, then for Lipschitz continuous functions, then for continuous functions, and finally for measurable functions. Each step provides a new result and is therefore a publishable effort, but one could argue that the economic content of these (mathematical) refinements is marginal.'[12]

2.   We may ask if the theory of knowledge presented in Part II can be put to work here, to dissolve or at least clarify certain aspects of this conflict, and indeed a number of observations are possible.

   First of all, a dispute over choice of methods is of course a dispute over a choice – that is to say, it is a *normative* dispute having to do with what economists *ought* to do or not do as economists. At once we would know from our theory of knowledge that this is a dispute capable of sustaining reasonable and open-ended and objective discussion. We may begin with the certainty that there are positive grounds to be contested here, that there will be scope for common reasoning to be put to work. Modern mathematical economists have typically argued that the use of mathematical methods has contributed to the removal of ambiguity surrounding economic concepts, to precision in reasoning, to clarity and economy of expression, to assisting the discovery of errors in economic analysis. They have charged the non-mathematical economist with speaking from ignorance, with not making or being capable of the requisite effort to learn the relevant methods, and so failing to see their benefits. The critics have typically argued that the growth of mathematical economics has led to impenetrability and not clarity, to a lack of critical thinking and imagination, to the mechanical churning out of results, to a lack of realism and practical application. They have charged the mathematical economist with irresponsibility in his choice of work. Yet here intellectual values may be finely poised! For there is nothing surely to disagree that greater clarity and precision and falsifiability are virtues to be encouraged, or that a lack of responsibility or critical thinking or imagination are failings to be discouraged in economic study. Like other long-standing normative disputes, the dispute over the use of mathematics in economics may be found to have substantive values poised on either side, and it is precisely in face of the complexity of the problem that we must not despair with reason. Where a humean epistemology might conclude the differences to be sheer and irreconcilable and that all we can do ultimately is choose our side and fight for it, the epistemology of Part II would warn us to expect strong dogmatisms pitted against strong scepticisms and advise us that there may be no single side to be chosen. Better perhaps to court the friendship and the enmity of both! Indeed the bitterness of the conflict could be explained by the fact each party has tended to deny the *legitimacy* of the other's work, as if the legitimacy of research in any complex field of inquiry and scholarship, whether science or literature or economics or philosophy or mathematics itself, can be universally legislated by some or other unique and general and exceptionless rule. Protagonists in divisions on substantive questions in economics have seldom charged one another with not being economists at all, in the way protagonists in this division on the choice of methods seem on occasion to have done.

A juster perspective may be possible by applying the model of the structure of concepts given in Chapter 5. Concepts like 'economist' or 'advance in economic understanding' may be better understood as family resemblance concepts, whose instances are objectively ascertainable and yet are of indefinite variety, requiring careful description of context and circumstance, of the particular 'language-game' within which they are intended to be understood. If we abandoned the idea, which seems to be shared by many mathematical economists as well as their critics, that there must exist some unique and identifiable criterion or set of criteria determining what makes an economist or what makes a piece of economic study, we would be able to take seriously the manifold diversity of economic thought *as it actually is*, and to recognize that just as the phenomena we are concerned to study are complex and various, so the methods we need may have to be complex and various. Here as elsewhere the antidote to dogmatisms of all kinds must be freedom of inquiry and expression. Whether the application of a particular method or technique to a particular economic problem indicates a lack of responsibility or imagination or critical thinking, or whether it has led to greater clarity or precision or falsifiability, or to what extent it has done a combination of these things, is a question capable of a disinterested and objective answer. While it may be hard work to determine the answer in some cases (for example the method of analogy may need to be applied, comparing and contrasting the question at hand with others whose answers are not presently in dispute), and even futile work in most cases, what we may be confident about is that it is *possible* for the answer to be determined in every case.

Second, in view of the seriousness of the economic controversy, it is remarkable that scant attention has been paid by either side to the discussions among mathematicians and mathematical philosophers about the ultimate character of mathematics itself. While there has been much abstract thinking in contemporary economics, perhaps we have not been abstract enough! For the relationship that the axioms and theorems of mathematical economics *can possibly* have to the reality of economic life and phenomena is certainly an abstract epistemological question, but one which has received little if any serious thought on the part of either mathematical economists or their critics. Russell wrote at one place of how in mathematics it is possible either to look telescopically forward 'towards gradually increasing complexity: from integers to fractions, real numbers, complex numbers; from addition and multiplication to differentiation and integration, and on to the higher mathematics', or to look microscopically 'backward to the logical foundations of the things that we are inclined to take for granted . . . . by analyzing, to greater and greater abstractness and logical simplicity; instead of asking what can be defined and deduced from what is assumed to begin with, we ask instead what more general ideas and principles can be found, in terms of which what was our starting-point can be defined or deduced.'[13] By this analogy mathematical economics has been telescopic, as when it is said by Debreu and Samuelson that the 'frontier refinements' of mathematics have been finding use in contemporary mathematical economics. But if we looked even briefly in the other direction in which Russell pointed, we would find a sight quite different from the one to which we have grown accustomed. Here are a rich assortment of continuing questions and controversies in which are engaged some of the great figures of modern logic, mathematics, science and philosophy. Here are leaders and loyalties, doctrines and dissenters, spirited attacks and exchanges, noble admissions of error and paradox and puzzlement – leading one participant to even remark 'it has proved not to be intuitively clear what is intuitively clear in mathematics'.[14]

In particular, mathematics most definitely treats of certain kinds of objects, such as points, lines, spaces, numbers, quantifiers, and so on. Yet these objects are surely not objects like the objects of natural science. For one thing, unlike the table in this room or the tree outside the window or the city of Paris or the planet Venus, mathematical objects evidently do not have any real location. 'Certainly there are such things as numbers, but surely there is no such *thing* as a number. What sort of a thing is it that is not a *thing* and yet is not nothing at all?'[15] Many kinds of answer have been offered in discussions in the philosophy of mathematics to this sort of question, and of these three may have special bearing upon an analysis of the economic debate: (i) that mathematics is an abstraction of the reality in which we actually live (empiricism); (ii) that mathematics is an abstraction of a transcendental reality in which we most definitely do not live (platonism); and (iii) that mathematics is an abstraction of no sort of reality at all (formalism).[16] Let us briefly consider each of these in turn.

The empiricist thesis, represented by Mill, would see mathematics as not differing in kind from empirical science but as a species of empirical science itself, just the most certain and general and abstract of all. Mathematical writing is a shorthand way of describing relationships between the actual objects of our universe. Thus Mill suggested that our understanding of a number like three would derive from our recognition that it corresponded to particular collections of physical objects like three horses or three pebbles: '[W]e may call "Three is two and one" a definition of three; but the calculations which depend on that proposition do not follow from the definition itself, but from an arithmetical theorem presupposed in it, namely that collections of objects exist, which while they impress the senses thus $^{\circ}{}_{\circ}{}^{\circ}$, may be separated into two parts, thus $\circ\circ$ $\circ$. This proposition being granted, we term all such parcels Threes, after which the enunciation of the above-mentioned physical fact will serve also as a definition of the word Three . . . . every number represents that particular number of all things without distinction. . . .' 'The mere written characters, *a*, *b*, *x*, *y*, *z*, serve as well for representatives of Things in general, as any more complex and apparently more concrete conception. That we are conscious of them, however, in their character of things, and not of mere signs, is evident from the fact that our whole process of reasoning is carried on by predicating of them the properties of things. . . . The inferences, therefore, which are successively drawn, are inferences concerning things, not symbols.'[17]

The criticism of Frege would appear to have been decisive in discrediting the empiricist view, at least in the form in which Mill had stated it. Mill seemed to have no place for zero or the imaginary numbers or the irrationals, all of which are legitimate objects of mathematical inquiry yet are not perceivable by the senses, and we surely do not have to perceive zero pebbles or $\sqrt{2}$ horses to understand the concepts of zero or $\sqrt{2}$. (Mill's view is to be contrasted however with the modern opinion of Professor Hilary Putnam, that mathematics does in fact employ empirical and 'quasi-empirical' methods.[18])

The second thesis is one we have met already in Chapter 5, namely, the highly influential thesis of platonism represented by G. H. Hardy, Kurt Gödel, and many others, possibly including Frege and Russell as well.[19] The things we find in the world would be taken by the platonist to be distorted and defective versions of ideal entities not given to experience. The dot on a piece of paper we call a point is but a defective image of the *ideal* point which has no parts or magnitude, the chalk mark on the blackboard we call a line is but a defective version of the *ideal* line without breadth or width, and so on. It is such ideal points, lines, spaces, etc., which are the true objects of mathematical inquiry. Mathematical objects do not have location in the world in which we live but instead inhabit a kind of transcendental parallel universe, a domain reachable through the reasonings of the pure mathematician, whose task it becomes to discover and chart its unobservable terrain in the way the geographer and astronomer discover and chart the observable earth and universe in which we live. As Michael Dummett puts it: 'Platonism, as a philosophy of mathematics, is founded on a simile: the comparison between the apprehension of mathematical truth to the perception of physical objects, and thus of mathematical reality to the physical universe.' It is 'the thesis that there really do exist such structures of abstract objects, and that we are capable of apprehending them by a faculty of intuition which is to abstract entities as our powers of perception are to physical objects.'[20] The platonist seeks to mentally grasp the ideal entities by his 'mind's hand' (in the phrase of Morton White) and once he believes himself to have done so, the expression of his understanding would amount to being not only an expression of objective knowledge but an expression of absolute knowledge as well, something necessarily free of error or exception.

In criticism, it may be said again as in Chapter 5 that the platonist's reference to a transcendental universe would appear to be no more than a declaration of faith – and one moreover which is unnecessary to questions in the theory of knowledge, since the question of the objectivity of mathematical knowledge and inquiry need not be made to depend on the existence of a transcendental mathematical reality.[21]

A third and again highly influential thesis has been that of formalism, represented by David Hilbert, Johann Von Neumann, Haskel Curry and many others. The formalist takes mathematical inquiry to be possible without reference to any and all realities, whether of our own world or that of the platonist or any other. Mathematics is independent of everything that is real or actual, and says nothing about anything that is real or actual. The pure mathematician does not abstract from reality – his theorems simply do not have reality as their concern and are incapable by themselves of having anything to say about it. The felicitous consequence of such a view is that the mathematician is liberated from having to justify in any way whatsoever the empirical plausibility of any of his axioms. In Russell's epigram: 'pure mathematics is the subject in which we do not know what we are talking about.'[22] The formalist requires himself first to state the 'vocabulary' he will use; that is to say, list all symbols and propositions to be defined as the 'primitives' or 'axioms' or 'tokens' for the project at hand. For instance

'$p \lor q$' will mean 'either $p$ or $q$'
'$f(x)$' will mean 'the property $f$ belongs to object $x$'
'$\exists x, f(x)$' will mean 'there exists an $x$ such that $f$ is its property'
'$\forall x, f(x)$' will mean 'for every $x$, $f$ is a property of $x$'
'$x = y$' will mean '$x$ and $y$ are names of the same object'

and so on. A list like this would be intended to be no more than a string of symbols, not signifying anything concrete, possessing only what meaning the mathematician shall choose to give each symbol. Then, 'rules of procedure' or 'operators' are to be stated, the use of which upon the axioms in the vocabulary will give rise to meaningful 'formulas'. Taking Von Neumann's illustrations, a combination of symbols

$$1 + 1 = 2$$

would be a meaningful formula which is true, while

$$1 + 1 = 1$$

would be a meaningful formula which is false, while

$$1 + \rightarrow = 1 \text{ or}$$
$$+ + 1 = \rightarrow$$

would remain meaningless strings of symbols. The act of 'proving a theorem' is that of deducing meaningful formulas thus defined via the successive application of the given rules of procedure to the given axioms. The 'consistency' of the axioms and rules of procedure with a theorem proved from them defines the truth of the theorem. A 'formal system' would be a set of theorems derived from given axioms by given rules such that no two theorems contradicted each other. To take a commonplace illustration, the axioms of chess would include that it is a game played by two on an 8 × 8 board, each player having sixteen pieces, of which eight are of one kind, two each are of three other kinds, and each of the remaining two is of one of two further kinds, and so on. The pieces may be called anything we wish and are not intended to refer to any real objects outside the game. The rules of procedure decree 'the King' may move one square in any direction, 'the Queen' may move any number of squares in any direction, 'the pawns' shall be on the second row of each player at the beginning of play, and so on. Given the axioms and the rules of procedure, it is then a trivial theorem to prove that White can move a pawn to the square called K4: we may say there *exists* a consistent move by White of pawn to K4. As a game proceeded, a theorem from a particular configuration of the pieces might be deduced like 'White is mate in three moves', i.e. there may be said to exist a set of consistent moves by Black which forces such an outcome. The 'formal system' of chess would be the set of all such provable theorems, given the axioms and the rules of the game.

The value of the formalist thesis lay in its liberation of the mathematician. It 'allowed mathematicians to investigate any kind of mathematical theory without asking whether any "reality" corresponded to it.'[23] As Hilbert put it in correspondence with Frege: 'As long as I have thought, written and lectured about these matters, I have always [believed]: if arbitrarily postulated axioms do not contradict each other with their collective consequences, then they are true and the things defined by means of the axioms exist. That, for me, is the criterion of truth and existence.'[24] The kind of 'existence' Hilbert meant was not one in the physical world as when we say there exists a table in this room, but rather the kind as when we say there exists a way for Black to mate White in three moves. The consistency of a set of axioms *is* all there is to the existence of a formal mathematical structure.[25] The formalist stresses the *independence* of mathematics from empirical science. Empirical experiments can neither prove nor disprove a mathematical theorem, and equally a mathematical theorem by itself can neither refute nor corroborate an empirical hypothesis. To take a famous example, the formal consistency of euclidean geometry and of the various non-euclidean geometries cannot by themselves tell us whether physical space is euclidean or non-euclidean, or euclidean in the small and non-euclidean in the large, and so on.

In criticism, it may be said that the recondite theorems of Gödel have cast doubt on the viability of the full formalist programme, and raised the question whether it too may not suffer from serious and fatal internal weaknesses.[26] Also, from the formalist's self-conscious assertion of the total independence of mathematical axioms and theorems from their interpretations, that mathematical symbols are intrinsically meaningless and only acquire any significance that they can in the context of a consistent mathematical structure, it would seem to follow that the formalist thesis must be silent on how mathematics may be in fact applied, on what grounds a particular theorem is or is not to be accepted. As Curry himself put it in a critique of Hilbert: the question of 'acceptability' is the question of the relationship of mathematical theorems to their applications, 'a matter of interpreting the theory in relation to some subject matter'; while the consistency of a formal system stressed by Hilbert is an internal criterion of acceptability, it is not the only one we may think of; in general, 'acceptability is relative to a purpose; discussion of the usefulness of a mathematical theory is pointless until a particular purpose has been stated.'[27] Insofar as this is true, it would seem our old friend, human judgement, in all its complexity, is found again to have to make a necessary reappearance, even in the otherwise austere terrain traversed by the formalist mathematician. If mathematics is to be useful, if it is to have a value or a utility, then there is *judgement* required in its use. And of course, as has been argued throughout in this work, there is every reason to suppose such judgements to be capable themselves of being objectively supported or criticized.

**3.** The possible bearing upon modern economic theory of these brief philosophical considerations may be illustrated in two specific contexts: the theory of probability and expected utility, and the theory of general equilibrium.

In the theory of probability, many contemporary economic theorists appear to have followed the extreme or moderated subjectivism represented in England by F. P. Ramsey's review of J. M. Keynes's *Treatise on Probability*, in Europe by Bruno de

Finetti's Poincaré Lectures, and in the United States by L. J. Savage's *Foundations of Statistics*.[29] According to such a theory, a judgement of probability would be understood as the personal degree of belief of an individual agent with respect to the uncertain occurrence of an event, constrained only by the weak requirement that the agent not be allowed to bet against himself – e.g., the agent may not assign a probability of one fourth to an event $S$ as well as a probability of one fourth to its contrary $\sim S$. Indeed the subjective probabilist may be seen to stand in close relationship with the humean and the emotivist in moral philosophy – as when Savage declared logic to be 'a crude but sometimes handy empirical psychological theory', or when de Finetti declared that while there might be 'rather profound psychological reasons which make the exact or approximate agreement that is observed between the opinions of different individuals very natural . . . there are no reasons, rational, positive, or metaphysical, that can give this fact any meaning beyond that of a simple agreement of subjective opinions.'[30] Subjectivist probabilists have been especially emphatic in rejecting any hint of a platonist ontology, as when de Finetti declared: 'Probability does not exist!' – by which he is taken to mean probability 'does not exist in an objective sense, in other words he denies the existence of physical probability.'[31] A small rebellion has been led for a number of years now against the subjectivist school by the French theorist Professor Maurice Allais, who declares to the contrary with as much emphasis as de Finetti: 'The probability of an event likely to occur repeatedly under the same conditions is a physical quantity corresponding to a physical reality.'[32] In view of our discussions, a possible means to the resolution of this dispute may be offered. *Viz.*, it is possible that de Finetti and other subjectivist probabilists have wanted to deny a platonist ontology *and so* have believed it necessary to deny the possible objectivity of probable knowledge; while Allais has wanted to defend the possible objectivity of probable knowledge *and so* has believed it necessary to accept a platonist ontology. In other words, it is possible that both sides have unwittingly shared the same epistemological assumption which we have found to be of questionable soundness, namely, that a claim to objective knowledge in a given context must go hand in hand with a platonist theory of existence. Moreover, relative to discussion of the concept of probability itself, there may have been a subtle reversal of philosophical positions when it comes to the theory of expected utility which has derived from the subjectivist view of probability. For subjectivist probabilists in economic theory have sometimes given the impression of maintaining the platonistic belief that the Von Neumann-Morgenstern model of an agent maximizing 'expected utility' defines or describes absolutely the behaviour of an *ideal* rational agent, whether or not it can find a counterpart in the actual world in which we live. On the other hand, Allais may be seen on this point to have launched an *anti*-platonist protest – rightly arguing that to move from the premise 'the only rational behaviour is behaviour conforming to the American [expected utility maximizing] School' to the conclusion 'anyone who does not conform to these axioms is irrational' would be dogmatic and unfounded.[33]

A juster alternative may be possible. The important truth the subjectivist probabilist has been concerned to emphasize may be seen as analogous to the important truth we have (in Part I) seen the humean economist to be concerned to emphasize, namely, that the circumstantial evidence on the basis of which an individual agent makes the probability judgement he does in a given case may be available peculiarly to the agent and not to others. In other words, it will usually be the case as a matter of fact that the individual agent has a kind of *privileged access* to the relevant evidence necessary for the decisions which happen to concern him most. Once we make such an observation about the availability of evidence, we may be led in rough discussion to treat a statement of probability as synonymous with the personal degree of belief that the individual agent, given his privileged access to the relevant evidence, happens to attach to an event. But that would not imply, as the subjectivist probabilist would have us believe it does, that such a probability judgement cannot be mistaken – *objectively* mistaken. Like other kinds of judgements, probability judgements may be thought of as liable to error regardless of who happens to be making them, and we have seen moreover that a recognition of this sort would not have to depend on any endorsement of a platonist ontology. Keynes remarked at one place 'a proposition is not probable because we think it is so'[34] – just as the theory of knowledge advanced in Part II would suggest that a proposition is not true because we happen to think it is so, or a proposition is not right because we happen to think it is so. Something may be true *and* we may believe it to be true; these are two separate things. Similarly something may be right *and* we may believe it to be right; these are again two separate things. Similarly something may be probable *and* we may believe it to be probable – that these are two separate things would seem to be the point of Keynes's remark. Things are not made probable or true or right merely because you or I or any number of persons happen to think them so. All the meteorological evidence may point to heavy rainfall being imminent, or all the medical evidence may point to a treatment being a fake cure for some disease, yet someone might choose to place a high subjective probability on the contrary and even be willing to bet sums of money in a consistent way as a token of the depth and sincerity of his belief. The subjective probabilist may have to say there is nothing unreasonable about such a belief even though there *is* something unreasonable about it. Like the humean and the emotivist, the subjective probabilist may have nothing to say to someone who refuses to reason or discuss or accept objective evidence for what it is.

Of course insofar as probability judgements guide our actions, it may be that it is the subjective probabilities of people, regardless of their accuracy, which need to be studied if we are to explain or predict actual behaviour, just as it is the subjective opinions of voters which interest the pollster trying to explain or predict the outcome of an election or the subjective preferences of consumers which interest the advertiser. Thus the subjectivist theory may be useful for purposes of description and prediction. In general however, if we grant knowledge to be well described as a family resemblance concept capable of indefinitely varied kind and instance, it may be preferable to take probable knowledge to be a particular species of it, one which, indeed, may be itself capable of varied kind and instance. Just as the way in which we can possibly know something about the present may differ in principle from the way in which we can possibly know something about the past, or the way in which we can know something about our own minds from the way in which we can know something about someone else's mind, so it may be that the way in which we can know something with certainty may differ in principle from the way in which we can know something with

probability.[35] Probable knowledge, like scientific knowledge or
moral knowledge or historical knowledge, may be something
objectively ascertainable and yet relative to the given circumstantial evidence available to the individual agent. Thus the concerns
of the subjectivist probabilist can be met even while we avoid the
paradoxes into which he would otherwise lead us. Indeed this
would seem to have been a main point of Keynes's line of
argument: 'The terms "certain" and "probable" describe the
various degrees of rational belief about a proposition which
different amounts of knowledge authorise us to entertain. All
propositions are true or false, but the knowledge we have of
them depends on our circumstances; and while it is often
convenient to speak of propositions as certain or probable, this
expresses strictly a relationship in which they stand to a *corpus* of
knowledge, actual or hypothetical, and not a characteristic of the
propositions in themselves. A proposition is capable at the same
time of various degrees of this relationship, depending upon the
knowledge to which it is related, so that it is without significance
to call a proposition probable unless we specify the knowledge to
which we are relating it.' Furthermore, given the particular
evidence available, judgements of probability are subject to
common reasoning and should not be seen merely as possible
expressions of caprice: 'When once the facts are given which
determine our knowledge, what is probable or improbable has
been fixed objectively, and is independent of our opinion. The
theory of probability is logical, therefore, because it is concerned
with the degree of belief which it is *rational* to entertain in given
conditions, and not merely with the actual beliefs of particular
individuals, which may or may not be rational.'[36] Ramsey's
review of *A Treatise on Probability* would seem to have missed
this line of argument, and the subsequent influence of the review
among modern economic theorists may have contributed to the
neglect of Keynes's original work. The purpose of this brief note
will have been served if it is seen that, once the Spell of Hume
has been broken, it is possible for this neglect to be redressed.

**4.** A second context in which our epistemological discussion
may have bearing is the theory of general equilibrium, which has
been the centrepiece of much economic study in recent decades.
Among the many distinguished economists who have contributed

to it in recent times have been Professor Debreu, Professor Arrow and Professor Hahn, with Debreu's *Theory of Value* and Arrow and Hahn's *General Competitive Analysis* being two important current statements of the theory. Yet Debreu appears to have taken a formalist perspective in mathematics with some hints at platonism, while Arrow and Hahn have appeared to be platonist with some hints at empiricism, when it is far from clear that these are points of view which are or can be made compatible with one another.

From *Theory of Value* onwards, Debreu has maintained as his purpose to treat economic subjects 'with the standards of rigor of the contemporary formalist school of mathematics'.[37] As we have seen, a formalist perspective would take individual mathematical objects and symbols to be meaningless in themselves, and not intended to refer to any actual economic events or phenomena. The task of the mathematical economist then would be to test by explicit rules of deductive procedure whether or not a given set of axioms is consistent. If so, the existence of a formal mathematical structure would be established, and the individual mathematical objects would find meaning within its defined context. Thus when Debreu says the mathematical propositions of *Theory of Value* are 'logically entirely disconnected' from their 'interpretations', and so from any reference to the actual world, he may be seen as being correctly formalist and hilbertian in particular.[38] The mathematics itself is independent of any of countless possible interpretations that can be given to it, real or imaginary, sensible or absurd, and does not by itself have anything to say about the actual world outside the window. We may posit axioms like:

Let $E^n$ be an $n$-dimensional Euclidean space.

Let there be a set $H$ with a finite number of elements.

Let each element $h \in H$ have attributed to it a closed and convex subspace $X_h \subset E^n$. . . .

Let a relation $R$ be defined for each $h$ such that for any pair $(x_1 x_2) \in X_h$, either $x_1 R x_2$, or $x_2 R x_1$, or $x_1 R x_2$ & $x_2 R x_1$. . . .

Let there be a set $F$ with a finite number of elements.

Let each element $f \in F$ have attributed to it a subspace $Y_f \subset E^n$. . . .

And so on. The meanings we happen to attach to the ciphers put down on paper are superfluous to the act of stating the axioms themselves. To have said '$E^n$' is the 'commodity space' or '$h \in H$' is 'a household' or '$f \in F$' is 'a firm' is as unnecessary to the mathematics itself as the giving of particular names to the pieces in chess is to the playing of chess itself. That we speak about the axioms of chess the way we do implies nothing about the axioms themselves, nor *a fortiori* about any actual armies engaged in real battle outside the game. Similarly the axioms of Debreu's theory can be stated and particular meanings attached to them without any reference to particular households or firms engaged in economic life in any real economy whatsoever. Then, the rules of procedure in chess decree that certain moves are permissible and others are not; whence we may deduce theorems like 'White can move a pawn to K4' or 'Black can mate in three moves'. Similarly we may apply to Debreu's stated axioms a theorem of Weierstrass:

'If $f$ is a continuous function from a non-empty compact set $S$ to the real line, $f\colon S \to R$, then $f(S)$ has a maximum'

to obtain

'If $U_h$ is a continuous function from a non-empty compact subspace $B_h \subset X_h$ to the real line, $U_h\colon B_h \to R$, then $U_h(X_h)$ has a maximum'.

Next by attaching specific connotations to $X_h$, $B_h$, and $U_h(X_h)$, we can read a theorem of economics:

'If there is a suitably defined utility function for the individual household then there exists a vector of consumption goods within the budget set which gives maximum utility'.

Or, we may take a theorem of Brouwer:

'If $A$ is a compact convex subspace and if $f\colon A \to A$ is a continuous function, then $f$ has a fixed point, i.e., there exists $a \in A$ such that $f(a) = a$'

and attach specific connotations appropriately to obtain

'There exists a vector of relative prices such that every agent solves its appropriate constrained optimization problem given this vector, and total excess demand is zero for each good'.

157

The existence of such a vector of prices may be referred to as the existence of an 'equilibrium' of the economy. But by that we would not imply – indeed according to the formalist perspective we *could* not imply – that we have said anything at all about any real economic phenomenon. A general equilibrium would 'exist' in the same sense that a way can exist for Black to mate White in three moves; it would not exist in the sense the table in this room or the city of Paris may be said to exist. Thus the formal (uninterpreted) structure presented in *Theory of Value* may be seen as standing to the simultaneous equations of Walras and Hicks and Samuelson rather in the way that Hilbert's *Foundations of Geometry* stands to Euclid: as a statement of consistent systems of axioms establishing the existence of particular formal mathematical structures. As such, both the formal (uninterpreted) theory of general equilibrium and Hilbert's axiomatization of geometry would be *internal* to mathematics. Neither would their correctness depend on any feature of the world in which we actually live, nor would anything in the world depend on the existence of these structures. The formal theory of general equilibrium may then be considered to consist of theorems which are unambiguously true; the theorems were true in the fifties, are true today, and will remain true at the millenium; they are true whether they are read in Tokyo or Cairo or on the moon or on Voyager II. Yet they are true in the same way that other theorems of mathematics are true, or the grand theorems of chess are true. By themselves they must be silent about any and all actual economic phenomena. Such, briefly, would be the consequence of a strict formalist perspective in mathematical economics.

In contrast, Arrow and Hahn have sought to place the significance of general equilibrium theory in a larger context in the history of economic thought. They have endorsed the widespread view that the primary intent of Adam Smith in *Wealth of Nations* was to make a universal claim of the allocative merits of a market economy, and furthermore that this claim did not begin to be examined by the standards of modern science until Walras's statement of a system of simultaneous equations of aggregate demands and supplies in relative prices. Walras's system was taken further by Hicks and Samuelson and others, but internal or technical weaknesses had remained. Specifically it had not been proven that $n-1$ independent excess demand equations in $n-1$ relative prices could have a solution. Through the use of newer and more fundamental mathematics, precise conditions sufficient for the existence of a general equilibrium came to be stated. Moreover, a general equilibrium could also be shown to be 'efficient' by the definition of Pareto, and so modern general equilibrium theory is to be seen to represent the culmination of the effort begun by Walras to examine the classical and neoclassical claims originating with Smith about the allocative merits of the market economy, and thus ultimately about the appropriate scope of the functions of civil government. Arrow and Hahn would add that there are numerous features of actual economies not accounted for within the basic model; for instance, forward contracts are less frequent in actual economies then they are assumed to be in the model. Such points of difference between reality and the model, Arrow and Hahn would argue, are grounds for believing the neoclassical belief to be subject to much qualification. The most famous alternative has been that of Keynes (as we have seen in Chapter 8) who had claimed to provide a general theory, a theory from which the neoclassical could derive but not conversely. The scope of general equilibrium analysis has been sought to be extended to ask whether Keynes's claim was justifiable, and until such a project is completed the question of the merits of neoclassical monetary theory may not be said to have been answered with the authority of economic science behind it.[39]

At the same time, as we have noted in Chapter 5, Professor Arrow was to remark in his Nobel Lecture: 'In my own thinking, the model of general equilibrium under uncertainty is *as much a normative ideal* as an empirical description. It is the way the actual world differs from the criteria of the model which suggests social policy to improve the efficiency with which risk bearing is allocated.'[40] And Professor Hahn has remarked that the model of general equilibrium 'serves a function similar to that which *an ideal and perfectly healthy body* might serve a clinical diagnostician when he looks at an actual body'; that although the model 'is known to conflict with the facts' and 'is not a description of an actual economy' it can still tell us 'what the world would have to look like' if the neoclassical view of the economy is to be plausible.[41] Thus it would seem the formal general equilibrium model is to be taken to describe some empirically possible economy though not any actual one, which is at the same time supposed to be the 'normative ideal' of actual market economies in the way the perfect point or line is supposed to be an idealization of the actual point or line we draw with chalk on the blackboard. It may be possible to identify where an actual economy is defective relative to this perfect structure, and thereby seek to improve it. In other words, Arrow and Hahn seem to have wished to endorse both a platonist ontology as well as something of a Millian empiricism – though it is far from clear that these can be made compatible either with one another or with the strict formalism embraced by Debreu (who hints at platonism as well at one place in speaking of the 'discovery' of axiomatic theories in economics[42]), let alone with their own subjectivism on the positive/normative relationship recorded in Chapter 2, or with the subjectivism which is to be found in the theory of social choice to be discussed in Chapter 10. If these are indeed accurate characterizations of some of the implicit philosophical premises which are to be found in parts of contemporary mathematical economics, then a conclusion we must be led to is that in some of the central theories of modern economic study, there may exist inconsistency at a more fundamental level of abstraction than we have been usually prepared to venture.

**5.** In sum, serious thought does not seem to have been given in modern economics to the nature of the relationship between mathematical economics and the reality of economic life and phenomena. This is an abstract and logical question descending in part from the question of the relationship between reality and mathematics itself. Neither mathematical economists nor their critics seem to have asked whether modern mathematical economics *can* be made to say all that has been claimed for it. If it is true that mathematics *by itself* is silent even about the great questions of physics such as whether or not actual space is euclidean or non-euclidean or euclidean in the small and non-euclidean in the large (as Hilbert and probably Frege and Russell and Wittgenstein would have maintained) then is it *logically* possible for it to be made to answer such momentous questions in political economy as to what happens to be the optimum scope of civil government everywhere or anywhere? Moreover if we take mathematics by itself to be silent about any and all actual phenomena, whether in physics or economics or anywhere else, would we have implied by that that mathematics was not *valuable* – indeed that it was not *indispensable* to empirical inquiry? Professor R. M. Solow remarks: 'I don't feel that I understand something until I have a (usually mathematical) model of it.'[43] Here would be a quite radical scepticism being expressed, which taken literally would mean we cannot know or understand anything in the actual world without a mathematical model of it. An associated dogmatism may be that mathematical models constitute the only truly legitimate route to knowledge and understanding in economic science. Yet here as elsewhere we need not take the sceptic's words at face value. Some Moorean commonsense can be a sufficient antidote. For it is clear that we can and do know any number of things perfectly well without any mathematics at all, such as that there is a table in this room or a tree outside the window or that here is a taxi driver who knows how to get his passengers from one place to another. Here as elsewhere the sceptic may be understood to mean something other than what he says: that the sheer scale and complexity of the actual phenomena which the economist is called upon to interpret and comment on often makes it necessary to employ *indirect* means, means which may be able to reduce both the scale and the complexity to reasonable and comprehensible proportions. And most notable among such means would be that of mathematical modelling.

Models in any discipline are created not for fun or private profit, and ought to have a serious purpose. (Part of the critics' protest has been that there is much mathematical modelling in contemporary university economics without serious purpose, that models *are* being created merely for fun or private profit.) Within pure mathematics itself, what would be meant by a 'model' is something like this: given such and such a set of axioms, is there any interpretation of these axioms such that they are consistent with one another? If so, this *interpretation* would be defined to be 'a model' for the particular set of axioms. And, within a formalist perspective, such a use of the concept 'model' would not be intended to say anything at all about real or actual objects.[44] By contrast, within an empirical science like physics or biology or

161

anthropology or economics a 'model' would have precisely the purpose of telling us something about reality which we happen to find greatly more difficult in telling by other means like direct observation. And the reality referred to would not be the transcendental heaven of the platonist but the actual world or universe in which we live. Thus a road map, a globe, the floor plan of an apartment, a calendar or diary, the blueprints for a bridge or a house, a scale model of an aircraft, a political caricature, Watson and Crick's double helix, Tolstoy's Kutusov – each has some informative utility that may be sought to be appreciated. A model which attempted a one-to-one correspondence with reality (if such a thing can be imagined) would not be a model of reality but reality itself; something closest to being identical with reality may be useless as a model, because it would tell us little or nothing we could not have found out by means like direct observation. For a model to have value or utility it may be necessary (though clearly it will not be sufficient) for some features of the 'original' phenomena to be suppressed, while other features are duplicated and therefore come to be exaggerated. Thus a scale model has the same three dimensions of the original but suppresses its true size, a blueprint or a contour map is a two-dimensional model of a three-dimensional original, and so on. Mathematical models in economics are evidently neither like physical scale models nor like two-dimensional maps of a three-dimensional reality. Rather they may be compared perhaps with what have been called 'analogue' models: where there would have to be first 'a change of medium' from the original objects and phenomena of economic life to the mathematical symbolism on paper, with an attempt being made to conserve 'truth value' in the sense 'every incidence of a relation in the original must be echoed by a corresponding incidence of a correlated relation in the analogue model.'[45] Theorems then may be established deductively from the axioms of the model. Finally the transformation must be applied in reverse, so the theorems of the model would be now sought to be interpreted as referring to the original economic phenomena which had been thought too complex to be understood by direct observation.

In a process of this sort, it will be our old friend *judgement* which must make an appearance once more, required first in making the abstraction from the actual phenomena of economic life to the mathematical symbolism on paper, and secondly in transforming in reverse the results of the model to ascertain their significance and upshot to actual economic phenomena. As Wittgenstein put it: 'in real life a mathematical proposition is never what we want. Rather, we make use of mathematical propositions only in inferences from propositions that do not belong to mathematics to others that likewise do not belong to mathematics.'[46] Or as Peirce put it in typical fashion: 'An engineer, or a business company . . . or a physicist, finds it suits his purpose to ascertain what the necessary consequences of possible facts would be; but the facts are so complicated that he cannot deal with them in his usual way. He calls upon a mathematician and states the question. Now the mathematician does not conceive it to be any part of his duty to verify the facts stated. . . . At the same time, it frequently happens that the facts, as stated, are insufficient to answer the question that is put. Accordingly, the first business of the mathematician, often a most difficult task, is to frame another simpler but quite fictitious problem . . . which shall be within his powers, while at the same time it is sufficiently like the problem set before him to answer, well or ill, as a substitute for it. This substituted problem differs also from that which was first set before the mathematician in another respect: namely, that it is highly abstract. All features that have no bearing upon the relations of the premises to the conclusion are effaced and obliterated. . . . Thus, the mathematician does two very different things: namely, he first frames a pure hypothesis stripped of all features which do not concern the drawing of consequences from it, and this he does without inquiring or caring whether it agrees with the actual facts or not; and secondly, he proceeds to draw necessary consequences from that hypothesis.'[47] Or in Carl Hempel's metaphor: 'in the establishment of empirical knowledge, mathematics (as well as logic) has, so to speak, the function of a theoretical juice extractor: the techniques of mathematical and logical theory can produce no more juice of factual information than is contained in the assumptions to which they are applied; but they may produce a great deal more juice of this kind than might have been anticipated upon a first intuitive inspection of those assumptions which form the raw material for the extractor.'[48] In any case of mathematical application, an exercise of judgement is necessarily called for – as to what does and what does not have bearing upon the relations of the premises to the conclusion, as to what is to be effaced and what is to be accentuated, as to what is relevant and what is not, as to whether or not the questions from the model to which we can give direct answers are sufficiently like those from the reality to which we happen to find we cannot. And again, according to the theory of knowledge advanced in Part II, every such judgement needs to be thought of not as a mere expression of subjective caprice or prejudice but as something which is open to reasonable and open-ended and objective discussion.

Thus it may be possible to take a view that while mathematics by itself cannot say anything about economic reality, and while nothing real or actual depends ultimately on the formal validity of any mathematical theorem, mathematics is nevertheless valuable – indeed that it is *in practice* indispensable to empirical inquiry, whether in economics or elsewhere. Whenever we ask questions of real phenomena, we must necessarily make use of concepts; and just as there are concepts of natural science like 'acceleration' and 'wavelength' and 'element' and 'isotope' and 'vertebrate' and 'anaerobic', or of psychology like 'neurosis' and 'intelligence' and 'retardation', or of mathematics like 'real number' and 'sequence' and 'continuous', or of jurisprudence like 'tort' and 'intent' and 'sovereignty', so too there are concepts necessary for an understanding of economic phenomena – such as 'relative price' and 'rate of interest' and 'utility' and 'diminishing returns to scale' and 'competitive market' and 'capital good' and 'human capital' and 'risk aversion' and so on. A constant feature of our reasoning involves judging by comparison and contrast such things as whether a particular concept is empty or has instances falling under it, whether these instances of our observations fall under this concept or that, whether a concept has been well defined or needs improvement. While mathematics by itself may not be able to say anything about real economic phenomena, it may have been indispensable in practice to the task of the clarification and elucidation of the conceptual basis of economic science, without which we would not be able to ask questions of economic reality at all or as readily. For example, a concept like 'rate of interest' is clarified when it is defined in terms of intertemporal relative prices, or 'production activity' when it is defined in terms of the transformation of inputs into outputs. And the activity of competition is elucidated to an extent by the metaphor of a '*tâtonnement*', as are the manifold and indefinitely complex relationships between markets by the metaphors of general equilibrium theory – and similarly in many scores of other cases. Many of our concepts may be hard to define and clarify, and equally hard to ascertain instances of. Thus it may be we shall continue to argue for many years over such questions as the best definition of a hard compound concept like 'involuntary unemployment in the long run', and whether it has any instances falling under it. Yet it frequently has been through the application of mathematical definitions and methods that we have succeeded in clarifying many of those concepts which are today part of the common vernacular when questions must be asked about the complex kinds of phenomena that we face. More generally it may be said: the primary task of economic theory or analytical economics is the clarification and elucidation of the conceptual basis of the science. When faced with a particular problematic situation, it is to the analytical economist, whether or not he or she is a mathematical economist, to whom we turn for conceptual guidance and criticism. Ultimately, all theory is (or ought to be) 'Critique of Language'.

It may be seen, then, that an argument can be developed which is at odds both with the received view of mathematical economists themselves about the upshot of mathematical economics, and with the received criticisms of that view. There may be positive consequences for economic science of courting the friendship and the enmity of both sides. And that perhaps is how it should be. Keynes wrote in one place that the student of economics needs to be 'mathematician, historian, statesman and philosopher – in some degree. He must understand symbols and speak in words. He must contemplate the particular in terms of the general, and touch abstract and concrete in the same flight of thought. He must study the present in the light of the past for the purposes of the future. No part of man's nature or his institutions must lie entirely outside his regard. He must be purposeful and disinterested in a simultaneous mood: as aloof and incorruptible as an artist, yet sometimes as near the earth as a politician.'[49] This is not an easy order to fulfil – yet if it had been taken more seriously by more in the last half-century, there would surely have been less of the kind of confusion and conflict that this chapter has sought to clarify and dissolve.

# 10

# *Remarks on the Foundations of Welfare Economics*

At the heart of the subject referred to as the foundations of welfare economics or theoretical welfare economics or most recently the theory of social choice, has been the question of the appropriate relationship between the positive and the normative, as have been wider questions of the scope of reason in the making of judgements and the role of the economic expert in society. A quite different perspective upon these questions will be seen to have been offered in the preceding chapters than is to be found in the post-war conventions of the subject. One point of difference which may be observed straightaway arises from the latter being premised for the most part on a quite radical moral scepticism, while one of the main purposes of the present work has been to show some of the logical difficulties with holding such a position. Following from an assumption of moral scepticism has been the belief that interpersonal comparisons of utility are not possible to be made objectively, and tied up to this belief has been the notion of the measurability or immeasurability of utility. It is this belief too, more than anything else, which seems to have motivated the entire theory of social choice; indeed the quintessential belief of the moral sceptic in economics may be that Professor Arrow's famous theorem proved, under seemingly weak but desirable conditions of individual freedom, the impossibility of the existence of a social good (or we might say following Frege, proved the emptiness of the concept of a social good). The purpose of this chapter will be to offer a few further suggestions towards helping to dissolve some of the conceptual puzzles faced in welfare economics, or at least to clarify their possible philosophical sources. The preceding chapters have advanced a theory of economic knowledge which is at the same time objectivist and explicitly anti-absolutist or anti-platonist. Insofar as the post-war conventions of welfare economics have been steeped in subjectivism and/or platonism, the interpretations given here will be found to be critical and even perhaps quite radical in nature. Yet Professor Arrow himself concluded his Nobel Lecture saying the philosophical implications of his theorem were not clear, and expressed a hope that his theorem would be seen 'as a challenge rather than as a discouraging barrier'.[1] It will be in such a spirit of a continuing and mutually critical tradition of scholarship that the remarks offered here are intended to be taken.

**2.** As the issues involved are well known to be slippery to the grasp, it may be useful to offer a synopsis of the argument at the outset.

*Remark A* The theory of demand given by Marshall was relatively direct, literal and commonsensical, whereas the theory of demand given by Hicks has been indirect, metaphorical and abstract. Marshall's use of a concept of utility was not unnatural since a part of his purpose was realistic description of the actual business of life. Hicks's theory has had innumerable uses in modern economics but one ill consequence: that of sending Marshall's theory into exile. The young Hicks's scepticism of the meaningfulness of the Marshallian concept of utility was misdirected, and this is something which the older Hicks has acknowledged.

*Remark B* Robbins's scepticism of interpersonal comparisons amounted to a species of solipsism. The problem of solipsism may have a relatively straightforward philosophical solution via establishing the possibility of different logical kinds of objective knowledge.

*Remark C* Interpersonal comparisons are a species of judgement, and are therefore open to objective reasoning (which itself may be various in kind and open-ended in scope and direction, as has been argued in previous chapters).

*Remark D* The question of whether a judgement *can be* made objectively is separate from (and prior to) the question of *who* should be making a judgement in a given case. Interpersonal comparisons are a species of judgement. The question of whether interpersonal comparisons *can be* made objectively is a separate question from the question of *who* should be making them in a given case.

*Remark E* For interpersonal comparisons to be possible to be made objectively in this sense does not say anything at all about the concept of utility being open to measurement or quantification. There is no such implication unless one made a link between an objectivist theory of knowledge and a platonist theory of existence – *viz.*, assuming that if the concept of utility is taken to be meaningful then measurements of utility would be meaningful as well (perhaps corresponding to distances defined in some sort of invisible, transcendental domain).

*Remark F* That such a link is unnecessary has been argued in previous chapters, especially in Part II. Yet the idea that objectivity is somehow tied up with platonism is widespread. It prevails both among subjectivists, who, wishing to reject platonism, go on to reject objectivity; and among absolutists, who, wishing to endorse objectivity, go on to embrace platonism. The philosophical malaise often found in contemporary economic theory of being alternately subjectivist and absolutist may be a result of an acceptance of this idea (as it may be also of an ambivalence between formalist and platonist views of mathematics).

*Remark G* Confounding objectivity with platonism may lead to a further malaise of supposing utility and interpersonal comparisons are meaningful if and only if the State should be making interpersonal comparisons (specifically redistributions such as via progressive income tax). This has either of two mutually exclusive symptoms, *viz.*, supposing *if* utility and interpersonal comparisons are meaningful *then* the State should be making redistributions; or supposing *if* the State should not be making redistributions *then* neither utility nor *a fortiori* interpersonal comparisons can be meaningful.

*Remark H* Whether or not the State should redistribute in a given case is a separate question from whether or not the State should be involved in making interpersonal comparisons. (For example the judiciary clearly makes interpersonal comparisons but not all of these involve redistributions.) Whether the State should redistribute in a given case and whether the State should be making interpersonal comparisons in a given case is each a distinct question from whether interpersonal comparisons can be meaningful.

*Remark I* The theory of social choice pioneered by Arrow has been motivated by the scepticisms of Hicks and Robbins. Central to Arrow's theory has been his idea of an all-encompassing 'social state', over which individual preferences are to be defined. Given moral scepticism and an assumption of 'objectivity *if and only if* platonism', this may be the only way for an individual to have social opinions. But consequently the normal concept of an individual is lost. The human beings of social choice theory, like the human beings of modern demand theory, are not normal human beings.

*Remark J* The definition of each of Arrow's axioms depends on the definition of the social state. The resulting interpretation of Arrow's theorem might be plausible when the size of the society is as small as that of a committee, but it is quite unnatural otherwise. In particular, Sen has defined liberalism following Arrow's route, and this definition comes to look very different from what has been traditionally recognized as liberalism.

These remarks may seem extraordinarily radical relative to certain trends in contemporary economic theory, so it will be important to tread with special care and as much attention to detail as possible.

**3.** Among the most vexing questions encountered in welfare economics have been ones of the form 'Should $X$ be done if (or even if) it benefits A more than it benefits B?' If this is to be considered meaningful at all, the notion of a benefit or loss to A and of a benefit or loss to B have to be considered meaningful in the first place, as must be the possibility of comparisons between these. A pair of parallel divisions can be identified among twentieth-century economists on the matter – with Marshall, Wicksell, Pigou and Robertson among others seeming to stand to the one side and broadly answering that the notions are meaningful, and Pareto, Robbins, Hicks, Samuelson and Arrow among others seeming to stand to the other side and broadly answering that they are not. It may be helpful to remind ourselves of a representative view of each side.

Marshall's description of the nature of human wants and their satisfaction went like this: 'There is an endless variety of wants, but there is a limit to each separate want. This familiar and fundamental tendency of human nature may be stated in the "law of satiable wants" or of "diminishing utility" thus: The "total utility" of a thing to anyone (that is, the total pleasure or benefit it yields him) increases with every increase in his stock of it, but not as fast as his stock increases. If his stock increases at a uniform rate the benefit derived from it increases at a diminishing rate. . . . That part of the thing which he is only just induced to purchase may be called his "marginal purchase", because he is on the margin of doubt whether it is worth his while to incur the outlay required to obtain it. And the utility of his marginal purchase may be called the "marginal utility" of the thing to him. Or, if instead of buying it, he makes the thing himself, then its marginal utility is the utility of that part which he thinks is only just worth his while to make. And thus the law just given may be worded: The marginal utility of a thing to anyone diminishes with every increase in the amount of it he already has.'[2] A famous neoclassical observation followed. 'If a person has a thing which he can put to several uses, he will distribute it among these uses in such a way that it has the same marginal utility in all. For if it had a greater marginal utility in one use than another, he would gain by taking away some of it from the second use and applying it to the first.'[3] Marshall went on to argue that the purchaser of a good may be seen as buying an amount up to which the utility to him of the last unit just equalled the price being quoted. If tea was selling at two shillings a pound and a person bought ten pounds, we might say the difference in utility to him of ten pounds of tea instead of nine was just above two shillings, and the difference in utility to him of eleven pounds instead of ten was just below two shillings. Add to this an observation that every world contains more than one good and so all prices must be relative prices, and we have the famous condition of consumer equilibrium, that the ratio of the marginal utilities to a particular trader of two goods equals the ratio of the prices of the goods being quoted in the marketplace.

Hicks's initial objective in launching a critique of this account would seem to have to have been a relatively limited one: 'My work on this subject began with the endeavour to supply a needed theoretical foundation for statistical demand studies; so that there is a definite relevance to that field. Other matters of fundamental methodological importance are thrown up as well.'[4] Hicks's aim was to derive the demand curve mathematically, at least partly in the belief that this would be valuable for the purposes of econometrics, and indeed his collaborator R. G. D. Allen would become a pioneer of the statistical study of demand. With such a purpose in mind, it was understandable that Hicks should be sceptical of Marshall's account: 'But now what is this "utility" which the consumer maximizes? And what is the exact basis for the law of diminishing marginal utility? Marshall leaves one uncomfortable on these subjects.'[5] Whence, putting the indifference curve analysis of Pareto to work in the way every economist now knows, Hicks and Allen showed how the downward sloping demand curve could be deduced without a mention of the word utility. Hicks concluded: 'The quantitative concept of utility is not necessary in order to explain market phenomena. Therefore, on the principle of Occam's razor, it is better to do without it. For it is not, in practice, a matter of indifference if a theory contains unnecessary entities. Such quantities are irrelevant to the problem in hand, and their presence is likely to obscure the vision. . . . We have . . . to undertake a purge, rejecting all concepts which are tainted by quantitative utility, and replacing them, so far as they need to be replaced, by concepts which have no such implication.'[6] The problem in hand had been to derive the demand curve from the fewest axioms, and Hicks and Allen – in a spirit of Russellian scepticism – showed how this could be done without any necessary reference to a concept of utility or that of a utility function.

It is remarkable how decisively the hicksian view has seemed to prevail over the marshallian in contemporary theory – as when Professor Samuelson declared 'the whole end and purpose' of the analysis of consumer behaviour to be the derivation of demand functions in prices and income, or when Professor Arrow reissued Hicks's occamist challenge: 'the proponents of measurable utility have been unable to produce any proposition of economic behavior which could be explained by their hypothesis and not by those of the indifference curve theorists.'[7] Yet it does not seem self-evident that an acceptance of a marshallian concept of utility would necessarily imply utility to be measurable or quantifiable, or even that Marshall himself had believed it to be so. Marshall did conclude that a quoted price for tea of two shillings a pound at which the buyer actually makes his purchase 'measures the utility to him of the tea which lies at the margin or terminus or end of his purchases; it measures the marginal utility to him.'[8] But this would seem to be the only sense in which Marshall believed the utility of a good to someone could be measured by the agent or anyone else. To the contrary it is said frequently enough in Book III of *Principles* that desires themselves 'cannot be measured directly', that the utility of a thing accrues only to a given individual, that 'price will measure the marginal utility of the commodity to each purchaser individually: we cannot speak of price as measuring utility in general, because the wants and circumstances of different people are different', that 'we cannot compare the quantities of two benefits, which are enjoyed at different times even by the same person.'[9] Marshall's purpose is mainly descriptive, to say how people actually 'live and move and think in the ordinary business of life', and any names and 'elaborate machinery' he invents in his study are intended 'only to bring to light difficulties and assumptions that are latent in the common language of the marketplace.'[10] Marshall's illustrations are commonplaces open to ordinary observation: a housewife must decide how much yarn should be put to making socks and how much to making vests so 'as to contribute as much as possible to family well being'; a clerk is in doubt whether to ride to work, or walk and save the cash for something extra at lunch; a pair of newlyweds plan all their expenditures carefully, 'weighing the loss of utility that would result from taking away a pound's expenditure here, with that which they would lose by taking it away there', and so on. Marshall's examples are about tea and salt and socks and vests and wool and wood and furniture and champagne and pineapples. And such goods are desired, delighted in, regretted, and enjoyed by flesh-and-blood human beings, who have appetites for and emotions about the things they find in the world, and senses with which to enjoy them. Moreover, the notion that in most cases, as a person comes to possess or consume more and more of a good, the marginal unit is enjoyed by less and less, may be capable of a physiological and psychological underpinning. It could be a natural limitation of the mind that it better understands and is better aware of what is proximate to it, and that such awareness and understanding diminishes as objects become remote or peripheral to ordinary experience. When this observation is considered in the context of property, it may suggest that the ownership of increasing quantities of goods gradually diminishes awareness of the whole. The person with very little is likely to be acutely conscious of what he does in fact possess, whereas no reader of these pages will be a Scrooge, with an exact inventory in mind of everything he or she owns, down to the last box of matches in the cupboard and the loose change in the pocket (though situations are easily imagined in which we would become acutely conscious of the utility of such things). In short, Marshall's account of the concepts of utility and marginal utility is one which may be understood by anyone by applying ordinary powers of reason and observation to experience.

For purposes of contemporary demand theory by contrast, axioms and theories about human beings need to be postulated but we do not need either to acknowledge the fact of our own humanity, or to observe human actions and motivations as these happen to be given to experience, or to look to the pleasures and pains of actual human beings. A logical cipher can substitute, to which we associate other sets of ciphers, defining the first to be 'the agent', the second to be the 'commodity space', the third to be 'the agent's preferences' which are 'complete', 'reflexive', 'transitive', 'continuous', and so on. In the previous chapter we have seen that a formalist approach in the philosophy of mathematics has the liberating effect of permitting the mathematician to proceed with the statement of formal systems without reference to any reality at all. A similar liberating effect may have been made possible in analytical economics by the Hicks/Allen approach to the theory of demand, permitting numerous new formal economic systems to be stated without any necessary reference being made to real economic phenomena. With respect to the theoretical purpose of deriving demand curves in prices and income, which had been Hicks's original purpose, it may be neither possible nor necessary to meet the occamist challenge that the marshallian theory has nothing to offer which cannot be offered by the hicksian and post-hicksian theories. Yet that does not mean the occamist challenge cannot be met with respect to the purpose the marshallians themselves may have had, namely, the purpose of description, requiring the use of our common powers of reasoning and observation to describe how human beings actually *are* in their economic behaviour. The ghost of Marshall might reply to the challenge of Hicks and Samuelson and Arrow on the following lines: 'Agreed that the paretian indifference curve theory, and in due course the axioms of revealed preference, have permitted more austere deductions of the demand curve from fewer and fewer axioms. Agreed too, if you wish, that an "ordinal" theory of demand is analytically more elegant than a "cardinal" theory of demand (though neither I nor my contemporaries were concerned to use such terms). Agreed too that your theory has been and continues to be greatly valuable in innumerable contexts in economic inquiry. But that does not mean you have described how people *are* – how they actually "live and move and think in the ordinary business of life." As a plain matter of fact, *everyone* with whom you or I have been actually acquainted, you and I included, has been a being who has experienced utility or disutility, pleasures or pains, whether of a mental or physical kind, from a wide variety of goods, whether tradeable at a positive price or not. At the same time, *no one* with whom you or I have been acquainted has ever given any evidence of having "preference orderings" of the kind you postulate. I am even prepared to say I know this to be true *for certain*, and moreover, not only do *I* know this but so do you and so does everybody else. We *know* we do experience pleasures and pains, and we know we do *not* define precise orderings between vast numbers of vectors of goods and skills.'

Where Hicks, Robbins, Samuelson, Arrow and others have written in the sceptical and occamist tradition of Russell (and

Russell is well known for a time to have been platonist as well!)
the replies of Marshall, Wicksell, Pigou, Robertson and others
may be in the critical and commonsensical traditions of Moore
and Peirce. And the true point of such a reply would be not to
decry in the slightest the achievements of the post-hicksian
theory, but rather to place it in juster perspective: to remind
ourselves that it is *literally* false, and that its value derives
precisely from its *metaphorical* use in contexts in which the
primary purpose is not a literal description of the individual agent
but something else, e.g. analysis of a backward-bending supply
curve of labour, or of the gains from trade, or 'Liquidity
Preference as Behavior Toward Risk', and so on in scores of
different contexts within economic study. Such a purpose is to be
contrasted with the marshallian account which did purport to be
literally true, and does succeed in being a more plausible literal
description. Indeed there appears to be quite firm evidence that
Professor Hicks's present opinion may be closer to such a
position than it is to the author of Chapter I of *Value and Capital*:
'the replacement of the old consumer theory – the marginal
utility theory – by the modern theory of ordinal preferences (a
replacement in which I myself have played a part) was not so
clear an advance as is usually supposed. Marshall's consumer,
who decides on his purchases by comparing the marginal utility of
what is to be bought with the marginal utility of the money he
will have to pay for it, is more like an actual consumer, at least so
far as some important purchases are concerned, than Samuelson's
consumer, who "reveals his preference".'[11] Professor Hicks has
confirmed in correspondence that his present view is indeed 'very
different from that which I took in '34 and '39', and has cited
further passages in his recent writings as evidence of a fresh
position.[12]

A conclusion we may provisionally register, then, is that it may
be possible the marshallian and hicksian theories of the consumer
have had subtly different purposes which need not be considered
incompatible. One result of such a recognition would be the
return of the marshallian account from wrongful exile and its
restoration as a plausible and literal description of individual
economic behaviour.

**4.** Where Hicks's scepticism seemed to derive from a premise that allowing utility and marginal utility to be meaningful notions would permit them to be in some sense 'quantitative', Robbins's scepticism seemed to derive from a premise that it would permit interpersonal comparisons and a numerical sum of individual utilities to be meaningful as well. And much contemporary opinion seemed to exist to such an effect. For example Wicksell had written in criticism of Cassel: 'He also repeats his old objection about the impossibility of "measuring utility", as though exchange and economic activity in general – even in a primitive economy – would be conceivable, if we could not estimate the utility of different goods to us. Similarly, the deliberation of members of Parliament on problems of taxation would be meaningless, if it were impossible to compare the utility of the same good to different persons.'[13] And Pigou had written that it was 'evident that any transference of income from a relatively rich man to a relatively poor man of similar tempera-ment, since it enables more intense wants to be satisfied at the expense of less intense wants, must increase the aggregate sum of satisfaction. The old "law of diminishing marginal utility" thus leads securely to the proposition: Any cause which increases the absolute share of real income in the hands of the poor, provided that it does not lead to a contraction in the size of the national dividend from any point of view, will in general, increase economic welfare.'[14] And Marshall himself had written of 'the fact that the same sum of money measures a greater pleasure for the poor than for the rich', that a tax of £20 on each of fifty incomes of £200 caused 'unquestionably far greater hurt' *ceteris paribus* than a tax of £1000 on one income of £10,000; that 'the utility, or benefit, that is measured in the poorer man's mind by twopence is greater than that measured in the richer man's mind. . . .'[15] It was to this body of opinion that Robbins replied: 'The Law of Diminishing Marginal Utility implies that the more one has of anything, the less one values additional units thereof. Therefore, it is said, the more real income one has, the less one values additional units of income. Therefore, the marginal utility of a rich man's income is less than the marginal utility of a poor man's income. Therefore, if transfers are made, and these transfers do not appreciably affect production, total utility will be increased. Therefore, such transfers are "economically justified". Q.E.D. At first sight, the plausibility of the argument is overwhelming. But on closer inspection it is seen to be merely specious. . . . [it] begs the great metaphysical question of the scientific comparability of different individual experiences.'[16]

How, if at all, can Robbins's challenge be met? The marshallian notion of utility did entail that 'the richer a man becomes the less is the marginal utility of money to him; every increase in his resources increases the price which he is willing to pay for any given benefit. And in the same way every diminution of his resources increases the marginal utility of money to him, and diminishes the price he is willing to pay for any benefit.'[17] I.e. given an income of fifty dollars a week the utility of me of the fiftieth dollar is much higher than the utility to me of the five thousandth dollar given an income of five thousand dollars a week. Or, if I experience a ten dollar cut in a fifty dollar income I shall be much more upset than if I experience the same in a five thousand dollar income. The statements refer to the individual's *own* experiences and feelings; i.e., they presume he is able himself to describe the state of his own mind when he experiences an increase or decrease in the quantity of the goods he owns and so a decrease or increase in their marginal utilities to him. Thus the philosophical question implicit in Robbins's challenge may appear to be: Is this not all the individual can possibly experience? In particular, how can it be possible for A to know – to know *objectively* – what B happens to feel or experience? Is not such a thing impossible?

Stated in this manner, it may be readily seen that what may have been implicit in Robbins's challenge is something close to the problem of solipsism discussed in the philosophy of mind and which we have met with briefly in Chapter 4. For the solipsist is someone who holds his own feelings and experiences to be indeed *all* that he can *possibly* experience: 'He goes to the limit of declaring that he has no reason for believing in the existence or occurrence of anything but the present state of his own mind.'[18] And, just as with the humean sceptic or the subjective probabilist, there may be truth in what the solipsist means even while there is not in what he says or believes himself to mean. I can *and* cannot know the pleasures or pains or joy or sorrow you feel, depending on which is being meant of two different senses in which there may be a knowledge of these feelings to be had. Wittgenstein remarked at one place: 'For what the solipsist means is quite correct',[19] and Bambrough has recently sought to make this clearer. I cannot know how you feel pain, pleasure, joy or sorrow *in the same way* you feel the pain, pleasure, joy or sorrow you do: the solipsist is right when he means that he and only he can know the state of his own mind in the way that *only* he can know it. But that does not mean I cannot know *at all* how you feel what you do: the solipsist is wrong when he means that the way he and only he knows the state of his own mind is the *only* way in which the state of his mind can be known. It is as if someone says we cannot really know what the Duke of Wellington saw or did at Waterloo if we are not the Duke of Wellington ourselves: 'When we say that the Duke of Wellington or the child with toothache or the man who had the dream or saw the play or the tomato knows in a way that we do not know, we must distinguish between two uses of these words: we may mean that the Duke or the child or the man does know something that we do not know, or we may mean that his *way* of knowing is different from ours.'[20] Just as the way in which it is possible for the eyewitness to know is different from the way in which it may be possible for the historian to know, so the way in which it is possible for you to know how you feel what you do is different from the way in which it may be possible for me to know how you feel what you do. Equally, just as the historian *can* know what happened at Waterloo or Borodino or Plassey without having to know it in the way someone who was there knows it, so I *can* know how you feel something without having to know it in the way you know how you feel it. Indeed such an argument may be able to sustain considerable generalization. No one can feel the labour pains of a woman during childbirth in the same way that she happens to feel them herself. Yet women who have themselves felt the pains of childbirth may be able to *understand* the pain in a way others cannot. Other women who have not given birth but who have miscarried may still understand the pain in a way yet others cannot. And yet other women who have neither given birth nor miscarried but who have experienced the pains of menstruation may still understand it better than someone, such as a man, who has not and cannot have done so, and yet who himself is capable of understanding it as well, though in a necessarily different way. In each case there would be a relevant sense in which an objective understanding is possible,

178

and yet there are a variety of different logical kinds of such understanding. Reframing the problem in the terms used in Chapter 6 in discussing liberalism and in Chapter 10 in discussing probability, we might say a person has a kind of *privileged access* to his or her own experience which is impossible for others to possess. The solipsist mistakes the fact of this privileged access for a signal that all access is closed, when it is instead a signal that access can be had in logically differing ways. Thus subjective experience, like subjective belief, may be possible without diminishing in the slightest the scope for objective understanding.

There are two further results of the theory of knowledge of Part II which may be relevant here. The first would be simply that questions of judgement, like all questions in general, once adequately described in particular context and circumstance, should be capable of sustaining reasonable and open-ended inquiry and discussion as to their answers; since interpersonal comparisons are a species of judgement, we may predict the same to hold for them as well. Secondly, questions of a given kind may need analysis into two separate senses: whether objective answers can *possibly* be given to such questions, and whether it is known *who* if anyone is in the best position of having an answer in a given case. It is possible that at least some of the discussion in theoretical welfare economics has been muddied by a general failure to make such a distinction, and a confounding of these senses into one. In previous chapters we have seen that Plato had certainly seemed to fail to make such a distinction, and ever since the proper fear or abhorrence of elitism or dictatorship may have contributed at the same time to the abandonment of objectivity. More specifically in the case of the economists' division, both parties may have agreed to the questionable assumption that the possibility of interpersonal comparisons entailed, and was entailed by, approval that it was the State which should be involved in the making of such judgements – where by the State is here meant legislature and executive, since the judiciary clearly has the task of judging already (e.g. to which parent, or which pair of parents, would it be better to give custody of the child?). This would not be to say the State cannot or should not attempt to make interpersonal comparisons as objectively as it can, but merely that there is no necessary connection between an argument that objective comparisons of this sort are possible, and substantive political questions about whether, in a given context, it is the State which happens to be in the best position to be making them. It is possible that Pigou and others were led from an assumption that interpersonal comparisons were not meaningless to a conclusion that, for example, redistributions by the State were thereby justified; while Robbins and others were led from an assumption that the State should not make such comparisons (or at least that the economist *qua* scientist could not advise the State to do so) to a conclusion that interpersonal comparisons of utility and the concept of utility itself were meaningless. Here as in other cases of seemingly irreconcilable difference, it is possible that 'one theory is in secret and mistaken agreement with another, where because they both agree on a false disjunction, each of them sacrifices a truth that the other strenuously guards, and embraces the paradox that it is the primary function of the other to controvert.'[21]

These simple philosophical observations may serve to dissolve at least some of the puzzlement over interpersonal comparisons which has vexed theoretical welfare economics for half a century now.[22]

**5.** The modern theory of social choice would seem clearly to have been premised upon the Hicks/Robbins approach to demand theory and welfare economics. For example, Professor Arrow has written forthrightly of how, upon setting out on his investigation, he had 'fully adopted' the viewpoint of *Value and Capital*, and also that his system has been motivated by an assumption that interpersonal comparisons are meaningless: 'The viewpoint will be taken here that interpersonal comparison of utilities has no meaning and, in fact, that there is no meaning relevant to welfare comparisons in the measurability of individual utility.'[23]

We have seen in the previous chapter that a view can be taken in the philosophy of mathematics that a logical or mathematical theorem does not, indeed cannot, have any factual significance by itself, merely as a valid theorem. Equally, the validity of a theorem does not depend on any feature of the actual world whatsoever. We may be led to such a view by endorsing for example a traditional *a priori*/empirical or logic/fact dualism, or a hilbertian formalism. So for example we could say that the fact that the people of Switzerland happen to have had a well-working constitution or the fact that the people of Lebanon have not, is evidence which cannot have any possible effect on the *formal* validity of Arrow's theorem. In other words, given a formalist point of view, a logical or mathematical symbolism would need to be kept quite distinct from the interpretations that it may be open to. The definition of a relation like $R$ between two objects $x$ and $y$ thus $xRy$, and subsequent definitions of $xPy$ as $xRy$ & $\sim yRx$, and of $xIy$ as $xRy$ & $yRx$, neither entail nor are entailed by specific interpretations of 'weak preference', 'preference', and 'indifference' given to them in contemporary theories. Indeed to free ourselves from habitual modes of thought, we might even consider briefly a highly unusual interpretation – let us imagine a psychologist to conduct an experiment on sensory perception, in which in each of a set of jars is put the same quantity of a liquid at a different or the same temperature, so in one jar the liquid is at 5°C, in another jar at 6°C, in a third jar at 7°C, and so on. Each of the psychologist's subjects is invited to take the jars two at a time, dip a different finger into each, and rank one as being colder than or as cold as the other – with the requirement that if jar A is ranked at least as cold as jar B and jar B is at least as cold as jar C then jar A must be ranked at least as cold as jar C. Every subject does as told and the psychologist hands in the results to a theorist familiar with Arrow's theorem. Clearly an interpretation of the axioms of that theorem may be possible in such a context – obtaining, for example, what has been called the Pareto principle as follows: 'If any two jars $(x, y)$ are ranked $xP_iy$ by at least one subject $i$ and $xR_jy$ by every other subject $j$ then $xPy$ is the social ranking'; and what has been called the condition of non-dictatorship as follows: 'There is no subject such that whatever his or her ranking of a pair of jars that is the social ranking, regardless of the rankings of the other subjects', and so on. The psychologist may be told that Arrow's theorem can be applied to deduce there to be no social ranking with respect to perception of the coldness of the liquid which would satisfy Arrow's four axioms. Examples of this sort, whether fanciful or plausible, clearly can be generated indefinitely, with the results of experiments on individual perceptions of colour, shades of the same colour, height, weight, sound, taste, and so on (as Piaget might have done in his experiments with the development of children). And the result would be a *multiplicity* of interpretations of Professor Arrow's theorem – informing us that there are difficulties perhaps not only with the concept 'social welfare' which had concerned Professor Arrow, but also with concepts like 'social coldness', 'social colour', 'social height', and so on.

The purpose of making such a contrasting interpretation would be to gain a juster perspective of the intended interpretation of the theorem – which of course is that of an economic and socio-political context, specifically 'a capitalist democracy' (perhaps the United States) as well as 'the emerging democracies with mixed economic systems (Great Britain, France and Scandinavia).'[24] If we followed such an intent and interpreted the theorem as one referring to the analysis of actual economic and socio-political contexts, then some reference to such a context – i.e. *an invitation to accept some empirical claim about the world* – would be necessary to be made, whether it happens in fact to be true about the world or not. Professor Arrow makes one such invitation in his definition of the 'objects of choice' being 'social states': 'The most precise definition of a social state would be a complete description of the amount of each type of commodity in the hands of each individual, the amount of labor to be supplied by each individual, the amount of each productive resource invested in each type of productive activity, and the amounts of various types of collective activity (such as municipal services, diplomacy and its continuation by other means, and the erection of statues to famous men). It is assumed that each individual in the community has a definite ordering of all conceivable social states in terms of their desirability to him. It need not be assumed that an individual's attitude toward different social states is determined exclusively by the commodity bundles which accrue to his lot under each. It is simply assumed that the individual orders all social states by whatever standards he deems relevant.'[25] This definition is one which happens to be indispensable to the purpose of interpreting the theorem in its intended context. For what has been meant is something to this effect: 'If $(p, q, r, s)$ obtain in the world then you will find $\sim t$ obtains' – where $p, q, r, s$ are the four axioms and $t$ would be a 'social ordering' which satisfied them. And it is in the definition of each of the axioms that the definition of a social state given above is necessarily presupposed. It is over *pairs of social states* defined as

above – and not jars of liquid at various temperatures or
something else – that each individual agent is to be pictured in
social choice theory as having and exercising a complete,
reflexive and transitive preference ordering symbolized by $R$. It is
only given such an interpretation that it becomes possible now to
get what is called the Pareto principle to read: 'If any two social
states $(x, y)$ are ranked $xP_iy$ by at least one citizen $i$ and $xR_jy$ by
every other citizen $j$ then $xPy$ is the social ranking'; and what is
called the condition of non-dictatorship to read: 'There is no
citizen such that whatever his or her ranking of a pair of states,
that is the social ranking, regardless of the ranking of the other
citizens', and so on. In Chapter 2 we have seen Professor Arrow
hold to a quite radical moral scepticism; yet the subjective
element in his theory of social choice does not have to do
with what the objects of choice facing the individual agent *are*,
but with how the individual agent chooses to rank them. The
individual agent is not free to say he is going to take alternative $x$
to be exactly what he pleases; the *same* set of alternatives is
presumed to be objectively known and understood by all agents:
$x$ is $x$ and $y$ is $y$ and $z$ is $z$, and everyone takes them to be so.
Where the subjective features of the theory appear is in every
agent being presumed to rank pairs of alternative social states in
any way that he or she pleases subject to transitivity: 'The
individual plays a central role in social choice as the judge of
alternative social actions according to his own standards. We
presume that each individual has some way of ranking social
actions according to his preference for their consequences. These
preferences constitute his value system. They are assumed to
reflect already in full measure altruistic, egoistic motivations, as
the case may be. . . .'[26] Yet before an individual may be said to
be in a position *to rank* one alternative as preferred to or
indifferent with another, it must be supposed necessary for him
or her *to know* of the existence of the alternatives, or at least for
the alternatives to be able to be distinguished. There must be two
distinct alternatives $(x, y)$ *known* to the agent before he or she is
able to rank them either $xRy$ & $\sim yRx$, or $yRx$ & $\sim xRy$, or $xRy$ &
$yRx$. For the intended interpretation to be viable, therefore, it
must be assumed *that every agent can and does know of every
alternative social state there is* – that he or she is able to
distinguish between them – if he or she is to be imagined as being

able to take them two at a time and rank them according to personal wishes as being either preferred to or indifferent with one another. The domain over which every individual's preferences are to be defined consists of every logically possible social state, and *every* element of this domain must be assumed to be known by the agent.

Now there may be contexts in which this could be imagined to be plausible. That is to say, where every agent could be imagined to have more or less the same uniform knowledge of the existence of each possible alternative social state. We can think of cases of the distribution of a fixed vector of goods between a small number of individual recipients where every agent knows of each possible collective distribution; e.g., a settlement between divorcing spouses, or a division of property between the children of someone who has died intestate, or the division of resources between the members of a federation. We could think also of contexts where although the number of agents is large, the number of alternatives happened to be small and proxied for social states; e.g., different candidates in an election being taken to be rough proxies for the different social states that may be expected in the event that they came to be elected. In contexts of this sort, where, so to speak, collective decisions are being made in the small, it could be of interest for the economist or political scientist to impose Professor Arrow's axioms and observe the result. However the same cannot be said to hold with respect to collective decisions in the large, which would seem to have been the intended context, where we would be asked to imagine a large number of alternative social states being ranked by each of a large number of individual agents. As discussed in Part II, the particularity of knowledge would render such a claim manifestly false – *as indeed Professor Arrow himself* has argued in his distinguished writings in the theory of general equilibrium: 'In defenses of the free enterprise system such as Hayek's, great emphasis is placed on the particularity of knowledge in different agents. . . . I suggest that the lessons of this observation are sometimes forgotten in current model building, particularly in the emphasis on rational expectations formed in a rather sophisticated way. . . . It is the essence of the decentralized economy that individuals have different information. Each individual is specialized in certain activities and has in general specialized knowledge about these activities.'[27] Of course the last two of these sentences express and endorse as clearly as anything the observation of Aristotle and Smith and Hayek that it would not be a claim of universal knowledge but its contrary which may be true of actual economies and polities. Yet the lessons of this observation seem to have been neglected in the theory of social choice!

This same definition of 'social state', over pairs of which the individual agent is supposed to have a preference, has been central to a notion of liberalism advanced and discussed by Professor Sen and endorsed by Professor Arrow and others. Professor Sen has interpreted his theorem on 'the impossibility of a paretian liberal' as implying that it is logically possible for there to be a contradiction for some sets of individual preferences between what has been called the Pareto principle (as defined previously), a condition of 'unrestricted domain' (i.e., that the domain of the mapping which is to give the social ordering is the product-set of all logically possible individual orderings), and a condition Sen named $L$ for liberalism, defined to the following effect: For every agent $i$, there exists at least one pair of alternative social states $(x, y)$, such that if the agent prefers $x$ to $y$ then $x$ is to be preferred to $y$ in the social ranking; $xP_iy$ implies $xPy$.[28] Professor Sen has claimed that while he does not wish to enter into questions in the history of thought, this kind of definition adequately captures what liberals in traditional political thought have meant when they have said they valued a 'protected sphere' for every person, within which the freedom and privacy of the individual is guaranteed. And he has cited J. S. Mill and Professor Hayek as two such liberals. But Professor Sen has said too that it is not necessary to be an archetypical liberal in order to agree to $L$, and he cites Gramsci and even Stalin as among those who might have agreed to $L$ as well. Furthermore, it is said to be not sufficient to hold to $L$ in order to be considered a liberal: 'Condition $L$ reflects only a small part of what a "liberal" or "libertarian" is typically concerned with.'[29] Therefore the precise extent of Professor Sen's claim would seem to be that it is necessary but not sufficient to accept $L$ in order to be considered an archetypical liberal. And Professor Arrow would seem to be found to be in agreement with such an understanding of the concept of liberalism: 'The only rational defense of what may be termed a liberal position, or perhaps more precisely a principle of limited social preference, is that it is itself a value judgment. In other words, an individual may have as part of his value structure precisely that he does not think it proper to influence consequences outside a limited realm. This is a perfectly coherent position but I find it difficult to insist that this judgment is of such overriding importance that it outweighs all other considerations. Personally, my values are such that I am willing to go very far indeed in the direction of respect for the means by which others choose to derive their satisfactions.'[30]

Yet a quite straightforward example may suffice to show a difficulty at the roots of such a concept of liberalism. Let us imagine two men, each of whom may be in one of two individual states – say whether or not to wear a moustache – giving a total of four possible 'social states' as follows:

social states

|  | $z^1$ | $z^2$ | $z^3$ | $z^4$ |
|---|---|---|---|---|
| individual $K$ | $a$ | $a$ | $b$ | $b$ |
| individual $S$ | $c$ | $d$ | $c$ | $d$ |

Individual state $a$ might be that $K$ wears a moustache and state $b$ that $K$ does not, while individual state $c$ might be that $S$ wears a moustache and state $d$ that $S$ does not. Thus, by the Arrow-Sen definition, $z^1$ would be the 'social state' in which both men wore moustaches, $z^4$ would be the social state in which neither man wore a moustache, and $z^2$ and $z^3$ would be social states in which one man wore a moustache and the other did not. By the condition of unrestricted domain, each man is to be permitted to have any preference he may wish over all the possible pairs of social states that there can be, *viz.*,

$$(z^1, z^2), (z^1, z^3), (z^1, z^4), (z^2, z^3), (z^2, z^4), (z^3, z^4).$$

And by Sen's definition of liberalism, each is to be 'decisive' over at least one pair of social states, in the sense that that individual's preference over two social states is to prevail.

Now it may well be that what Sen and Arrow have *meant* to say is that by a liberal criterion, each man should be allowed to decide whether *he himself* wears a moustache or not, regardless of what the other does. But that is not what follows from the

186

formulation actually given. For if $K$ decided to be 'decisive' over $(z^1, z^2)$ or $(z^3, z^4)$, i.e., over social states which differed due to differences in $S$'s individual state, or if $S$ decided to be 'decisive' over $(z^1, z^3)$ or $(z^2, z^4)$, i.e., over social states which differed due to differences in $K$'s individual state, the Arrow-Sen notion of liberalism would have to admit these decisions, even though they plainly contradict traditional liberal premises. Put differently, the Arrow-Sen concept of liberalism is one which is unable to specify *which* social states are or should be in *whose* 'protected sphere'. The question seems to have been overlooked whether or not it is a liberal tenet that the individual be free to choose which pair of 'social states' he or she wishes to be 'decisive' about, among every conceivable pair of such states that there happens to be. Indeed if we agreed with Frege that when a concept is made to extend to every instance its content must vanish altogether, and if the Arrow/Sen concept of liberalism is such that it extends to both liberal cases and to manifestly anti-liberal cases, we may ask if its content does not vanish altogether.[31] Certainly Professor Sen has claimed that since, given a restriction of the domain, his definition happens to include liberal cases we have to accept $L$ as a necessary condition of liberal thought. But what we may observe instead is not only that the theory of social choice has happened to neglect that the claim of universal knowledge is false, but also that archetypical liberals did not neglect it and in fact built part of their normative arguments precisely on the observation that it *is* false. Modern social choice theory appears to have neglected one of the main positive observations upon which traditional argument in support of liberal institutions has rested. In the Arrow-Sen perspective, the liberal position is one of 'limited social preference' (i.e., a particular kind of 'restriction of the domain'). We would be asked to assume the agent *knows of* every possible social state as defined above, *and then* chooses to be indifferent with respect to those which do not happen to affect his individual state. In contrast, traditional liberal political thought premised itself *inter alia* on an observation that the individual does not and cannot know of every possible 'social state', and so *a fortiori* cannot be said to have preferences defined over such a domain. If it is a plain fact that $K$ knows only about his own individual state, while $S$ knows only about his, then $K$ would have to define preferences over only a partition of 'social states' thus $\{z_k = [(z^1, z^2), (z^3, z^4)] = [z_{k1}, z_{k2}]\}$ and $S$ over a different partition thus $\{z_s = [(z^1, z^3), (z^2, z^4)] = [z_{s1}, z_{s2}]\}$. Indeed the procedure of defining individual preferences over a set of uniformly known 'social states' may have had the inadvertent result of making trivial the very concept of an individual. For it would seem to have been central to the procedure employed in the theory of social choice for practically every action of any individual to be a possible subject of the deliberation of anyone at all: 'The fundamental fact which causes the need for discussing public values at all is that every significant action involves the joint participation of many individuals. Even the apparently simplest act of individual decision involves the participation of a whole society. It is important to note that this observation tells us all non-trivial actions are essentially the property of society as a whole, not of individuals. . . . [W]e must in a general theory take as our unit a social action, that is, an action involving a large proportion or the entire domain of society. At the most basic axiomatic level, individual actions play little role. The need for a system of public values then becomes evident; actions being collective or interpersonal in nature, so must the choice between them. A public or social value system is essentially a logical necessity.'[32] But we are not told which 'trivial' actions the individual might call his own and are not 'the property of society as a whole', nor whether what is and what is not trivial may vary with context. Practically any action by anyone at all would seem to be supposed 'the property of society as a whole'. We are then invited to ascribe to each individual, thus defined, knowledge of all social states as well as preferences over them. And in such an unusual construction, the only way it might come out that the individual acts *as* an individual in at least some matters may be by saying that it is a fortuitous matter of subjective preference – when all along traditional liberalism has been premised on an observation of the particularity of the availability of knowledge.

In sum, the usual interpretations of Professor Arrow's theorem and Professor Sen's theorem as having put into serious question the possibility of answering questions about the existence or definition of the social good, may be themselves brought into question when a scrutiny is made of how each of their axioms is intended to be interpreted, and whether such interpretations are reasonable. In particular, an observation that individual knowledge may be of a particular and diverse kind (which may be found to have been accepted in general equilibrium theory) and not of a general or uniform kind (as has been supposed in social choice theory) would give us enough reason not to accept an invitation that the 'objects of choice' faced by the individual agent are or even can be 'social states'. Where Arrow's theorem may be said to be of possible interest would be not with respect to large-scale democratic decision-making in civil societies, but instead with respect to very small-scale democratic decison-making. It would seem to be more relevant to a theory of committees, where each member of a committee can be presumed to have the same uniform knowledge of the alternative 'social states' and therefore the axioms can be made to have relatively plausible interpretations. The graver consequences of employing such procedures have been the misdescriptions of liberalism and the individual. Where liberalism as well as its rival traditions in political thought have been sought to be given objective justifications by their proponents, the modern theorists of social choice have been under the Spell of Hume. These brief critical remarks have been intended to break that spell.

# 11

# *Envoy*

Where the modern foundations of welfare economics and the received theory of economic knowledge and policy in general, have been founded on a quite extreme scepticism about our ability to answer questions of the social good, even about the meaningfulness of a concept of a social good, the theory advanced in this work would yield the result that questions of the social good, like questions of other kinds, can indeed be framed coherently; can indeed be made the subject of reasonable and open-ended discussion; can indeed sustain objective inquiry and investigation as to their answers. We have seen more generally that all questions need to be understood within as careful descriptions as possible of their implicit and explicit contexts. Also we have seen it to be of central importance to distinguish the question whether there *can be* an objective answer to a given question from the question of *who*, if anyone, should be thought of as possessing the best or most reasonable answer to give to it. Both these considerations may take on an acute significance when it is the determination of the social good which is under discussion. The former would imply that while we can bring to bear all and any principles and precedents that we need in answering a given question of the social good, there may be no universal or absolute theories either necessary or possible from which all answers about the social good have to be derived regardless of particular context and circumstance. The latter would imply that once a question of the social good has been carefully framed within its implicit and explicit context, the true political question which it becomes necessary to address is that of identifying who in the given context should be thought of as having the best answer to it, who should be considered the expert, who should be thought to have the authoritative opinion about it, who should be granted the authority to decide upon it. And this may be the more fruitful way to interpret how most actual discussions of economic and public policy do in fact proceed. Here is a question as to what should be done in a given context – now the question is, who has the best answer to it? – who should make the decision – mother or father, child or parent, parents or judge, judiciary or executive, executive or legislature, legislature or electorate, government or private sector, local government or state government or federal government, rule or discretion, and so on indefinitely. It may be that political discussions take on the vehemence they sometimes do precisely because the answers to questions of the social good, whether in the family or in public life, are *not easy* to determine – there may be manifold and complex considerations needing to be accounted for, often within a fleeting span of time, without either principles or precedents or evidence readily at hand, with the private interests and emotions and mutual bigotry and mistrust of the participants all inextricably involved. Certainly Pareto's idea that if an outcome can be made to obtain in which the positions of some are improved while the positions of no others are worsened then that would be a good thing, may be part of the considerations entering into an inquiry of what is the right thing to be done in given circumstances. But it would be at most one among any of a number of considerations which may be relevant to the matter at hand, and must be required to weigh in with them as well and not assumed to be the only or absolute or supreme value – as the humean economist, struck by his debilitating scepticism, would have us believe.

Rather, we have seen in this study, once the concept of reason is recognized in its full range of kind and instance, the scope of reason may be recognized to be indefinite in principle. We have seen too that it is the active exercise of freedom of thought and inquiry and expression which is of integral importance to the theory of knowledge, and so to the theory of reasonable action. It is through an exercise of freedom, perhaps only through an exercise of freedom, that the complex and sometimes momentous questions of political economy may find their most reasonable answers; that we may aspire towards objectivity and knowledge and understanding – in all their manifold diversity.

# Notes and References

---

## 1 Introduction

1 On the influence of economic knowledge in the twentieth century, see, for example, John Maynard Keynes, *The Economic Consequences of the Peace* (London: Macmillan, 1919); Robert Skidelsky, *John Maynard Keynes, 1883–1920, Hopes Betrayed* (New York: Viking, 1986); Milton Friedman and Anna Jacobson Schwartz, *A Monetary History of the United States, 1867–1960* (Princeton, NJ: Princeton University Press, 1963); Charles Kindleberger, *The World in Depression 1929–1939*, revised edition (Berkeley, California: University of California Press, 1986). It is reported by Leszek Kolakowski that following the failure of the Great Leap Forward in China, Mao Zedong was to admit his ignorance of economics, saying 'it had not occurred to him that coal and iron do not move of their own accord but have to be transported.' *Main Currents of Marxism, Vol. III, The Breakdown* (Oxford: Clarendon Press, 1978), p. 504.

2 David Hume, *A Treatise of Human Nature*, 1739, 2nd edition of 1888, edited by L. A. Selby-Bigge, revised by P. H. Nidditch (Oxford: Clarendon Press, 1978), p. xiv.

3 Quoted by Ernest Nagel and James R. Newman in *Gödel's Proof* (London: Routledge & Kegan Paul, 1958), p. 13.

4 Ludwig Wittgenstein, *Philosophical Investigations*, translated by G. E. M. Anscombe (Oxford: Blackwell, 1978), §133, p. 51e. The metaphor of philosophy being like 'a machine to think with' is attributed to the British philosopher C. K. Ogden. The author is indebted to Renford Bambrough for this information.

5 'Two dogmas of empiricism', in *Philosophy of Mathematics*, edited by Paul Benacerraf and Hilary Putnam (Englewood Cliffs, NJ: Prentice Hall, 1964), p. 362. See also Note 2 to Chapter 4 on pp. 201–203 below.

6 *Collected Papers of Charles Sanders Peirce*, edited by Charles Hartshorne and Paul Weiss (Cambridge, Mass.: Harvard University Press, 1931), §5.264, p. 156.

7 Let us say about one hundred years if we count from Alfred Marshall's inaugural lecture at the University of Cambridge in 1885, with Marshall then becoming the prime mover in England of an independent economics syllabus.

8 The small letter shall be used where it is not intended to be said that a major exponent of a point of view would accept all or much that may have been said by others who have followed him. This useful convention is suggested by Morton White in *Toward Reunion in Philosophy* (Cambridge, Mass.: Harvard University Press, 1956), p. 9.

9 Professor Alexander has said it is clear to him the results of the present work had been arrived at completely independently. See also Notes 24 and 25 to Chapter 6, pp. 209–210 below. See also the critique of Sen with respect to the theory of social choice in Chapter 10, pp. 180–189.

## 2 *Hume and the Economists*

1 *'Positive' Economics and Policy Objectives* (London: Allen & Unwin, 1964). Hutchison discusses the opinions of Nassau Senior, J. S. Mill, J. E. Cairnes, Henry Sidgwick, Neville Keynes, Vilfredo Pareto, Max Weber, and others.

2 C. L. Stevenson, *Ethics and Language* (New Haven, Conn.: Yale University Press, 1944); *Facts and Values* (New Haven, Conn.: Yale University Press, 1963); A. J. Ayer, *Language, Truth and Logic*, 1937 (New York: Dover, 1952); *Freedom and Morality and Other Essays* (Oxford: Oxford University Press, 1984); R. M. Hare, *The Language of Morals* (Oxford: Oxford University Press, 1952); *Freedom and Reason* (Oxford: Oxford University Press, 1963); *Moral Thinking* (Oxford: Clarendon Press, 1981); Karl Popper, *Conjectures and Refutations* (London: Routledge & Kegan Paul, 1962).

3 *Treatise of Human Nature*, III. 1. pp. 469–470.

4 This may be compared with the rule stated by Hare: 'No imperative conclusion can be validly drawn from a set of premises which does not contain at least one imperative' (*Language of Morals*, p. 28). Among contemporary moral philosophers, Hare has been among the most steadfast and influential to have taken a humean point of view, recently reiterating his commitment in *Moral Thinking*, p. 6.

5 *Enquiries Concerning Human Understanding and Concerning the Principles of Morals*, 1777, 3rd edition, edited by P. H. Nidditch (Oxford: Clarendon Press, 1975), Appendix I, §240, p. 290.

6 *Moral Thinking*, p. 6. Hare adds that if we could have had 'a perfect command of logic and of the facts' then we would be found 'in

practice' to be unanimous in our evaluations. The intended meaning
of this remark is not clear to the present author.

7 'The methodology of positive economics', in *Essays in Positive
Economics* (Chicago: University of Chicago Press, 1953), p. 5, pp.
39–40.

8 *The Political Element in the Development of Economic Theory*,
Swedish original 1929, translated from the German by Paul Streeten
(Cambridge, Mass.: Harvard University Press, 1953), p. 2. In the
preface to the English edition, p. vii, Myrdal seemed to want to
withdraw the propositions quoted here, taking them to be a
concession to those of whom he was critical. Myrdal's position will be
further discussed in Chapter 6.

9 *Ibid.*, pp. 192–193.

10 *An Essay On the Nature and Significance of Economic Science*, 2nd
edition (London: Macmillan, 1935), pp. 142–150.

11 *Foundations of Economic Analysis*, 1947, enlarged edition
(Cambridge, Mass.: Harvard University Press, 1983), pp. 219–220.

12 'The foundations of welfare economics', in *Economic Journal*,
December 1939, reprinted in *Wealth and Welfare* (Cambridge, Mass.:
Harvard University Press, 1981), pp. 59–61.

13 Nicholas Kaldor, 'Welfare propositions and interpersonal comparisons
of utility', in *Economic Journal*, September 1939; Harold Hotelling,
'The general welfare in relation to problems of taxation and of
railway and utility rates', in *Econometrica*, July 1938.

14 Vilfredo Pareto, *Manual of Political Economy*, 1927, translated from
the French by Ann S. Schwier, edited by Ann S. Schwier and Alfred N.
Page (New York: Augustus M. Kelley, 1971), see especially §33 p.
261, §89 p. 451. See also related entries on the Pareto criterion listed
in the index.

A clear survey of the new welfare economics is to be found in J. de V.
Graaff, *Theoretical Welfare Economics* (Cambridge: Cambridge
University Press, 1963), pp. 84–90.

15 *Wealth and Welfare*, p. 61. Parentheses in the original around the full
sentence have here been dropped.

16 'The scope and status of welfare economics', in *Oxford Economic
Papers*, 1975, reprinted in *Wealth and Welfare*, p. 219.

17 *Introduction to the Theory of Employment*, 2nd edition (London:
Macmillan, 1969), pp. 99–100. Robinson also wrote some obscure
passages in an explicitly methodological work, which seemed to grope
towards the same effect. The interested reader may refer to
*Economic Philosophy* (Chicago: Aldine, 1962), pp. 2–13.

18 'Socialism and science', in *New Studies in Philosophy, Politics,
Economics and the History of Ideas* (Chicago: University of Chicago
Press, 1978), p. 297.

19 'Socialist calculation I: the nature and history of the problem', 1935,
reprinted in *Individualism and Economic Order* (London: Routledge

& Kegan Paul, 1949), p. 120.

20 'Socialism and science', in *New Studies*, p. 298.

21 *The Road to Serfdom* (London: Routledge & Kegan Paul, 1944), p. 26.

22 'The use of knowledge in society', in *American Economic Review*, September 1945, reprinted in *Individualism and Economic Order*, p. 79.

23 'The scope and method of economics', in *Review of Economic Studies*, 1945–46; reprinted in *Readings in the Philosophy of Science*, edited by Herbert Feigl and May Brodbeck (New York: Appleton, 1953), pp. 748–749.

24 *History of Economic Analysis*, edited by Elizabeth Boody Schumpeter (New York: Oxford University Press, 1954), pp. 805–806.

25 *Ibid.*, p. 805.

26 'A difficulty in the concept of social welfare', 1951, reprinted in *Collected Papers of Kenneth J. Arrow 1, Social Choice* (Cambridge, Mass.: Harvard University Press, 1983), p. 13.

27 'Values and collective decision making', 1967, reprinted in *ibid.*, p. 60.

28 *Ibid.*, p. 67, the first two quotations; 'Some ordinalist-utilitarian notes on Rawls's theory of justice', 1973, in *ibid.*, pp. 98–99, p. 106, the third and fourth quotations respectively.

29 *Economic Theory in Retrospect*, 3rd edition (New York: Cambridge University Press, 1978), pp. 708–709; *The Methodology of Economics* (New York: Cambridge University Press, 1980), pp. 133–134.

30 *Methodology of Economics*, p. 126.

31 *Philosophy and Economic Theory*, edited and with an introduction by F. H. Hahn and Martin Hollis (Oxford: Oxford University Press, 1979), p. 2.

32 'Economic theory and policy' in *Equilibrium and Macroeconomics* (Cambridge, Mass.: The MIT Press, 1984), p. 344.

33 Robert Sugden, *The Political Economy of Public Choice* (Oxford: Martin Robertson, 1981), p. 10; W. J. Baumol and Alan S. Blinder, *Economics, Principles and Policy*, 2nd edition (New York: Harcourt Brace Jovanovich, 1983), p. 16; James Quirk, *Intermediate Microeconomics* (Chicago: SRA Inc., 1976), p. 8; Jack Hirschleifer, *Price Theory and Applications*, 2nd edition (Englewood Cliffs, NJ: Prentice Hall, 1980), p. 526.

## 3 *Understanding the Consensus*

1 Gottlob Frege, *The Foundations of Arithmetic*, 1884, translated from the German by J. L. Austin (Evanston, Ill.: Northwestern University Press, 1980), p. x. Two other principles were 'always to separate sharply the psychological from the logical, the subjective from the objective', and 'never to lose sight of the distinction between concept and object'.

2 'For naming and describing do not stand on the same level: naming is a preparation for description. Naming is so far not a move in the language-game – any more than putting a piece in its place on the board is a move in chess. We may say: *nothing* has so far been done, when a thing has been named. It has not even *got* a name except in the language-game. This is what Frege meant too, when he said that a word has meaning only as part of a sentence.' *Philosophical Investigations*, §49, p. 24e. Of relevance too is Max Black, 'Wittgenstein's language-games', in *Dialectica*, 33.3/4, 1979, pp. 337–353.

3 This may not be a drawback peculiar to the economist; for example, the archaeologist or the astronomer must face similar difficulties in giving summary interpretations of ancient civilizations relative to more recent ones, or more distant planets and stars relative to nearby ones.

4 *The Collected Dialogues of Plato including the Letters*, edited by Edith Hamilton and Huntington Cairns, Bollingen Series LXXVI (Princeton, NJ: Princeton University Press, 1961). See especially *Republic*, translated by Paul Shorey, §383c, §375e, §404, §464c, §484.

5 The most influential contemporary critic of Plato has been Karl Popper in *The Open Society and Its Enemies, Volume 1, The Spell of Plato* (Princeton, NJ: Princeton University Press, 1962). For a field report of the controversy which followed Popper's critique, see Renford Bambrough, 'Plato's modern friends and enemies', in *Philosophy*, 1962, reprinted with a number of other relevant papers in *Plato, Popper and Politics: Some Contributions to a Modern Controversy*, edited by Renford Bambrough (New York: Barnes and Noble, 1967).

   Plato's experience with the training of Dionysius II of Syracuse is given in his *Letters*; see especially *Letter VII*, translated by L. A. Post, in *Collected Dialogues*, pp. 1574–1598. See also A. E. Taylor, *The Mind of Plato*, 1922 (Ann Arbor, Mich.: University of Michigan Press, 1960), pp. 15–17.

6 Immanuel Kant, *Critique of Pure Reason*, 1781, translated from the German by J. D. Meiklejohn (New York: Dutton, 1934), pp. 220–221. For a modern illustration, we may think of the perfect firm in which all management was redundant. See also Note 9 to Chapter 6.

7 Two dissident schools remain, however, both dismayed at the actual course of the nineteenth century and how it was being thought about by economists. The first is the historical school led by Wilhelm Roscher, Friedrich List and later Gustav Schmoller – who denounce the smooth deductivism growing in England, Vienna and Lausanne with an alleged failure to take seriously the concrete realities of the Industrial Revolution in Europe, and an accompanying failure to imbibe economic thinking with suitable moral purpose. Moderators looking for a compromise were Adolph Wagner from the one side

and Marshall and Neville Keynes from the other. See 'Wagner on the present state of political economy', translated in *Quarterly Journal of Economics*, Vol. I, 1886, pp. 113–133; Alfred Marshall, *Principles of Economics*, 1920, 9th (Variorum) edition (London: Macmillan, 1961) Appendix B, pp. 754–769; John Neville Keynes, *The Scope and Method of Political Economy*, 4th edition (London: Macmillan, 1917). The second dissident school arises out of the hegelian thesis of a complete determinism – taking the notion of history unfolding itself not merely to be a complex metaphor but as the literal description of the story of man. It is Karl Marx and Friedrich Engels who mould out of this hegelian clay a new doctrine which says society and economy cannot but evolve through progressive historical stages, and that in particular the burgeoning capitalism of the times is destined to be transformed through revolution into a classless utopia. The literature on marxism is of course vast; the single best reference known to the author is Leszek Kolakowski, *Main Currents of Marxism: Vol. I, The Founders; Vol. II, The Golden Age; Vol. III, The Breakdown* (Oxford: Clarendon Press, 1978).

The reader is cautioned again that no more than a thumbnail intellectual history has been attempted to be given here. It has drawn in part upon the account given by Karl Pribram (1877–1973) in *A History of Economic Reasoning* (Baltimore, Md.: Johns Hopkins University Press, 1983), although it differs from it in very significant ways as well. Pribram was an erudite economist who had been a co-speaker with J. M. Keynes at an important conference on unemployment at the University of Chicago in 1931, and whom Hayek is reported to have considered 'without exception, the most learned man in the field'. Yet his name is practically unknown to economists today, possibly because he did not have a permanent university affiliation. The main thesis of Pribram's *History* is that the currents and cross-currents of economic thought need to be seen within the larger currents and cross-currents of European thought in general. Those who have addressed themselves to political and economic questions have done so not only with contingent problems in mind, but also in the context of contemporary philosophical movements, and especially the contemporary understanding of the Realist/Nominalist dualism. Such a thesis that the economists of any generation may be expected to be influenced in some degree by contemporary intellectual movements is to be contrasted with that of Schumpeter in *History of Economic Analysis*, a work which is equalled in scope by Pribram's but which has been vastly more influential upon the thinking of economists today given the fame of its author and the much earlier date of its publication. Schumpeter claimed that economics and philosophy had proceeded independently, but he gave as argument only that the philosophical writings of Leibniz and Hume seemed distinct from their writings on economic subjects. In the opinion of the present author, Pribram's *History* is a splendid work, although it seems mistaken in its characterization and assessment of the Realist/Nominalist dualism; see Chapter 5, pp. 73–89.

8 'Utopia and violence' in *Conjectures and Refutations*, p. 359.

9 *Principles*, pp. 117–118.

10 Jan Tinbergen, *On the Theory of Economic Policy* (Amsterdam: North Holland, 1952). Henri Theil, *Economic Forecasts and Policy*, 2nd edition (Amsterdam: North Holland, 1970).

11 Theil, *ibid.*, p. 374.

12 Even among Tinbergen's close followers, the relationship between the popular choice and the policy-maker's choice appears to have remained quite obscure. On the one hand, it is said that the policy-maker will in his own interest want to reflect the popular choice, or lose the next election: 'The first element of [Tinbergen's] framework is the postulation of an objective welfare or preference function reflecting the general interest of the people. To circumvent the difficulties inherent in any attempt at making interpersonal and intertemporal utility comparisons, as well as the possible intransitivity of the community welfare function, Tinbergen replaces the aggregate social welfare function of the community by the policy-maker's preference function, which normally should approximate the welfare function of the citizens rather closely. If this were not the case, the government (of the party in power) would be replaced in the next general elections by a more representative state.' Karl Fox, J. K. Sengupta and Erik Thorbecke, *The Theory of Quantitative Economic Policy* (Amsterdam: North Holland, 1966), pp. 448–449. Such a view must presuppose a parliamentary process, and of course that the policy-maker is interested in winning the next election. On the other hand, Theil suggests the policy-maker need not give much heed to the popular choice as this may be 'unsophisticated': an assumption that a policy-maker can define a social utility function is said to be at least as good as an assumption that consumers have individual utility functions 'because the policy-makers we have in mind, like Government officials, entrepreneurs, labour-union officials etc., are usually more "rational" than unsophisticated consumers, so that the existence of stable indifference curves seems to be a more realistic assumption for our present case' (Theil, *Economic Forecasts*, p. 377).

13 For example, in reviewing the Klein-Goldberger model in 1956, Professor C. F. Christ was to refer to Tinbergen's 'pioneering' theory, and to write of 'the series of aggregate econometric models of the U.S. economy that have followed in the footsteps of Tinbergen.' 'Aggregate economic models', in *American Economic Review*, June 1956, reprinted in *Readings in Business Cycle Theory*, edited by L. R. Klein and R. A. Gordon (Homewood, Ill.: Richard D. Irwin, 1965), p. 308.

14 'The objectives of equilibrium business cycle theory are taken, without modification, from the goal which motivated the construction of the Keynesian macroeconomic models: to provide a scientifically based means of assessing, quantitatively, the likely effects of alternative economic policies.' R. E. Lucas, Jr, and T. J. Sargent, 'After Keynesian macroeconomics', in *Rational Expectations and Econometric Practice*, edited by R. E. Lucas Jr, and T. J. Sargent (Minnesota: University of Minnesota Press, 1981), p. 317. 'The idea is to use historical data to estimate the model and then to utilize the estimated version to obtain estimates of the consequences of alternative policies.' (*ibid.*, p. 297). 'Our task as I see it . . . is to write a Fortran program that will accept specific economic policy rules as "input" and will generate as "output" statistics describing the operating characteristics of time series we care about, which are predicted to result from these policies. For example, one would like to know what average rate of unemployment would have prevailed since World War II in the United States had M1 grown at 4% per year during this period, other policies being as they were.' R. E. Lucas, Jr, 'Methods and problems in business cycle theory', in *Studies in Business Cycle Theory* (Cambridge, Mass.: MIT Press, 1981), p. 288.

## 4 *Difficulties with Moral Scepticism*

1 A brief bibliography may include Stephen Toulmin, *An Examination of the Place of Reason in Ethics* (Cambridge: Cambridge University Press, 1958); J. R. Searle, 'How to derive "ought" from "is" ', in *Philosophical Review*, Vol. 73, 1964, pp. 43–58, reprinted in *Theories of Ethics*, edited by Phillipa Foot (Oxford: Oxford University Press, 1967); Max Black, 'The gap between "is" and "should" ', in *Philosophical Review*, Vol. 73, 1964, pp. 165–181, reprinted in *Margins of Precision* (Ithaca, NY: Cornell University Press, 1970); Renford Bambrough, *Reason, Truth and God* (London: Methuen, 1969) and *Moral Scepticism and Moral Knowledge* (London: Routledge & Kegan Paul, 1979); *The Is-Ought Question*, edited by W. D. Hudson (London: Macmillan, 1969); *Skepticism and Moral Principles*, edited by Curtis L. Carter (New University Press, 1973); Roger N. Hancock, *Twentieth Century Ethics* (New York: Columbia University Press, 1974); Richard B. Brandt, *A Theory of the Good and the Right* (Oxford: Clarendon Press, 1979); Hilary Putnam, *Reason, Truth and History* (Cambridge: Cambridge University Press, 1981); Morton White, *What Is and What Ought To Be Done* (Oxford: Oxford University Press, 1981); Bernard Mayo, *The Philosophy of Right and Wrong* (Routledge & Kegan Paul, 1986).

2 It may be worth taking a moment to consider this 'is-is' dualism

further, since it will have some bearing upon the discussion in Chapter 9 and Chapter 10.

Hume himself distinguished between the use of 'is' as an identity or an equals-sign as in 'the Sciences of Geometry, Algebra and Arithmetic', and the use of 'is' as a copula between subject and predicate referring to 'matters of fact' (*Enquiries*, pp. 25–26). This would be in line with the traditional dualism between the *a priori* or logical on the one hand, and the contingent or empirical on the other. To an *a priori* question a true answer must be given necessarily, with an internal contradiction being entailed by every false answer. For example: 'What is the twelfth day after Christmas?' by this definition would be a logical or *a priori* question, the only possible answer to it without contradiction being 6 January. Other examples: 'If all $S$ is $P$ and if $x$ is $S$ then $x$ is $P$'; 'In the geometries of Euclid, Reimann and Lobachevski respectively, the angles of a triangle equal, are greater than, and are less than two right angles'; 'In the model of consumer demand, the demand for a good is inversely related to its relative price unless there is a perverse income effect'. On the other hand, an empirical question would be one admitting several answers without contradiction, only one of which is true in the sense of being in agreement with what is the case. Thus it is empirically true that Truman defeated Dewey in 1948 even though the headline could say 'Dewey defeats Truman' with no necessary contradiction of the question as to who had won. Other examples: 'Red blood corpuscles are the carriers of oxygen'; 'The atomic weight of carbon is 12'; 'The speed of light is constant'; 'The economic decisions of human beings are determined in part by the relative prices of the goods they wish to trade'. Each of these would have at least one contrary, and there would be some test to establish it to be true and the contraries false.

A dualism of this sort seems to have been endorsed by a long line of philosophers from Aristotle through Leibniz to Frege and Wittgenstein. See, for example, Aristotle, *Prior Analytics* translated by A. J. Jenkinson, in *Basic Works*; G. W. Leibniz, 'Monadology', 1714, in *Philosophical Writings*, edited by G. H. R. Parkinson (London: J. M. Dent, 1973), p. 184; *Translations from the Philosophical Writings of Gottlob Frege*, edited by Peter Geach and Max Black (Oxford: Basil Blackwell, 1952), pp. 43–44. Ludwig Wittgenstein: 'Why are the Newtonian laws not axioms of arithmetic? Because we could quite well imagine things being otherwise. But . . . this only assigns a certain role to those propositions in contrast to another one. I.e. to say of a proposition: "This could be imagined otherwise" or "We can imagine the opposite too", ascribes the role of an empirical proposition to it.' *Remarks on the Foundations of Mathematics*, edited by G. H. von Wright, R. Rhees, G. E. M. Anscombe, translated by G. E. M. Anscombe, 1956 (Cambridge, Mass.: MIT Press, 1978), p. 225. In the philosophy of mathematics, the dualism finds acceptance within the logicist school of Frege, Russell, Carnap and Hempel, and the formalist school of Hilbert, Von Neumann, and Curry. See, for example, Bertrand Russell, 'Selections from *Introduction to Mathematical Philosophy*', 1919, reprinted in *Philosophy of Mathematics*, 2nd edition, edited by Paul Benacerraf and Hilary Putnam (Cambridge: Cambridge University Press, 1983), pp. 160–182; Rudolf Carnap, 'The logicist foundations of mathematics', 1931, translated by Erna Putnam and Gerald I. Massey, in *ibid.*, pp. 41–52; Carl Hempel, 'On the nature of mathematical truth', 1945, in *ibid.*, pp. 377–393; Johann Von Neumann, 'The formalist foundations of mathematics', 1931, translated by Erna Putnam and Gerald I. Massey, in *ibid.*, pp. 61–65; Haskel B. Curry, 'Remarks on the definition and nature of mathematics', 1939, in *ibid.*, pp. 202-206. Karl Popper's definition of a scientific proposition as one capable of refutation or falsification may be understood as requiring the conclusion of a scientific project to be a claim to fact; that is, something whose contrary might be the case but is being alleged by the scientist as being not the case, it being left open to anyone to show him to be mistaken. See *The Logic of Scientific Discovery* (London: Hutchinson, 1959), pp. 27–48. The dualism would also seem to be implicitly or explicitly endorsed when we contrast 'form' with 'content' or 'theory' with 'evidence' or 'hypothesis' with 'test' or 'conjecture' with 'refutation'.

Yet there has been an important undercurrent of criticism as well. For example, J. S. Mill seems to have argued the subject matter of mathematics not to be ultimately different in kind from that of empirical science, that mathematical propositions are ultimately only very general propositions about the world. *A System of Logic*, 1843, 9th edition (London: Longmans, 1975), Book II, Chapter VI. See also Note 17 to Chapter 9 below. A merit of such a view is that it is a reminder of non-deductive ways of reasoning, which may be a useful corrective to a pure deductivism. W. V. O. Quine has argued: 'Any statement can be held true come what may if we make drastic enough adjustments elsewhere in the system. . . . Conversely, by the same token, no statement is immune to revision.' ('Two dogmas of empiricism', 1953, in Benacerraf and Putnam, *Philosophy of Mathematics*, p. 362). Quine takes an *a priori* statement to be a claim which is supposed to be unrevisable in principle, and concludes that there are by this definition no *a priori* truths, not even the law of excluded middle. See also Hilary Putnam, 'The logic of quantum mechanics', in *Mathematics, Matter and Method, Philosophical Papers Vol. 1*, 2nd edition (Cambridge: Cambridge University Press, 1979); and 'Two Dogmas Revisited', in *Reason and Reality, Philosophical Papers, Vol. 3* (Cambridge: Cambridge University Press, 1983).

3 *Moral Scepticism and Moral Knowledge*, p. 87.

4 'Thought, language and objectivity', in *The Living Principle: 'English' as a Discipline of Thought* (Oxford: Oxford University Press, 1975), pp. 35–36.

5 Bambrough has challenged sceptics in moral philosophy to produce such a case; to this may be added here a challenge to humean economists.

6 Aristotle, *On Sophistical Refutations*, translated by W. A. Pickard-Cambridge, in *The Basic Works of Aristotle*, edited by Richard McKeon (New York: Random House, 1941), §165a21–23, p. 209.

7 For a fuller discussion of emotivism, see G. J. Warnock, *Contemporary Moral Philosophy* (New York: St. Martin's Press, 1967), pp. 18–29; and J. O. Urmson, *The Emotive Theory of Ethics* (London: Hutchinson, 1968). Also Bambrough, *Moral Scepticism and Moral Knowledge*, pp. 51–58, 69–70, and 157–158.

8 *Freedom and Reason*, pp. 157–185.

9 *Conjectures and Refutations*, p. 357–359.

10 'Why should I be rational?' in *The Prevalence of Humbug and Other Essays* (Ithaca, NY: Cornell University Press, 1983), pp. 27–28.

11 A joke some years ago about a certain military dictatorship went 'They are having a General Election – and everyone knows which generals are going to be elected!'

12 Aleksandr I. Solzhenitsyn, *The Gulag Archepelago*, translated from the Russian by Thomas P. Whitney (New York: Harper & Row, 1973), p. 208.

13 *Open Society*, pp. 121–125.

14 *Collected Papers*, I, p. 67.

15 *Enquiries* §126, pp. 158–159.

16 'The metamorphosis of metaphysics', in *Proceedings of the British Academy*, Vol. XLVII, reprinted in *Paradox and Discovery* (Berkeley: University of California Press, 1970), pp. 65–66.

17 *Moral Scepticism and Moral Knowledge*, p. 128.

18 *Treatise*, p. 89 and pp. 651–652 respectively. See also Karl Popper, *The Logic of Scientific Discovery* (London: Hutchinson, 1959), p. 369, and a review of it by I. J. Good, in *Mathematical Reviews*, 21, 1960, No. 6318.

19 A reader has observed that the present work does not consider why moral scepticism 'has seemed to many . . . to be a much more compelling and practically significant doctrine than other forms, such as inductive scepticism. In particular, why is the problem of induction usually described as not whether but how to justify inductive inference, while the problem in ethics is both whether *and* how to justify ethical claims?' This is a most interesting question which has not received attention either in this work or elsewhere. The criticism is that no comparison or contrast has been made between the explanation of moral scepticism and the explanation of other forms of scepticism. The previous chapter has offered a brief political and

historical explanation of why moral scepticism may have seemed compelling, but no attempt has been made in this work to discuss a parallel explanation of other forms of scepticism. On the question of statistical inference in its philosophical aspects, see Ian Hacking, *The Logic of Statistical Inference* (Cambridge: Cambridge University Press, 1965).

20 Bambrough, *Moral Scepticism and Moral Knowledge*, p. 142.
21 Renford Bambrough, 'Thought, word, and deed', in *Proceedings of the Aristotelian Society*, Supplementary Volume LIV, 1980, pp. 109–110.

## 5 *Objectivity and Freedom*

1 The original passage is as follows:
'Consider for example the proceedings that we call "games". I mean board-games, card-games, ball-games, Olympic games, and so on. What is common to them all? – Don't say: 'There *must* be something in common, or they would not be called "games" ' – but *look and see* whether there is anything in common to all. – For if you look at them you will not see something that is common to *all*, but similarities, relationships, and a whole series of them at that. To repeat: don't think, but look! – Look for example at board-games with their multifarious relationships. Now pass to card-games; here you find many correspondences with the first group, but many common features drop out, and others appear. When we pass next to ball-games, much that is common is retained, but much is lost. – Are they all "amusing"? Compare chess with noughts and crosses. Or is there always winning and losing, or competition between players? Think of patience. In ball-games there is winning and losing; but when a child throws his ball at the wall and catches it again, this feature has disappeared. Look at the part played by skill and luck; and at the difference between skill in chess and skill in tennis. Think now of games like ring-a-ring-a-roses; here is the element of amusement, but how many other characteristic features have disappeared! And we can go through the many, many other groups of games in the same way; can see how similarities crop up and disappear.' (*Philosophical Investigations*, §66, pp. 31e–32e).
2 'Some consequences of four incapacities', in *Collected Papers*, §5.264, p. 156.
3 For a critical appreciation of the scholastic doctors, see Peirce, 'Lessons from the history of philosophy', in *Collected Papers* §1. 28–34, pp. 10–14; and 'Review of *The Works of George Berkeley*', in *Collected Papers* §8.7–38, pp. 9–38.
4 The argument given here is due to Renford Bambrough in

## Notes and References

'Universals and family resemblances', in *Proceedings of the Aristotelian Society*, Vol. LXI (1960–61), pp. 207–222, reprinted in *Wittgenstein*, edited by George Pitcher (Notre Dame, Ind.: University of Notre Dame Press, 1968). See also by Bambrough, *Reason, Truth and God*, pp. 95–98, and 'Objectivity and Objects', in *Proceedings of the Aristotelian Society*, Vol. LXXII (1971–72).

5 *Philosophical Investigations*, §67, p. 32e. See also, for example,. Rudolf Carnap, 'Empiricism, semantics and ontology', in *Meaning and Necessity*, 2nd edition (Chicago: University of Chicago Press, 1956), pp. 205–221; H. A. Price, *Thinking and Experience*, 2nd edition (London: Hutchinson, 1969); D. M. Armstrong, *Universals and Scientific Realism* (Cambridge: Cambridge University Press, 1978); D. W. Hamlyn, *Metaphysics* (Cambridge: Cambridge University Press, 1984); *The Problem of Universals*, edited by Charles Landesman (New York: Basic Books, 1971).

6 *Philosophical Investigations* §67, p. 32e.

7 Max Black, 'Wittgenstein's language-games', in *Dialectica*, 1979, p. 347.

8 *Moral Scepticism and Moral Knowledge*, p. 143. See also Hans Reichenbach, 'The philosophical significance of the theory of relativity', in *Readings in the Philosophy of Science*, edited by Herbert Feigl and May Brodbeck (New York: Appleton, 1953), p. 201.

9 *The Blue and Brown Books* (Oxford: Basil Blackwell, 1958), pp. 17–18.

10 'Lessons from the history of science', in *Collected Papers* §1.59, p. 26.

11 G. H. Hardy, *A Mathematician's Apology* (Cambridge: Cambridge University Press, 1967), pp. 123–124 and p. 126. Michael Dummett, 'Platonism', 1967, in *Truth and Other Enigmas* (Cambridge, Mass.: Harvard University Press, 1978), p. 207. See also A. E. Taylor, *Plato*, pp. 49–50.

12 Kenneth J. Arrow, 'General economic equilibrium: purpose, analytic techniques, collective choice', in *Les Prix Nobel en 1972* (Stockholm: Nobel Foundation, 1973), reprinted in *Collected Papers of Kenneth J. Arrow 2, General Equilibrium* (Cambridge, Mass.: Harvard University Press, 1983), p. 222, italics added; Frank Hahn, 'Why I am not a monetarist', in *Equilibrium and Macroeconomics*, p. 308, italics added.

13 *Toward Reunion in Philosophy*, p. 6.

14 'On what there is', in *From a Logical Point of View* (Cambridge, Mass.: Harvard University Press, 1953), reprinted in Benacerraf and Putnam *Philosophy of Mathematics*, 1964, p. 183–184.

15 'A feature of Wittgenstein's technique', in *Proceedings of the Aristotelian Society*, Supplementary Volume, 1961, reprinted in *Paradox and Discovery*, p. 102.

16 Such an argument may remind the reader of the way an assumption of the continuity of a function can be used in mathematical analysis. For example, if $f(x)$ is a continuous function over its domain, and if

for some value of $x$, $f(x)$ is positive and for some other value of $x$, $f(x)$ is negative, then by the intermediate value theorem there must exist some value of $x$ for which $f(x)$ is zero. An analogous assumption in the present context would have to be that the function (or correspondence) mapping the domain of possible questions to the range of their true or right answers is continuous.

17 'Some consequences of four incapacities', in *Collected Papers* §5.265, pp. 156–157.

18 'What pragmatism is', in *Collected Papers* §5.416, p. 278.

19 *On Certainty*, edited by G. E. M. Anscombe and G. H. von Wright, translated by Denis Paul and G. E. M. Anscombe (Oxford: Basil Blackwell, 1969), §115, p. 18e. It is in the same vein that Bambrough remarks: 'Nothing can be proved to a man who will accept nothing that has not been proved.' (*Moral Scepticism and Moral Knowledge*, p. 23), and: 'I cannot tell you where something is unless you already know where something is. I can give you directions for finding the Guildhall only if you can already find some other building or some other object to which I can relate it. We cannot discuss the spatial location of any object unless there are other objects whose location we do not need to discuss. But anything that we can agree to use as a landmark or point of reference is something that is itself *locatable* by the same procedure; it is something into whose location somebody else, or you and I on another occasion, might need to inquire. And *any* object may be used as a landmark. There are no particular objects or locations which are *the* ultimate, fundamental landmarks or base-lines for the location of all other objects. There *could* not be such ultimate landmarks, and we do not *need* such landmarks. They are neither necessary nor possible.' (*Reason, Truth and God*, pp. 94–95).

Bambrough has investigated the possible influence of Peirce upon Wittgenstein, via F. P. Ramsey who had read and admired Peirce's work and who at the same time was an influence upon Wittgenstein. See Wittgenstein, *Philosophical Investigations* §81, p. 38e; Renford Bambrough, 'Peirce, Wittgenstein and systematic philosophy', in *Midwest Studies in Philosophy, Vol. VI, The Foundations of Analytical Philosophy*, edited by Peter A. French, Theodore E. Euhling Jr, and Howard K. Wellstein (Minneapolis, Minn.: University of Minnesota Press, 1981), pp. 263–272. See also Chapter 6, pp. 110–111.

## 6 *Expertise and Democracy*

1 'Proof of an external world', in *Philosophical Papers* (London: Allen & Unwin, 1959), pp. 127–150. See also 'A defence of commonsense',

in *ibid.*, pp. 52–59. See also *The Philosophy of G. E. Moore* edited by Paul Arthur Schlipp (La Salle, Ill.: Open Court, 1942); Wittgenstein, *On Certainty*; Norman Malcolm, *Ludwig Wittgenstein, A Memoir* (Oxford: Oxford University Press, 1958), pp. 66–68, pp. 87–93.

2 *Moral Scepticism and Moral Knowledge*, p. 15.

3 Ludwig Wittgenstein, *Tractatus Logico-Philosophicus*, German original 1921, translated from the German by D. F. Pears and B. F. McGuinness (London: Routledge & Kegan Paul, 1961), §6.5, p. 73.

4 Gottlob Frege, 'Logic', 1897, in *Posthumous Writings*, edited by Hans Hermes, Friedrich Kambartel and Friedrich Kaulbach, translated from the German by Peter Long and Roger White (Oxford: Basil Blackwell, 1979), pp. 132–133.

5 *Gorgias* §482c, translated by W. D. Woodhead, in *Collected Dialogues*, p. 265. In the same vein Hannah Arendt wrote: 'Insofar as man carries within himself a partner from whom he can never win release, he will be better off not to live with a murderer or a liar; or: since thought is the silent dialogue carried out between me and myself, I must be careful to keep the integrity of this partner intact, for otherwise I shall surely lose the capacity for thought altogether.' 'Truth and politics', in *Philosophy, Politics and Society*, 2nd Series, edited by Peter Laslett and W. G. Runciman (Oxford: Basil Blackwell, 1967), p. 118. This essay has had a greater influence on the present work than may be apparent.

6 'Conceive the sailors to be wrangling with one another for control of the helm, each claiming that it is his right to steer though he never learned the art and cannot point out his teacher or any time when he studied it. And what is more, they affirm that it cannot be taught at all, and they are ready to make mincemeat of anyone who says it can be taught . . . . they praise and celebrate as a navigator, a pilot, a master of shipcraft, the man who is most cunning to lend a hand in persuading or constraining the shipmaster to let them rule, while the man who lacks this craft they condemn as useless. They have no suspicion that the true pilot must give his attention to the time of the year, the seasons, the sky, the winds, the stars, and all that pertains to his art if he is to be a true ruler of a ship . . . . do you not think that the real pilot would in very deed be called a stargazer, an idle babbler, a useless fellow by the sailors in ships managed after this fashion?' (*Republic*, §488, in *Collected Dialogues*, pp. 724–725).

7 'Unless either philosophers become kings in our states or those whom we now call our kings and rulers take to the pursuit of philosophy seriously and adequately, and there is a conjunction of these two things, political power and philosophical intelligence . . . . there can be no cessation of troubles, dear Glaucon, for our states, nor, I fancy, for the human race either. Nor, until this happens, will this constitution which we have been expounding in theory ever be put

into practice within the limits of possibility and see the light of the sun.' (*Republic* §473d–473e, in *Collected Dialogues*, pp. 712–713). See also *Statesman*, §292e, translated by J. B. Skemp, and *Letter VII*, §326b, translated by L. A. Post, in *Collected Dialogues*, pp. 1061–1062 and p. 1576 respectively.

8 Immanuel Kant, *Groundwork of the Metaphysic of Morals*, §77–78, in H. J. Paton, *The Moral Law* (London: Hutchinson, 1948), pp. 96–97. The actions of a rational being have dignity when such a being has placed self-imposed constraints on its own freedom in recognition of the similar freedom of other rational beings. When a rational being does this of which it is capable, Kant would speak of a state of 'autonomy', *ibid.*, §86–88, pp. 101–102. (And if we take the concept of rationality to be a family resemblance concept, there seems no reason why it may not refer to the rationality of other forms of life besides homo sapiens – think of photosynthesis!)

In the course of a defence of Plato, Kant extended the argument to a constitutional context as follows: 'A constitution of the greatest possible human freedom according to laws, by which the liberty of every individual can consist with the liberty of every other (not of the greatest possible happiness, for this follows necessarily from the former), is, to say the least, a necessary idea, which must be placed at the foundation not only of the first plan of the constitution of a state, but of all its laws.' *Critique of Pure Reason*, translated by J. M. D. Meiklejohn (London: J. M. Dent, 1934), p. 220. If we call a law just when it allows the liberty of every individual to consist with the liberty of every other, then the rational being has no duty to obey laws which are not just, but is committed to obey just laws under pain of self-contradiction: 'if a certain use to which freedom is put is itself a hindrance to freedom in accordance with universal laws (i.e. if it is contrary to right) any coercion which is used against it will be a hindrance to a hindrance of freedom, and will thus be consonant with freedom in accordance with universal laws – that is, it will be right. It thus follows by the law of contradiction that right entails the authority to apply coercion to anyone who infringes it.' 'The metaphysics of morals' in *Kant's Political Writings*, edited by Hans Reiss, translated from the German by H. B. Nisbet (Cambridge: Cambridge University Press), p. 134.

9 *Economic Theory in Retrospect*, p. 709.

10 J. S. Mill, *On Liberty* (1859), in *Utilitarianism, Liberty and Representative Government*, edited by H. B. Acton (London: J. M. Dent, 1972), p. 79.

11 *The Logic of Scientific Discovery* (London: Hutchinson, 1959). See also *Criticism and the Growth of Knowledge*, edited by Imre Lakatos and Alan Musgrave (Cambridge: Cambridge University Press, 1967).

12 George Orwell, *1984* (New York: Harcourt Brace Jovanovich, Signet Classics, 1949), I.7. p. 69. The essays and fiction of Orwell have had

a greater influence on the present work than may be apparent.

13  *Gulag Archipelago*, p. 202.
14  Bambrough, *Moral Scepticism and Moral Knowledge*, p. 33.
15  'Individualism: true and false', in *Individualism and Economic Order*, p. 14.
16  *Nicomachean Ethics*, in *The Basic Works* §1104a2–1104a9, p. 953; §1112a28–30, p. 969. In a letter to the author dated 13 February 1981, Professor Hayek said he had not for some time looked at this source in Aristotle.
17  Hahn and Hollis, *Philosophy and Economic Theory*, p. 12.
18  See for example Leonid Hurwicz, in *Studies in Resource Allocation Processes*, edited by Kenneth J. Arrow and Leonid Hurwicz (Cambridge: Cambridge University Press, 1977), p. 8; Roy Radner, 'Competitive equilibrium under uncertainty', in *Econometrica*, 36, January 1968, pp. 31–58.
19  'The use of knowledge in society', in *Individualism and Economic Order*, p. 80.
20  Adam Smith, *An Inquiry into the Nature and Causes of the Wealth of Nations*, 1776, edited by R. H. Campbell, A. S. Skinner and W. D. Todd (Oxford: Oxford University Press, 1976), Book IV.ii, §10, p. 456.
21  See also J. S. Mill *Principles of Political Economy* (New York: Appleton, 1892), Book V, Chapter XI, especially §2, pp. 560–561.
22  *Foundations of Arithmetic*, p. 40.
23  *Nicomachean Ethics*, in *The Basic Works*, §1145a15–1152a35, pp. 1036–1053. See also Bambrough, *Moral Scepticism and Moral Knowledge*, pp. 112–116.
24  *Collective Choice and Social Welfare* (San Francisco, Calif.: Holden-Day, 1970), pp. 59–64.
25  In March 1985 the existence of Alexander's work on this subject came to the author's attention for the first time. In subsequent communication and conversation, both parties were surprised at the similarity of some of their findings and the independence of the routes that had been taken. It was agreed that this independence should be maintained, and therefore it may be best for the reader to be referred to Alexander's work directly for comparison and contrast. Alexander's two main papers on the subject are 'Human values and economists' values', in *Human Values and Economic Policy*, edited by Sidney Hook (New York: New York University Press, 1967), and 'Public television and the "ought" of public policy', in *Washington University Law Quarterly*, Winter 1968, pp. 35–70. See also 'The impersonality of normative judgements', in *Induction, Growth and Trade, Essays in Honour of Sir Roy Harrod*, edited by W. A. Eltis *et al.* (Oxford: Clarendon Press, 1970); 'Comment on K. J. Arrow's "Political and economic evaluation of social effects and externalities" ', in *The Analysis of Public Output*, edited by Julius Margolis (New

York: National Bureau of Economic Research, 1970); and 'Social evaluation through notional choice', in *Quarterly Journal of Economics*, November 1974, pp. 597–624.

Alexander has drawn upon a North American tradition which includes John Dewey, William James, Sidney Hook, W. V. O. Quine, Morton White and others, where the present work has drawn upon a line of thought from Wittgenstein as interpreted and developed especially by John Wisdom and Renford Bambrough in England. C. S. Peirce was an acknowledged influence on the North American tradition and at the same time could have had some tenuous influence on Wittgenstein (see Note 19 to Chapter 5 above); if a common lineage is desired to be traced between the present work and that of Alexander, it could go back to Peirce in the first instance.

26  Gunnar Myrdal, *Values in Social Theory: A Selection of Essays on Methodology*, edited by Paul Streeten (New York: Harper, 1958), pp. 1–2.

27  Paul Streeten, *ibid.*, p. xliii.

28  Solzhenitsyn, *Gulag Archipelago*, p. 174.

29  'Letters to Lady Welby', 1909, in *Selected Writings (Values in a Universe of Chance)*, edited by Phillip P. Weiner, 1958 (New York: Dover, 1966), p. 415. See also the letter to William James in *Collected Papers*, §8.255, p. 188, where Peirce speaks of 'the proof that logic must be founded on ethics'.

30  *Posthumous Writings,* p. 4. See also *ibid.*, p. 128 and p. 252.

31  *Remarks on the Foundations of Mathematics*, §I.121, p. 84; §III.55, p. 187, and §VII. 61, p. 425, respectively. See also *ibid.*, §III.9. p. 149; §III.39, p. 171; §VI.46, p. 350; §VI.49, p. 353; §VII. 67, p. 431. With respect to the comparison with Peirce, see also Note 19 to Chapter 5 above.

## 7 *An Example from Microeconomics*

1  'Fuss over phone rates', *The MacNeil-Lehrer NewsHour*, 19 December 1984, PBS Station, WNET/Thirteen, New York. The published transcript has been very slightly abbreviated here.

## 8 *A Dialogue in Macroeconomics*

1  The text of this chapter has drawn from the works of Knut Wicksell, J. M. Keynes, F. A. Hayek, John Hicks, Lionel Robbins, Milton Friedman, Don Patinkin, L. A. Metzler, James Tobin, Harry G. Johnson, Frank Hahn, Robert Clower, Axel Leijonhufvud, James Buchanan, Kenneth J. Arrow, R. E. Lucas, Jr, T. W. Hutchison, C. J. Bliss, J. M. Grandmont and others in modern macroeconomics

and monetary theory. Selected references may be found in the bibliography.

## 9 *Mathematical Economics and Reality*

1 J. S. Mill, 'On liberty', in *Utilitarianism*, p. 112.
2 Augustin Cournot, *Researches into the Mathematical Principles of the Theory of Wealth*, 1838, translated by Nathaniel T. Bacon with an introduction by Irving Fisher (New York: Macmillan, 1897), pp. 2–5. William Stanley Jevons, *The Theory of Political Economy* (London: Macmillan, 1871), pp. 3–9. Léon Walras, *Elements of Pure Economics*, 1874, translated by William Jaffé, 1954 (New York: Augustus M. Kelley, 1977), pp. 47–48.
3 L. R. Klein, 'The contributions of mathematics to economics', in *Review of Economics and Statistics*, November 1954, p. 360. P. A. Samuelson, *Foundations*, p. 6.
4 Nicholas Georgescu-Roegen, 'Methods in economic science', in *Journal of Economic Issues*, June 1979, p. 317.
5 John Maynard Keynes, *The General Theory of Employment, Interest and Money* (London: Macmillan, 1936), p. 298.
6 Samuelson, *Foundations*, p. xviii.
7 Gerard Debreu, 'The axiomatization of economic theory', 1977, quoted by Werner Hildenbrand in *Mathematical Economics: Twenty Papers of Gerard Debreu* (Cambridge: Cambridge University Press, 1983) with an introduction by Werner Hildenbrand, pp. 5–6. See also Gerard Debreu, 'Theoretic models: mathematical form and economic content', in *Econometrica* Vol. 54, No. 6, November 1986, pp. 1259–1270.
8 P. T. Bauer, 'Reflections on the state of economics' in *Equality, the Third World and Economic Delusion* (Cambridge, Mass.: Harvard University Press, 1981), p. 265.
9 Nicholas Kaldor, 'The irrelevance of equilibrium economics', in *Economic Journal*, December 1972, p. 180.
10 Hildenbrand, *Mathematical Economics*, pp. 2–3; Bertrand Russell, *The Scientific Outlook* (London: Allen & Unwin, 1931), no page cited, quoted by Frank Hahn in *On the Notion of Equilibrium in Economics* (Cambridge: Cambridge University Press, 1973), pp. 3–4, reprinted in *Equilibrium and Macroeconomics*, p. 45.
11 W. W. Leontief, in *Science* Vol. 217, 9 July 1982, pp. 104–105; reprinted as the Foreword to *Why Economics is Not Yet a Science*, edited by Alfred S. Eichner (Armonk, New York: M. E. Sharpe, 1983).
12 Salim Rashid, 'Methods in economic science: a comment', in *Journal of Economic Issues*, Spring 1981, p. 187. This was a thoughtful and moderate reply to Georgescu-Roegen's article referred to in Note 4

above, but provoked a harsh rejoinder.

13 'Selections from *Introduction to Mathematical Philosophy*', in Benacerraf and Putnam, *Philosophy of Mathematics*, 2nd edition, p. 173.

14 Arend Heyting, 'After thirty years', in *Logic, Methodology and the Philosophy of Science*, edited by Ernest Nagel, Alfred Tarski and Patrick Suppes (Stanford, Calif.: Stanford University Press, 1962), p. 195.

15 Renford Bambrough, 'Objectivity and objects', in *Proceedings of the Aristotelian Society*, Vol. LXXII (1971–72), p. 66.

16 The philosophy of mathematics is a complex and erudite field, in which there is available much specialist work of high quality. Some volumes which may be profitably consulted are: *From Frege to Gödel: A Source Book in Mathematical Logic, 1879–1931*, edited by Jean Van Heijenoort (Cambridge, Mass.: Harvard University Press, 1967); the two editions of *Philosophy of Mathematics*, edited by Benacerraf and Putnam; Max Black, *The Nature of Mathematics* (London: Routledge & Kegan Paul, 1933); Nagel and Newman, *Gödel's Proof*; Dummett, *Truth and Other Enigmas*; Michael D. Resnik, *Frege and the Philosophy of Mathematics* (Ithaca: Cornell University Press, 1980); Mark Steiner, *Mathematical Knowledge* (Ithaca: Cornell University Press, 1975).

17 *A System of Logic*, 1843, 9th edition (London: Longmans, 1975), p. 296, pp. 293–294. See also Note 2 to Chapter 4 above, and also Resnik, *Frege*, pp. 137–160.

18 Frege, *Foundations of Arithmetic*, pp. 9–14. Hilary Putnam, 'What is mathematical truth?', in *Mathematics, Matter and Method*, 2nd edition (Cambridge: Cambridge University Press, 1979), pp. 60–78.

19 Hardy, *A Mathematician's Apology*, see Note 11 to Chapter 5 above, p. 205. Kurt Gödel is considered to have endorsed platonism, and the following passage has been given as evidence: 'Evidently the "given" underlying mathematics is closely related to the abstract elements contained in our empirical ideas. It by no means follows, however, that the data of this second kind, because they cannot be associated with actions of certain things upon our sense organs, are something purely subjective, as Kant asserted. Rather they, too, may represent an aspect of objective reality, but as opposed to the sensations, their presence in us may be due to another kind of relationship between ourselves and reality.' ('What is Cantor's continuum problem', in Benacerraf and Putnam, *Philosophy of Mathematics*, 2nd edition, p. 484).

20 *Truth and Other Enigmas*, p. 202; p. 207.

21 This is a point made by Bambrough in 'Objectivity and objects'. Putnam attributes the same to Georg Kreisel without specific reference, in *Mathematics, Matter and Method*, p. 70. Also Benacerraf and Putnam, 'Introduction' to *Philosophy of Mathematics*, 2nd edition, pp. 30–33.

22 Nagel and Newman, *Gödel's Proof*, p. 13.

23  Resnik, *Frege*, p. 78.

24  Gottlob Frege, *On the Foundations of Geometry and Formal Theories of Arithmetic*, translated from the German with an introduction by Eike-Henner W. Kluge (New Haven: Yale University Press, 1971), p. 12. See also David Hilbert, 'On the foundations of logic and arithmetic', 1904, in Heijenoort, *From Frege to Gödel*, pp. 129–138, and 'The foundations of mathematics', 1927, in *ibid.*, pp. 464–479.

25  This remark may be an improvement on that of Resnik: 'The consistency of an axiom set *is* all there is to the mathematical existence of such structures.' (*Frege*, p. 116).

26  Nagel and Newman, *Gödel's Proof*, pp. 68–102.

27  Haskel B. Curry, 'Remarks on the definition and nature of mathematics', 1939, in *Dialectica*, 8, 1954; reprinted in Benacerraf and Putnam, *Philosophy of Mathematics*, 2nd edition, p. 205.

28  The reader is cautioned that the survey of opinions given here is highly simplified, and reference must be made to specialist works for proper appreciation of the philosophy of mathematics. In particular, no mention has been made of three other major points of view on number, namely, psychologism, intuitionism and logicism. For discussion of psychologism see Resnik, *Frege*, pp. 25–54. For discussion of intuitionism, see Arend Heyting, 'The intuitionist foundations of mathematics', 1931, in Benacerraf and Putnam, *Philosophy of Mathematics*, 2nd edition, pp. 52–61, and 'Disputation', 1956, in *ibid.*, pp. 66–75; L. E. J. Brouwer, 'Intuitionism and formalism', 1912, in *ibid.*, pp. 77–89; Black, *Nature of Mathematics*, pp. 169–210.

The logicist school is represented most significantly by Frege, and it may be worth stating the outlines of Frege's thesis of number as first stated in *Foundations of Arithmetic*, which has been deservedly accepted by many in contemporary mathematics. Frege proposed 'the content of a statement of number is an assertion about a concept' (§46, p. 59). The difficulty of formulating this simple maxim for the first time is perhaps hidden from us today who can understand it without difficulty. To say 'Jupiter has four major moons' or 'the number of major moons of Jupiter is four' is not to have attributed a property or a sign to the four largest objects actually in Jupiter's orbit; instead it is to have said something about the *concept* 'major moons of Jupiter'. Similarly, to say 'this car has four wheels' or 'this family has four members' or 'this animal has four legs' is to say something about the concepts 'wheels of this car', 'members of this family', 'legs of this animal'. If we define 'major moons of Jupiter' as concept F and 'wheels of this car' as concept G, then 'there exists a relation φ which correlates one to one the objects falling under concept F with the objects falling under concept G.' (§71, pp. 83–84). Frege defines concept F as being 'equal' to concept G. The objects encompassed by a concept define its 'extension'. Frege proposes to define the 'number' of a concept such as F as the extension of a certain concept derived from the concept F. From the major moons of Jupiter we derive a new concept 'equal to "major moons of Jupiter"'. We then define the number belonging to the original concept 'major moons of Jupiter' as the extension of this derived concept. Thus although the original concepts are very different from one another in sense, the extension of each of the concepts derived from them – 'equal to "major moons of Jupiter"', 'equal to "wheels of this car"', 'equal to "members of this family"', 'equal to "legs of this animal"' – is precisely the same, and defines the number four. In particular, the number nought is defined as the extension of the derived concept 'equal to "not identical with itself"', for there is nothing which is not identical with itself, and the number one is defined in contrast with nought: 'Affirmation of existence is in fact nothing but denial of the number nought.' (§53, p. 65; also §74–§77, pp. 87–91).

It had been shown by Guiseppe Peano before Frege how arithmetic may be reduced to the natural numbers. Frege, and A. N. Whitehead and Russell, showed how the natural numbers themselves could be derived from logical concepts. The important recognition of the logicists was that number was the objective attribute of a concept, and not of a physical thing or a collection of objects. Both the concept and its attribute of number are capable of being objectively understood, and this without any necessary reference to a transcendental mathematical universe. 'Not every objective object has a place' (*Foundations of Arithmetic* §61, p. 72). The broader logicist programme was one of deriving all the concepts used in mathematics from logic, using only explicit definitions and purely deductive reasoning. The ambition was to show that no specifically mathematical concepts are ultimately required in the construction of mathematics. Mathematics was seen as not merely the cousin of logic but its direct progeny. It seems to have been widely accepted that this is something of a dogmatic position and cannot be sustained. The axiom of infinity (for every natural number there is a greater one) and the multiplicative axiom (for every set of disjoint non-empty sets, there is at least one set which has exactly one member in common with each of the member sets) cannot be derived from logic alone. Also Russell's paradox of impredicative definition gave further reason for scepticism, leading Frege himself at the end of his life to doubt and decry his own achievement. (See Frege's 'Letter to Russell', 1902, in Heijenoort, *From Frege to Gödel*, pp. 126–128 – a document which must remain one of the most noble in all of modern scholarship; a fact recorded in Russell's letter to Heijenoort.) Nonetheless, the value of the logicist thesis to the development of modern mathematics hardly can be overestimated. It was able to show at least the intimate relationship that mathematics had to logic. From then on, mathematics hardly could be thought of as being any less objective than logic itself. Moreover, it did this without having to embrace a platonist ontology of a world of perfect mathematical entities somewhere outside spatio-temporal reality. Finally, logicism was to set the stage for the formalism which presently prevails in contemporary mathematics. See Rudolf Carnap, 'The logicist foundations of mathematics', 1931, in Benacerraf and Putnam, *Philosophy of Mathematics*, 2nd edition, pp. 41–52; Russell, 'Selections from *Introduction to Mathematical Philosophy*', in *ibid.*, pp. 160–182; Black, *Nature of Mathematics*, pp. 15–144; Steiner, *Mathematical Knowledge*; Resnik, *Frege*, pp. 161–234.

29 F. P. Ramsey, 'Truth and probability', 1926, in *The Foundations of Mathematics* (London: Routledge & Kegan Paul, 1931), reprinted in *Studies in Subjective Probability*, edited by Henry E. Kyburg, Jr, and Howard E. Smokler (New York: John Wiley, 1964). Bruno de Finetti, 'Foresight: its logical laws, its subjective sources', in *Annales de l'Institut Henri Poincaré*, 7, 1937, translated by Henry E. Kyburg, Jr, and reprinted in Kyburg and Smokler, *Subjective Probability*. L. J. Savage, *The Foundations of Statistics*, 2nd revised edition (New York: Dover, 1954); and also 'The foundations of statistics reconsidered', 1961, in Kyburg and Smokler, *Subjective Probability*. For the influence of subjectivism in probability theory on economic theory, see Kenneth J. Arrow, 'Alternative approaches to the theory of choice in risk-taking situations', in *Econometrica*, 19, 1951, reprinted in *Collected Papers of Kenneth J. Arrow, 3, Individual Choice Under Certainty and Uncertainty* (Cambridge, Mass.: Harvard University Press, 1984), pp. 5–41; Jacques H. Drèze, 'Axiomatic theories of choice, cardinal utility and subjective probability: a review', in *Allocation Under Uncertainty: Equilibrium and Optimality*, edited by Jacques H. Drèze (London: Macmillan, 1974), pp. 3–23. Of relevance too is Hacking, *Logic of Statistical Inference*, pp. 208–227.

30 Savage, *Foundations of Statistics*, p. 20; de Finetti, 'Foresight', in Kyburg and Smokler, *Subjective Probability*, p. 152 (original in italics).

31 Bruno de Finetti, *The Theory of Probability*, Vol. I. (New York: John Wiley, 1974), p. x; original in full capitals. I. J. Good, 'Review of de Finetti', in *Bulletin of the American Mathematical Monthly*, 83, 1977, p. 94.

32 Maurice Allais, 'The so-called Allais paradox and rational decisions under uncertainty', in *Expected Utility Hypotheses and the Allais Paradox*, edited by Maurice Allais and Ole Hagen (Dordecht, Holland: D. Reidel, 1979), p. 660; original in italics.

33 *Ibid.*, p. 517; see also p. 467 and pp. 507–517. Of possible relevance is Max Black, 'Making intelligent choices: how useful is decision theory?', in *Bulletin of the American Academy of Arts and Sciences*, November 1984, No. 2, pp. 30–49.

215

34 John Maynard Keynes, *A Treatise on Probability*, 1921, (London: Macmillan, 1973), p. 4.
35 See pp. 177–179 in Chapter 10 for development of this line of argument in the context of welfare economics.
36 *Treatise on Probability*, pp. 3–4.
37 *Theory of Value* (New Haven, Conn.: Yale University Press, 1959), p. x.
38 More recently: 'If one removes the economic interpretation of the primitive concepts, of the assumptions, and of the conclusions of the model, its bare mathematical structure must still stand.' (Gerard Debreu, 'Theoretic models: mathematical form and economic content', in *Econometrica,* November 1986, p. 1265). Another clear statement of hilbertian formalism in economic theory is to be found in Tjalling C. Koopman's remark: 'The test of mathematical existence of an object of analysis postulated in a model is in the first instance a check on the absence of contradictions among the assumptions made.' *Three Essays on the State of Economic Science* (New York: McGraw Hill, 1957), p. 55.
   These remarks may be compared with those of Hilbert to Frege referred to in Note 24 above.
39 Kenneth J. Arrow, 'Economic equilibrium', 1968; 'General economic equilibrium', 1972, both in *Collected Papers of Kenneth J. Arrow, 2, General Equilibrium*, (Cambridge, Mass.: Harvard University Press, 1983). Frank Hahn, 'On the notion of equilibrium in economics', 1973; 'General equilibrium theory', 1981; 'Reflections on the invisible hand', 1982; 'Keynesian economics and general equilibrium theory: reflections on some current debates', 1977; all reprinted in *Equilibrium and Macroeconomics* (Cambridge, Mass.: The MIT Press, 1984). See also Kenneth J. Arrow and F. H. Hahn, *General Competitive Analysis* (San Francisco: Oliver and Boyd, 1971), Chapter 1.
40 Arrow, *Collected Papers, 2, General Equilibrium*, p. 222.
41 Hahn, *Equilibrium and Macroeconomics*, p. 308, p. 136 and p. 142 respectively.
42 'The divorce of form and content immediately yields a new theory whenever a novel interpretation of a primitive concept is discovered. . . . Although an axiomatized theory may flaunt the separation of its mathematical form and content in print, their interaction is sometimes close in the discovery and elaboration phases.' (Debreu, 'Theoretic models: mathematical form and economic content', in *Econometrica* November 1986, p. 1265–1266). What is being meant in the first sentence seems clear in the context, namely, that the same mathematical structure may have more than one economic interpretation; in this sentence, the reference to the idea of 'discovery' may be incidental. But the same may not be said of the reference in the second sentence, where instead it seems quite possible to take Debreu to be making, like Arrow and Hahn, an obscure and implicit

216

reference to a platonist ontology.

It ought to be said that an earlier work by the present author may be open to criticism on similar lines. The interested reader may wish to refer to John Toye, *Dilemmas of Development* (Oxford: Basil Blackwell, 1987) p. 124, and 'Political economy and the analysis of Indian development', *Modern Asian Studies*, Vol. 22, 1, 1988, p. 105.

43 Robert M. Solow, in 'Economic development and the development of economics', edited by George Rosen, *World Development, Special Issue*, 11, October 1983, pp. 892–893.

44 Nagel and Newman, *Gödel's Proof*, p. 13.

45 Max Black, 'Models and archetypes', in *Models and Metaphors: Studies in Language and Philosophy* (Ithaca, New York: Cornell University Press, 1962) p. 22. See also Mary B. Hesse, *Models and Analogies in Science* (Notre Dame, Ind.: University of Notre Dame Press, 1966). Of possible relevance is Allan Gibbard and Hal R. Varian, 'Economic models', in *Journal of Philosophy*, 1978, pp. 664–677; Alexander Rosenberg, 'The puzzle of economic modelling', in *Journal of Philosophy*, 1978, pp. 679–683; Michael D. Intriligator, 'Economic and econometric models', in *Handbook of Econometrics, Volume I*, edited by Z. Griliches and M. D. Intriligator (Amsterdam: North Holland, 1983), pp. 182–220.

46 *Tractatus*, §6.211, p. 65.

47 'The logic of mathematics in relation to education', in *Collected Papers*, §3.559, pp. 348–350.

48 'On the nature of mathematical truth', in *American Mathematical Monthly*, 52, 1945, reprinted in Benacerraf and Putnam, *Philosophy of Mathematics*, 2nd edition, p. 391.

49 John Maynard Keynes, 'Alfred Marshall, 1842–1924' in *Memorials of Alfred Marshall*, edited by A. C. Pigou (London: Macmillan, 1925), p. 12.

## 10 *Remarks on the Foundations of Welfare Economics*

1 *Collected Papers, 2, General Equilibrium*, p. 225.

2 *Principles*, p. 93.

3 *Ibid.*, pp. 117–118.

4. J. R. Hicks, *Value and Capital*, 2nd edition (Oxford: Clarendon Press, 1946), p. 5.

5 *Ibid.*, p. 12.

6 *Ibid.*, pp. 18–19.

7 Samuelson, *Foundations*, p. 97. Kenneth J. Arrow, *Social Choice and Individual Values*, 2nd edition (New Haven, Conn.: Yale University Press, 1963), p. 9.

8 *Principles*, p. 95.

9 *Ibid.*, p. 92, p. 100, p. 121.

10 *Ibid.*, p. 129.

11 John Hicks, 'Time in economics', 1975, in *Money, Interest and Wages, Collected Essays on Economic Theory*, Vol. II (Cambridge, Mass.: Harvard University Press, 1982), pp. 285–286. 'Samuelson's consumer' is of course the natural successor to Hicks's own, if we should apply Occam's Razor too keenly in this place.

12 Letter to the author dated 1 May 1984. Besides the passage quoted here, Hicks cites as evidence of a fresh position the Introduction and pp. 114–52, 238, and 284 in *Wealth and Welfare, Collected Essays on Economic Theory,* Vol. I (Cambridge, Mass.: Harvard University Press, 1981). It may be a sign of the times that economists, great and small, rarely if ever disclaim their past opinions; it is therefore an especially splendid example to have a great economist like Hicks doing so in this matter.

13 Knut Wicksell, *Lectures on Political Economy, Vol. I. General Theory*, translated from the Swedish by E. Classen, edited by Lionel Robbins (London: Routledge, 1935), p. 221. For Wicksell's concept of marginal utility, see *ibid.*, pp. 29–35.

14 A. C. Pigou, *The Economics of Welfare*, 4th edition (London: Macmillan, 1932), p. 89.

15 'The present position of economics', 1885, in *Memorials*, p. 162; 'The Equitable Distribution of Taxation', 1917, in *ibid.*, p. 348; *Principles*, p. 95.

16 *Nature and Significance of Economic Science*, p. 137.

17 Marshall, *Principles*, p. 96.

18 Bambrough, *Moral Scepticism and Moral Knowledge*, pp. 62–63.

19 *Tractatus*, §5.62, p. 57.

20 Bambrough, *Moral Scepticism and Moral Knowledge*, p. 65.

21 *Ibid.*, p. 6. See also Bambrough, *Reason, Truth and God*, p. 10, where the maxim is named Ramsey's Maxim after F. P. Ramsey: 'In such cases it is a heuristic maxim that the truth lies not in one of the two disputed views but in some third possibility which has not yet been thought of, which we can only discover by rejecting something assumed as obvious by both the disputants.' (*Foundations of Mathematics*, pp. 115–116).

22 A part of these arguments has been taken from the author's 'Considerations on utility, benevolence and taxation', in *History of Political Economy,* Fall 1984, 16(3), pp. 349–362. Of possible relevance are D. Ellsburg, 'Classic and current notions of "measurable utility" ', *Economic Journal*, September 1954; Robert Cooter and Peter Rappoport, 'Were the ordinalists wrong about welfare economics?', in *Journal of Economic Literature*, June 1984, 22(2), pp. 507–530; subsequent criticism by Pieter Hennipman, 'A tale of two schools, comments on a new view of the ordinalist revolution', in *De Economist*, June 1987, 135(2), pp. 141–162; and the interchange between Hennipman and Rappoport in 'Communications',

in *Journal of Economic Literature*, March 1988, 26(1), pp. 80–91.

23 Arrow, *Collected Papers, 1, Social Choice*, pp. 2–3; *Social Choice and Individual Values*, p. 9. For a recent summary and extensive bibliography of the theory of social choice, see Amartya Sen, 'Social choice theory', in *Handbook of Mathematical Economics*, Vol. III, edited by Kenneth J. Arrow and Michael D. Intriligator (Amsterdam: North Holland, 1986), pp. 1073–1181.

24 *Social Choice and Individual Values*, p. 1; *Collected Papers, 1, Social Choice*, p. 4.

25 *Social Choice and Individual Values*, p. 17; *Collected Papers, 1, Social Choice*, pp. 10–11.

26 *Collected Papers, 1, Social Choice*, p. 66.

27 'The future and the present in economic life', in *Economic Inquiry*, 16, 1978, reprinted in *Collected Papers, 2, General Equilibrium*, p. 283.

28 Amartya Sen, 'The impossibility of a paretian liberal', in *Journal of Political Economy*, 78, 1970; reprinted in *Choice, Welfare and Measurement* (Cambridge, Mass.: MIT Press, 1982), p. 286.

29 'Liberty, unanimity and rights', in *Economica*, 43, August 1976; reprinted in *Choice, Welfare and Measurement*, p. 316. Mill, Hayek and Gramsci are cited on p. 292 and Stalin on p. 316.

30 *Collected Papers, 1, Social Choice*, p. 67.

31 That the Arrow-Sen concept of liberalism extends to both liberal cases and to anti-liberal ones appears to have been noticed by Christian Seidl in 'On liberal values', in *Zeitschrift für Nationalokonomie*, 35, 1975, p. 279; D. K. Osborne, 'On liberalism and the pareto principle', in *Journal of Political Economy*, 83, 1975, pp. 1285–86; and M. J. Farrell, 'Liberalism and the theory of social choice', in *Review of Economic Studies*, 43, 1976, pp. 8–9. The argument which is given in the present work was arrived at independently, and derives from two unpublished papers, 'Knowledge, social choice theory and liberalism: A critique of Professors Arrow and Sen' (April 1984), and 'Knowledge and freedom in economic theory Part II', (August 1982). In an unpublished paper dated 3 September 1976 titled 'An ambiguity in Sen's alleged proof of the impossibility of a pareto libertarian', Professor James Buchanan raised a similar objection to Sen's procedure. In terms of the example given in the text, if $K$ chose to be decisive over $(z^1, z^3)$ then individual state $d$ has been effectively ruled out as an option for $S$; or if $S$ chose to be decisive over $(z^1, z^2)$ then the individual state $a$ has been effectively ruled out as an option for $K$. A similar argument seems to be made implicitly by Peter Bernholz in 'Is a paretian liberal really impossible?', in *Public Choice*, 20, 1974, pp. 99–107.

 On a related point, the definition of the Pareto criterion in the theory of social choice would seem to be substantively different from the criterion by the same name in the theory of price, insofar as it

219

requires acceptance of the definition of the 'social state', where it is a major if implicit observation of the theory of price that most trading normally takes place under conditions of 'informational privacy'.
32 Arrow, *Collected Papers, 1, Social Choice*, pp. 63–65.

# Select Bibliography

For the convenience of the reader, a division has been made into *Works by Economists*, and *Works by Philosophers and Others*.

## Works by Economists

Alexander, Sidney S. 'Human values and economists' values'. In *Human Values and Economic Policy*. Edited by Sidney Hook. New York: New York University Press, 1967.

——. 'Public television and the "ought" of public policy'. In *Washington University Law Quarterly*. Winter 1968.

Allais, Maurice. *Expected Utility Hypotheses and the Allais Paradox*. Edited by Maurice Allais and Ole Hagen. Dordecht, Holland: D. Reidel, 1979.

Arrow, Kenneth J. *Social Choice and Individual Values*. 2nd edition. New Haven, Conn.: Yale University Press, 1963.

——. *Collected Papers of Kenneth J. Arrow, 1, Social Choice*. Cambridge, Mass.: Harvard University Press, 1983.

——. *Collected Papers of Kenneth J. Arrow, 2, General Equilibrium*. Cambridge, Mass.: Harvard University Press, 1983.

——. *Collected Papers of Kenneth J. Arrow, 3, Individual Choice Under Certainty and Uncertainty*. Cambridge, Mass.: Harvard University Press, 1984.

Arrow, Kenneth J. and F. H. Hahn. *General Competitive Analysis*. San Francisco: Oliver & Boyd, 1971.

Bliss, C. J. *Capital Theory and the Distribution of Income*. Amsterdam: North Holland, 1975.

Buchanan, James M. *Public Principles of Public Debt*. Homewood, Ill.: Richard D. Irwin, 1958.

——. 'Public finance and public choice'. In *National Tax Journal*. 1975.

Clower, Robert. 'The Keynesian counter-revolution: A theoretical reappraisal'. In *The Theory of Interest Rates* edited by F. H. Hahn and F. P. R. Brechling. London: Macmillan, 1965.

De V. Graaff, J. *Theoretical Welfare Economics*. Cambridge: Cambridge University Press, 1963.

Debreu, Gerard. *Theory of Value*. New Haven, Conn.: Yale University Press, 1959.

———. *Mathematical Economics: Twenty Papers of Gerard Debreu*. With an Introduction by Werner Hildenbrand. Cambridge: Cambridge University Press, 1983.

Friedman, Milton. *Essays in Positive Economics*. Chicago: University of Chicago Press, 1953.

———. *The Optimum Quantity of Money and Other Essays*. Chicago: Aldine, 1969.

———. *Milton Friedman's Monetary Framework*. Edited by Robert J. Gordon. Chicago: University of Chicago Press, 1974.

———. *Studies in the Quantity Theory of Money*. Edited by Milton Friedman. Chicago: University of Chicago Press, 1956.

Friedman, Milton and Anna Jacobson Schwartz. *A Monetary History of the United States, 1867–1960*. Princeton, N.J.: Princeton University Press, 1963.

Grandmont, Jean-Michel. *Money and Value*. Cambridge: Cambridge University Press, 1983.

Hahn, Frank. *Money and Inflation*. Oxford: Basil Blackwell, 1982.

———. *Equilibrium and Macroeconomics*. Cambridge, Mass.: MIT Press, 1984.

———. *Money, Growth and Stability*. Cambridge, Mass.: MIT Press, 1985.

———. *Philosophy and Economic Theory*. Edited by F. H. Hahn and Martin Hollis. Oxford: Oxford University Press, 1979.

Hayek, F. A. *The Road to Serfdom*. London: Routledge & Kegan Paul, 1944.

———. *Individualism and Economic Order*. London: Routledge & Kegan Paul, 1949.

———. *New Studies in Philosophy, Politics, Economics and the History of Ideas*. Chicago: University of Chicago Press, 1978.

Hicks, J. R. *Value and Capital*. 2nd edition. Oxford: Clarendon Press, 1946.

———. *Critical Essays in Monetary Theory*. Oxford: Clarendon Press, 1967.

———. *Wealth and Welfare*. Cambridge, Mass.: Harvard University Press, 1981.

———. *Money, Interest and Wages*. Cambridge, Mass.: Harvard University Press, 1982.

Hutchison, T. W. *'Positive' Economics and Policy Objectives*. London: George Allen & Unwin Ltd., 1964.

——. *On Revolutions and Progress in Economic Knowledge*. Cambridge: Cambridge University Press, 1978.

Johnson, Harry G. *Macroeconomics and Monetary Theory*. London: Gray Mills, 1971.

Keynes, John Maynard. *A Treatise on Probability*. 1921. London: Macmillan, 1973.

——. *The General Theory of Employment, Interest and Money*. London: Macmillan, 1936.

Keynes, John Neville. *The Scope and Method of Political Economy*. 4th edition. London: Macmillan, 1917.

Kindleberger, Charles. *The World in Depression 1929–1939*. Revised edition. Berkeley, Calif.: University of California Press, 1986.

Koopmans, Tjalling C. *Three Essays on the State of Economic Science*. New York: McGraw Hill, 1957.

Leijonhufvud, Axel. *On Keynesian Economics and the Economics of Keynes*. New York: Oxford University Press, 1968.

Lucas, R. E., Jr. *Studies in Business Cycle Theory*. Cambridge, Mass.: MIT Press, 1981.

——. *Models of Business Cycles*. Oxford: Basil Blackwell, 1987.

Marshall, Alfred. *Principles of Economics*. 1920, 9th (Variorum) edition. London: Macmillan, 1961.

——. *Memorials of Alfred Marshall*. Edited by A. C. Pigou. London: Macmillan, 1925.

Metzler, Lloyd. 'Wealth, saving, and the rate of interest'. In *Journal of Political Economy*, April 1951.

Myrdal, Gunnar. *The Political Element in the Development of Economic Theory*. Swedish original, 1929. Translated from the German by Paul Streeten. Cambridge, Mass.: Harvard University Press, 1953.

——. *Values in Social Theory: A Selection of Essays on Methodology*. Edited by Paul Streeten. New York: Harper, 1958.

Pareto, Vilfredo. *Manual of Political Economy*. 1927. Translated from the French by Ann S. Schwier. Edited by Ann S. Schwier and Alfred N. Page. New York: Augustus M. Kelley, 1971.

Patinkin, Don. *Money, Interest, and Prices*. 2nd edition. New York: Harper & Row, 1965.

Pigou, A. C. *The Economics of Welfare*. 4th edition. London: Macmillan, 1932.

——. *Employment and Equilibrium*. 2nd revised edition. London: Macmillan, 1949.

Pribram, Karl. *A History of Economic Reasoning*. Baltimore, Md: Johns Hopkins University Press, 1983.

Robbins, Lionel. *An Essay On the Nature and Significance of Economic Science*. 2nd edition. London: Macmillan, 1935.

——. *The Theory of Economic Policy in English Classical Political Economy*. London: Macmillan, 1952.

Samuelson, Paul A. *Foundations of Economic Analysis*. 1947. Enlarged edition. Cambridge, Mass.: Harvard University Press, 1983.

Schumpeter, Joseph A. *History of Economic Analysis*. Edited by Elizabeth Boody Schumpeter. New York: Oxford University Press, 1954.

Sen, Amartya. *Collective Choice and Social Welfare*. San Francisco: Holden-Day, 1970.

——. *Choice, Welfare and Measurement*. Cambridge, Mass.: MIT Press, 1982.

Smith, Adam. *An Inquiry into the Nature and Causes of the Wealth of Nations*. 1776. Edited by R. H. Campbell, A. S. Skinner and W. D. Todd. Oxford: Oxford University Press, 1976.

Theil, Henri. *Economic Forecasts and Policy*. 2nd edition. Amsterdam: North Holland, 1970.

Tinbergen, Jan. *On the Theory of Economic Policy*. Amsterdam: North Holland, 1952.

Tobin, James. 'Inflation and unemployment'. In *American Economic Review*, 1972.

——. *Asset Accumulation and Economic Activity*. Chicago: University of Chicago Press, 1980.

Walras, Léon. *Elements of Pure Economics*. 1874. Translated from the French by William Jaffé, 1954. New York: Augustus M. Kelley, 1977.

Wicksell, Knut. *Lectures on Political Economy*. Translated from the Swedish by E. Classen. Edited by Lionel Robbins. London: Routledge, 1935.

## Works by Philosophers and Others

Arendt, Hannah. 'Truth and politics'. In *Philosophy, Politics and Society*, 2nd Series. Edited by Peter Laslett and W. G. Runciman. Oxford: Basil Blackwell, 1967.

——. *The Life of the Mind*. New York: Harcourt Brace Jovanovich, 1978.

Aristotle. *The Basic Works of Aristotle*. Edited by Richard McKeon. New York: Random House, 1941.

Armstrong, D. M. *Universals and Scientific Realism*. Cambridge: Cambridge University Press, 1978.

Ayer, A. J. *Language, Truth and Logic*. 1937. New York: Dover, 1952.

——. *Freedom and Morality and Other Essays*. Oxford: Oxford University Press, 1984.

Bambrough, Renford. *Reason, Truth and God*. London: Methuen, 1969.

——. *Moral Scepticism and Moral Knowledge*. London: Routledge & Kegan Paul, 1979.

——. *Plato, Popper and Politics: Some Contributions to a Modern*

*Controversy*. Edited by Renford Bambrough. New York: Barnes and Noble, 1967.

Benacerraf, Paul. *Philosophy of Mathematics*. 2nd edition. Edited by Paul Benacerraf and Hilary Putnam. Cambridge: Cambridge University Press, 1983.

——. *Philosophy of Mathematics*. Edited by Paul Benacerraf and Hilary Putnam. Englewoods Cliffs, N.J.: Prentice Hall, 1964.

Black, Max. *The Nature of Mathematics*. London: Routledge & Kegan Paul, 1933.

——. *Margins of Precision*. Ithaca, N.Y.: Cornell University Press, 1970.

Brandt, Richard B. *A Theory of the Good and the Right*. Oxford: Clarendon Press, 1979.

Carnap, Rudolf. *Meaning and Necessity*. 2nd edition. Chicago: University of Chicago Press, 1956.

De Finetti, Bruno. 'Foresight: its logical laws, its subjective sources'. In *Annales de l'Institut Henri Poincaré*. 7, 1937. Translated from the French by Henry E. Kyburg, Jr. Reprinted in Kyburg and Smokler, *Studies in Subjective Probability*, 1964.

Dummett, Michael. *Truth and Other Enigmas*. Cambridge, Mass.: Harvard University Press, 1978.

Feigl, Herbert. *Readings in the Philosophy of Science*. Edited by Herbert Feigl and May Brodbeck. New York: Appleton, 1953.

Frege, Gottlob. *Translations from the Philosophical Writings of Gottlob Frege*. Translated, compiled and edited by Peter Geach and Max Black. Oxford: Basil Blackwell, 1952.

——. *On the Foundations of Geometry and Formal Theories of Arithmetic*. Translated from the German and with an introduction by Eike-Henner W. Kluge. New Haven: Yale University Press, 1971.

——. *Posthumous Writings*. Edited by Hans Hermes, Friedrich Kambartel and Friedrich Kaulbach. Translated from the German by Peter Long and Roger White. Oxford: Basil Blackwell, 1979.

——. *The Foundations of Arithmetic*. 1884. Translated from the German by J. L. Austin. Evanston, Ill.: Northwestern University Press, 1980.

Hacking, Ian. *The Logic of Statistical Inference*. Cambridge: Cambridge University Press,1965.

Hamlyn, D. W. *Metaphysics*. Cambridge: Cambridge University Press, 1984.

Hancock, Roger N. *Twentieth Century Ethics*. New York: Columbia University Press, 1974.

Hardy, G. H. *A Mathematician's Apology*. Cambridge: Cambridge University Press, 1967.

Hare, R. M. *The Language of Morals*. Oxford: Oxford University Press, 1952.

——. *Freedom and Reason*. Oxford: Oxford University Press, 1963.

——. *Moral Thinking*. Oxford: Clarendon Press, 1981.

Hesse, Mary B. *Models and Analogies in Science*. Notre Dame, Ind.:

University of Notre Dame Press, 1966.

Hume, David. *A Treatise of Human Nature*. 1739. 2nd edition of 1888. Edited by L. A. Selby-Bigge. Revised by P. H. Nidditch. Oxford: Clarendon, 1978.

——. *Enquiries Concerning Human Understanding and Concerning the Principles of Morals*. 1777. 3rd edition. Edited by P. H. Nidditch. Oxford: Clarendon Press, 1975.

Janik, Allan, and Stephen Toulmin. *Wittgenstein's Vienna*. New York: Simon and Schuster, 1973.

Kant, Immanuel. *Critique of Pure Reason*. Translated by J. M. D. Meiklejohn. London: J. M. Dent, 1934.

——. *Groundwork of the Metaphysic of Morals*. In H. J. Paton, *The Moral Law*. London: Hutchinson, 1948.

——. *Kant's Political Writings*. Edited by Hans Reiss. Translated from the German by H. B. Nisbet. Cambridge: Cambridge University Press, 1970.

Kolakowski, Leszek. *Main Currents of Marxism, Vol. I, The Founders*. Oxford: Clarendon Press, 1978.

——. *Main Currents of Marxism, Vol. II, The Golden Age*. Oxford: Clarendon Press, 1978.

——. *Main Currents of Marxism, Vol. III, The Breakdown*. Oxford: Clarendon Press, 1978.

Kyburg, Henry E., Jr. *Studies in Subjective Probability*. Edited by Henry E. Kyburg, Jr. and Howard E. Smokler. New York: John Wiley, 1964.

Lakatos, Imre. *Criticism and the Growth of Knowledge*. Edited by Imre Lakatos and Alan Musgrave. Cambridge: Cambridge University Press, 1967.

Landesman, Charles. *The Problem of Universals*. Edited by Charles Landesman. New York: Basic Books, 1971.

Leavis, F. R. *The Living Principle: 'English' as a Discipline of Thought*. Oxford: Oxford University Press, 1975.

Leibniz, G. W. *Philosophical Writings*. 1714. Edited by G. H. R. Parkinson. London: J. M. Dent, 1973.

MacIntyre, Alasdair. *After Virtue: A Study in Moral Theory*. 2nd edition. Notre Dame, Ind.: University of Notre Dame Press, 1984.

Mill, J. S. *A System of Logic*. 1843. 9th edition. London: Longmans, 1975.

——. *Utilitarianism, Liberty and Representative Government*. Edited by H. B. Acton. London: J. M. Dent, 1972.

Moore, G. E. *Philosophical Papers*. London: Allen & Unwin, 1959.

——. *The Philosophy of G. E. Moore*. Edited by Paul Arthur Schlipp. La Salle, Ill.: Open Court, 1942.

Nagel, Ernest and James R. Newman. *Gödel's Proof*. London: Routledge & Kegan Paul, 1958.

Nagel, Ernest, Alfred Tarski and Patrick Suppes (eds) *Logic, Methodology and the Philosophy of Science*. Stanford: Stanford University Press, 1962.

Odegard, Douglas. *Knowledge and Scepticism*. Totowa, N.J.: Rowman & Littlefield, 1982.

Peirce, C. S. *Collected Papers of Charles Sanders Peirce*. Edited by Charles Hartshorne and Paul Weiss. Cambridge, Mass.: Harvard University Press, 1931.

——. *Selected Writings (Values in a Universe of Chance)*. Edited by Phillip P. Weiner, 1958. New York: Dover, 1966.

Plato. *The Collected Dialogues of Plato including the Letters*. Edited by Edith Hamilton and Huntington Cairns, Bollingen Series LXXVI. Princeton, N.J. : Princeton University Press, 1961.

Popper, Karl. *The Logic of Scientific Discovery*. London: Hutchinson, 1959.

——. *The Open Society and Its Enemies, Vol. 1, The Spell of Plato*. Princeton, N.J. : Princeton University Press, 1962.

——. *Conjectures and Refutations*. London: Routledge & Kegan Paul, 1962.

Price, H. A. *Thinking and Experience*. 2nd edition. London: Hutchinson, 1969.

Putnam, Hilary. *Mathematics, Matter and Method, Philosophical Papers, Vol. 1*. 2nd edition. Cambridge: Cambridge University Press, 1979.

——. *Reason, Truth and History*. Cambridge: Cambridge University Press, 1981.

——. *Reason and Reality, Philosophical Papers, Vol. 3*. Cambridge: Cambridge University Press, 1983.

Quine, W. V. O. *From a Logical Point of View*. Cambridge, Mass.: Harvard University Press, 1953.

Ramsey, F. P. *The Foundations of Mathematics and Other Logical Essays*. Edited by R. B. Braithwaite. London: Routledge & Kegan Paul, 1931.

Resnik, Michael D. *Frege and the Philosophy of Mathematics*. Ithaca, New York: Cornell University Press, 1980.

Russell, Bertrand. *Introduction to Mathematical Philosophy*. London: Allen & Unwin, 1919.

Savage, L. J. *The Foundations of Statistics*. 2nd revised edition. New York: Dover, 1954.

——. 'The foundations of statistics reconsidered.' 1961. In Kyburg and Smokler, *Subjective Probability*. Edited by Henry E. Kyburg and Howard E. Smokler.

Searle, J. R. 'How to Derive "Ought" from "Is" '. In *Philosophical Review*. Vol. 73, 1964.

Solzhenitsyn, Aleksandr I. *The Gulag Archipelago*. Translated from the Russian by Thomas P. Whitney. New York: Harper & Row, 1973.

Stevenson, C. L. *Ethics and Language*. New Haven: Yale University Press, 1944.

——. *Facts and Values*. New Haven: Yale University Press, 1963.

Taylor, A. E. *The Mind of Plato*. 1922. Ann Arbor, Michigan: University of Michigan Press, 1960.

Toulmin, Stephen. *An Examination of the Place of Reason in Ethics*. Cambridge: Cambridge University Press, 1958.

Urmson, J. O. *The Emotive Theory of Ethics*. London: Hutchinson, 1968.

Van Heijenoort, Jean. *From Frege to Gödel: A Source Book in Mathematical Logic, 1879–1931*. Edited by Jean Van Heijenoort. Cambridge, Mass.: Harvard University Press, 1967.

Warnock, G. J. *Contemporary Moral Philosophy*. New York: St. Martin's Press, 1967.

White, Morton. *Toward Reunion in Philosophy*. Cambridge, Mass.: Harvard University Press, 1956.

Wisdom, John. *Paradox and Discovery*. Berkeley: University of California Press, 1970.

Wittgenstein, Ludwig. *Tractatus Logico-Philosophicus*. 1921. Translated from the German by D. F. Pears and B. F. McGuinness. With an Introduction by Bertrand Russell. London: Routledge and Kegan Paul, 1961.

——. *Philosophical Investigations*. c. 1929–1949. Translated by G. E. M. Anscombe, 1953. Third edition. Oxford: Blackwell, 1967.

——. *The Blue and Brown Books*. c. 1933–1935. Oxford: Basil Blackwell, 1958.

——. *Remarks on the Foundations of Mathematics*. c. 1937–1944. Edited by G. H. von Wright, R. Rhees and G. E. M. Anscombe. Translated from the German by G. E. M. Anscombe, 1956. Revised edition, Cambridge, Mass.: MIT Press, 1978.

——. *On Certainty*. c. 1949–1951. Edited by G. E. M. Anscombe and G. H. von Wright. Translated by Denis Paul and G. E. M. Anscombe. Oxford: Basil Blackwell, 1969.

# Index

229